BISHOP MORLEY OF WINCHESTER
1598–1684: *Politician Benefactor Pragmatist*

~ *Andrew Thomson* ~

A volume in THE WINCHESTER SERIES

Winchester University Press takes as a special interest the hinterland of Winchester, a city whose reach in time and space goes a great way. The scope of that hinterland provides the topics and titles for books in the Press's Winchester Series.

The beginnings of Winchester are suggested by the evolution of its name from suppositious Celtic through attested Latin to everyday English. Caergwinntguic becomes Cair-Guntin, Caergwintwg, Caer Gwent, Venta Belgarum, Venta Castra, Wintanceastre, Wincestre, Vincestre and finally Winchester. The names chart the city's passage over a thousand years from Britonic through Roman to Saxon possession, and they give a historical and linguistic starting point for the Winchester Series.

From the sixth to the eleventh century, Winchester was in the Westseaxna Rice, the kingdom of Wessex, the home of the West Saxons. They ruled land between the south coast and the River Thames. They contested their northern and eastern boundaries with the kingdom of Mercia; what are now the counties of Oxfordshire, Sussex and Kent were sometimes part of the one kingdom and sometimes part of the other. To the west, Wessex was bounded by the River Taw or by the River Tamar as today's Devon was contested with the British kingdom of Dumnonia. At highpoints, the West Saxon kings claimed rule over the whole of England, but the heart of their kingdom was Hampshire, the Isle of Wight, Berkshire, Wiltshire, Dorset, and Somerset. This is the heartland of the Winchester Series.

Under the Normans, the hinterland of Winchester was given new boundaries. It remained a place where kings held court, but it no longer had its own kingdom; instead, it became the cathedral city of a diocese that extended northeast through Surrey to border the River Thames at Southwark and southwest to Dorset. It still includes the Channel Islands, but it lost Surrey and Portsmouth in 1927. Within the Anglican Church, the bishops of Winchester are second only to the archbishops of Canterbury and York, and Winchester Cathedral is one of the architectural glories of Europe. This diocese is a dimension of the Winchester Series.

In the nineteenth century, Thomas Hardy revived the name of the ancient kingdom of Wessex and created through his novels a new notion of the hinterland of Winchester. The heart of his imaginary land is Wiltshire, his Mid-Wessex, and the other counties in his Wessex are Berkshire, Devon, Dorset, Hampshire, and Somerset. Hardy brings attention to the literary riches of the Winchester hinterland within which have lived and written Jane Austen, William Blake, William Cobbett, Charles Dickens, Benjamin Franklin, Elizabeth Gaskell, Edward Gibbon, William Hazlitt, George Herbert, John Keats, John Keble, Alfred Tennyson, Izaak Walton, H.G. Wells, Gilbert White, Charlotte Mary Yonge. The territory of these writers provides another focus for the Winchester Series.

In the twentieth century, Winchester was placed in what was described in various official documents as the South East England Region. Originally designated as a Civil Defence Area, the Region has expanded and contracted but presently includes the counties of Buckinghamshire, Oxfordshire, Berkshire, Hampshire, the Isle of Wight, Surrey, East Sussex, West Sussex and Kent. Hampshire and Winchester now look east and associate with Sussex and Kent. The old associate counties, Wiltshire, Dorset and Somerset, have been designated part of the South West England Region. Hampshire was once the place where the West Country began but no longer. The expansion of London has made it more a Home than a Shire county, and European Route 5 - running from Greenock to Algeciras by way of Southampton and Le Havre – makes twenty-first-century Hampshire more immediately part of Europe than it has been since the end of the Hundred Years War. The South East England Region too shapes the Winchester Series.

DEDICATION

I dedicate this book to Rosemary, Anna, Ethan Elijah, Elowen Eve, Jeremy, and Sebastian, who have had to suffer years of neglect and irritable responses to interruptions when the telephone rang or another trip to the supermarket was necessary and who have, in spite of all that and more, always shown interest and support for the project in which they say I have been absorbed for up to twenty-seven hours a day. I can only hope that the finished product comes somewhere near to making it all worthwhile.

Published by Winchester University Press 2019.

The Author hereby asserts the moral right always to be identified as such in accordance with the provisions of the Copyright, Designs and Patents Act 1988.

All rights reserved. No part of this publication may be reproduced in any form whatsoever or by any method whatsoever without prior permission of Winchester University Press. Quotations may however be taken for unpublished academic essays and newspaper and magazine reviews. Enquiries should be made direct to the Press. This book is published subject to the condition that it shall not be resold without prior written consent from the Winchester University Press.

First published globally in 2019
by Winchester University Press Winchester SO22 4NR.

British Library Cataloguing-in-Publication Data
A CIP catalogue record for this book is available from the British Library.

ISBN: 987-1-906113-27-8

Designed and typeset by All Caps

CONTENTS

Acknowledgements 6
Abbreviations 8
Introduction 9

Chapter 1   Birth, Education, and Early Career 15
Chapter 2   Exile 22
Chapter 3   Mission to England 29
Chapter 4   The Search for a Settlement: Part 1 38
Chapter 5   The Search for a Settlement: Part 2 54
Chapter 6   Morley at Worcester: his Stewardship of the Diocese 63
Chapter 7   Morley at Winchester: Part 1, Recovery 81
Chapter 8   Morley at Winchester: Part 2, Reform 101
Chapter 9   Death and Benefactions 115

Conclusion 125
Appendices 128
Bibliography 130
Index 136

ACKNOWLEDGEMENTS

Bishop Morley first captured my interest while researching my doctoral thesis on the clergy of the seventeenth-century Diocese of Winchester. I have had cause to mention and discuss aspects of 'Morley' frequently over the last twenty years or so and, for the last three or four, I have made him the central focus of my work.

Most writers state at some point in their acknowledgements that they could not have made anything like progress, completing the research, and finishing the book without the help of numerous academics, librarians, and archivists; and without the support of family and friends through such a time of trial, while taking upon themselves responsibility for all errors and misjudgements. The reason for these 'clichéd' comments is that they are mostly only too true, and this is certainly so in my case.

Libraries are *sine qua non* for any research of this kind and I have made countless visits to the Bodleian Library, the British Library, the House of Lords, the Institute of Historical Research, Lambeth Palace, and the National Archives; likewise to the record offices of Hampshire, Oxford, Somerset, West Sussex, Wiltshire, and Worcester; and at all of them I have had a warm welcome and much assistance. I am particularly grateful to Martin Robson Riley of the National Library of Wales, Rachael Laburn of the National Library of Scotland, and David Morrison of Worcester Cathedral. They all found the document in question almost immediately, sent photographs, checked details – a most efficient and personal service in all three cases – and saving me long and expensive journeys. I must thank also the young assistant at the Bodleian Library who went to the trouble of emailing an article to my home address – I hope she will know who she is!

I have to mention one archivist in particular – David Rymill at Hampshire Record Office – for truly outstanding help whenever I have sought it. I have been sustained in my researches by knowing that I can always count on David to resolve my problem – a perplexing Latin phrase or the intricacies of leasehold arrangements – and when we have occasionally reached 'impasse', I am confident I have at least sought the best advice available. He undertook, moreover, a preliminary reading of the text in spite of all his other commitments.

Next is the company of scholars – experts all of them in various aspects of church history – who regularly take part in the Religious History Seminars at Senate House in the University of London: among them, Pauline Ashbridge, David Crankshaw, Ken Fincham, Andrew Foster, George Gross, Graham Hart, Valerie Hitchman, Tom Reid, Nicholas Tyacke, and Rebecca Warren. Where two or three academics are gathered together, there will always be controversy and 'Morley' seems to have provoked, among some of them at least, more than the usual comment, some of it inevitably more constructive than others; and it would be true to say that the final version of his 'life' has emerged as much in spite of, as because of, their criticisms. Nonetheless, with a comment here, a document there, they have often 'set me right' and, although they may not know it, they have at times been inspirational.

I must also acknowledge the interest and support of two other friends – James Atwell (sometime Dean of Winchester) and John Hare (historian in his own right) – who have, in their different ways, sustained me. James took some interest in Morley, encouraged my research into Morley's ministry, and once delivered a sermon about him; while John can always be relied upon to make a useful comment, from his knowledge of the archives, about anything from bishops' palaces to the pipe rolls stored at Hampshire Record Office.

Three other people, at least, must be thanked: Phil Ferris for translation of the inscription on Morley's tomb and for his advice about its use for calculating Morley's age; John Crook for his photograph of Morley; Paul Thomson for suggesting ways to disentangle obscurities within the text; and David Rollason for help and advice on numerous occasions while the book was in gestation.

I am also hugely in debt to Stephen Greenhalgh and Neil McCaw of Winchester University Press. It is only through their good works – their wisdom and patience – that the book has emerged in anything like acceptable form.

I should add that none of these people – friends and colleagues – can be held responsible in any way for any errors which have crept into the book.

Finally, I must end with another cliché-looking, but nonetheless heartfelt, tribute to Rosemary, my wife, who has shown unfailing interest in the project and much patience, as I have said in the dedication, when stress has provoked an irritable response at some critical moment. Without her domestic ministerings, initial proofreading, and interjection of opinions, this work would never have been done or, at least, not within its present timescale.

ABBREVIATIONS

BIHR	*Bulletin of the Institute of Historical Research*
BCP	*Book of Common Prayer*
BL	British Library
Bod	Bodleian Library, Oxford
CR	*Calamy Revised,* ed. A. G. Matthews, Oxford, 1934
CSPD	*Calendar of State Papers Domestic*
DNB	*Dictionary of National Biography*
EconHR	*Economic History Review*
EHR	*English Historical Review*
HMC	*Historical Manuscripts Commission*
HRO	Hampshire Record Office
JEH	*Journal of Ecclesiastical History*
JF	*Alumni Oxonienses,* ed. J. Foster, Oxford, 1891-92
JMH	*Journal of Modern History*
LI	*Liber Institutionum,* TNA
LMA	London Metropolitan Archives
LPL	Lambeth Palace Library
NLofS	National Library of Scotland
NLofW	National Library of Wales
ODNB	*Oxford Dictionary of National Biography*
OHC	Oxfordshire History Centre
SCC	Southampton Civic Centre
SH	*Southern History*
SHC	Somerset Heritage Centre
STC	*Short Title Catalogue*
TNA	The National Archives
TAPS	*Transactions of the American Philosophical Society*
TRHS	*Transactions of the Royal Historical Society*
VENN	*Alumni Cantabrigienses,* ed. J. and J. A., Venn, Cambridge, 1922-27
WOOD *ATHENAE*	*Athenae Oxonienses,* ed. A. Wood, London, 1721
Winchester CL	Winchester Cathedral Library
Worcester CL	Worcester Cathedral Library
WR	*Walker Revised,* ed. A. G. Matthews, Oxford, 1948
WRO	Worcestershire Record Office
WSHC	Wiltshire and Swindon History Centre

INTRODUCTION

This book attempts to offer an authoritative account of the life and achievements of George Morley. Morley was for years a teacher at Christ Church, Oxford, subsequently Dean of the College, then Bishop of Worcester and, finally, Bishop of Winchester. These appointments would, in themselves, have made him an important figure in the history of seventeenth-century England; but Morley in fact played a huge part, far beyond the confines of the University of Oxford and the Dioceses of Worcester and Winchester, nationally, in the political and religious developments of his time. He played key roles in the restoration of the king in 1660 and in the subsequent attempts to achieve a settlement - the beginnings of the search for church unity - in the 1660s and 1670s.

Morley was an Elizabethan - just - born at the end of the 1590s into the world of Whitgift[1] and Hooker,[2] the scandal of Marprelate[3] barely over, the controversies of the Hampton Court Conference[4] and the outrage of the Gunpowder Plot[5] soon to come. These events alone signal the religious divisions of the times. He died in the 1680s, just before Charles II himself, amid more tensions of this kind in the crises of the Popish Plot and 'Exclusion'.[6]

The world was stirred and shaken many times in the seventeenth-century and in England even 'turned upside down' in the 1650s. There were other 'issues' - social, economic, and financial, let alone a clash of personalities - but religion was one of the most divisive and potent forces in Early Modern England. The Church of England, from its beginnings in the Henrician Reformation, faced challenges from Catholics, who wished to return to the 'true faith', from 'puritans' who wished to press forward with further, Calvinistic, change; and then, in the 1630s, from the 'Laudians' who wished for more order and more ceremonies - more formality - in the life and worship of the Church. Civil war in three kingdoms followed in the 1640s and, with the execution of the king and the abolition of the Church of England, 'a great overturning

---

1 John Whitgift (1530-1604), Archbishop of Canterbury 1583-1604, and instrumental in the production of the body of canons (1604) which governed the beliefs and practices of the Church of England, its people and its clergy.
2 Richard Hooker (1554-1600), theologian and outstanding proponent of the essence of the Church of England in his *Laws of Ecclesiastical Polity* (1590s).
3 A series of pamphlets issued in 1588-89 in which the author, disguised under the name 'Martin Marprelate', attacked bishops in person and the whole system of church government by bishops.
4 A conference at Hampton Court of 1604, comprising bishops and Puritans, presided over by James I, to consider Puritan demands for reform of the Church of England; its main achievement was to commission a new translation of the bible (the King James or Authorised Version) but by the time of its appearance the conference had long since collapsed in disunity.
5 The Gunpowder Plot was an abortive Catholic conspiracy to blow up the Houses of Parliament and the 'establishment' (including James I) in 1605 (Guy Fawkes was in charge of the explosives).
6 The Popish Plot of 1678 began with allegations of a Catholic conspiracy to overthrow Charles II, install his Catholic brother James as king, and restore the Catholic Church to England; 'Exclusion' was a campaign (1679-81) to alter the succession and exclude James, Duke of York (next in line after Charles II), from the throne.

of everything in England'.⁷ The Interregnum saw an explosion of religious groups and sects - Presbyterians, Independents, Congregationalists, Seekers, Ranters, Quakers, Fifth Monarchy Men, and Anabaptists - with radical social, economic, and political agendas, as well as their extraordinary religious views. Even in the 1660s and 70s religion could still generate conspiracies - or rumours of conspiracies - such as the Popish Plot and rebellions of Lambert, Venner, and the Yorkshire Revolt.

England and its Civil Wars in particular should be seen in the context of Europe where there were major conflicts, arising at least in part from the Reformation, in the sixteenth and seventeenth centuries: the Wars of the German Princes (1546/47 and 1552-55), the French Wars of Religion (1562-1598), the Revolt of the Netherlands (1568-1648) and the Thirty Years War (1618-1648).

The trouble lay, at root, in a mental framework which, whether in England or on the Continent, did not accept, let alone welcome, the notion of toleration. Such a notion was but dimly conceived. The Treaties of Augsburg in 1555 and of Westphalia in 1648, ending the conflict among the German states and in the Netherlands, together with the Edict of Nantes in 1598 which brought war to a close in France, were all, in their own particular ways, steps towards toleration and were in fact reluctant concessions by both Catholics and Protestants faced with the appalling alternative of more and more war. These conflicts demonstrate how widespread and complex was the issue of religion in the sixteenth and seventeenth centuries and how difficult it was to reach a settlement.

In England the solution was uniformity - one form of religion as expressed and practised by the Church of England - and this was laid down in the Acts of 1549, 1552, and 1559, and was still where the law stood in 1660, whatever the practice particularly in the 1650s. It could be said that all English monarchs of the sixteenth and early seventeenth century, whether Catholic or Protestant, agreed on one thing: that the nation could have only one religion, either Catholic or Protestant. The Restoration of 1660 involved a new settlement of a whole range of issues, of which religion was but one. It was a 'moment for review' and an opportunity to resolve religious divisions which stretched back to the Reformation. The choice was either another dose of 'Anglican' uniformity; or comprehension, still one church but achieved by uniting, through discussion and compromise, some, if not all, of the Protestant religions; or toleration, allowing the different religions to exist side by side. To the seventeenth-century mind it was uniformity first, comprehension second, with toleration very much a reluctant third; but the stark warning of the alternative - strife and war, abolition of kings and bishops, a world of Seekers, Ranters, and Fifth Monarchy Men - brought home to at least some of the men of the hour the failure of uniformity and the need to explore alternatives.

---

7 W. Haller, *Liberty and Reformation in the Puritan Revolution* (New York, 1955), p. xiv.

It was at this point, the Restoration of 1660, that George Morley rose to prominence for just short of the next quarter of a century. Although moving in noble and royal circles and, indeed, forced into exile by the mid-century upheavals in England, he had, hitherto, been rather an observer than a director of those events at home and abroad. From 1660, however, he was a central figure: in religious terms, as Bishop of Winchester; and politically as a member of the House of Lords and, for a time, the Privy Council. Morley faced, in common with all the other bishops, an array of problems – appointments, discipline, repairs, finance, and how much to restore or what to reform – at diocesan level. The greater question of national import – the nature of the religious settlement – faced king, Chancellor, Parliament, the bishops, and other divines in the early 1660s. That was the agenda, in sum, at the conferences at Worcester House, Savoy, and Convocation in the early 1660s. Morley was a member of all three conferences and, when final decisions passed to king and Parliament, Morley was there again as participant in the deliberations in the Lords and the Privy Council.

Surprisingly, in view of the centrality of the religious issue in 1660 and the efforts to achieve a settlement, little has been written or researched on the lives of the bishops at that time. W. G. Simon's is the only survey of the episcopate as a whole during the years of the Restoration. Anne Whiteman, Edward Carpenter, and Victor Sutch have reviewed the careers of three of Morley's contemporaries: Seth Ward, Bishop in turn of Exeter and Salisbury; Henry Compton, Bishop first of Oxford and then of London; and Gilbert Sheldon, Bishop of London before elevation to the Archbishopric of Canterbury.[8]

These studies all throw some light on Morley or invite comparisons of their respective episcopates with his, but there is no specific full-scale study of Morley himself. The entries by John Spurr in the *ODNB* and Ruth Paley and Beverly Adams in the relevant volume of the *History of Parliament* summarise his life and achievements; but neither of these accounts could enjoy the freedom, within the confines of a collection of articles, to discuss in detail efforts to achieve a measure of religious unity; nor the freedom likewise to tackle, beyond a few generalities, his role as enforcer and reformer within his two dioceses; and both, placing their faith ultimately in the writings of Roger Morrice[9] and Richard Baxter,[10] conclude that he was a deceiver and betrayer of the cause of church unity. Three other writers, Robert Bosher, Norman Sykes, and Ian Green, though not writing primarily about Morley, have important things to say about him. Bosher's command of sources is undoubtedly impressive and he gives much attention to Morley in the early 1660s at the time of Worcester House, Savoy, and Convocation; but, to him, Morley was part of the 'Anglican' conspiracy to outwit the 'Presbyterians' and restore a 'Laudian' church. Sykes, focusing, in particular, on the

---

8   See the bibliography for details of these and other works mentioned in this Introduction.
9   Roger Morrice (1628-1702), a religious minister and political journalist who suffered ejection from the Church of England in 1662 and who wrote his *Entring Book,* which is an important commentary on national events in 1677-1691.
10 Richard Baxter (1615-1691), thinker, writer, and leader of the Presbyterians, who was expelled by Morley from his parish at Kidderminster and who clashed repeatedly with Morley in conferences and by pamphlet; but whose autobiography, *Reliquiae Baxterianae,* is a key source, treated with caution, for the attempts at church unity (or comprehension) in the 1660s and 1670s.

attempts at *rapprochement* in the mid-1670s, presents Morley likewise as a schemer bent on the destruction of the dissenters; while it is left to Green to emphasise the pragmatic streak in Morley.

Justification for the subject matter of this books lies, in the first place, then, in the shortcomings, or at least the dearth, of other research. There are few full-scale 'lives' of bishops of the Restoration, none of Morley himself, and this study offers an account as complete as surviving evidence allows, all in one place, of his life and achievements. Secondly, this study offers the first thorough account of the administration of his dioceses, for some of which, ordinations and confirmations in particular, the bishop alone - Morley in this case - was responsible. Winchester, covering a large part of southern England and commanding enormous wealth, ranked fifth, if not higher, in the national ecclesiastical hierarchy. It was a diocese which could command notice and the administration of which, restored and reformed, had the potential to act as a model for the country. Analysis of 'the Winchester experience' will reveal something of the strengths and weaknesses of the Church as it faced a world, first of persistent division in the 1660s and then, after 1689, of toleration. Thirdly, the 'premier status' of the Diocese of Winchester allowed the bishop to speak with a powerful voice among other bishops in Convocation, among politicians in Parliament and, from time to time, before the king in the Privy Council; hence to play an important part, if he chose, in the affairs of the kingdom. The search for a national settlement of religious divisions was a central theme of the 1660s and 1670s and, though much of this is well known, this account moves Morley centre-stage, putting the stress on his initiatives in 1660-62 and 1674/75 and offering a new - more sympathetic - assessment of his achievements. A review of his efforts at those times highlights the obstacles to such plans; and consequently, where there might have been unity, division prevails to this day.

Specific questions this book will attempt to answer in the course of the narrative are: how and why did Morley rise to prominence? What did he contribute to the Restoration? What was his role in the search for a settlement between 1660 and 1662 and, later, in the 1670s? What was his stance on the repression of dissent in the 1660s? What did he achieve as Bishop of Worcester? What was the nature of his record - his jurisdiction - at Winchester, both spiritual and secular? Was he a restorer or a reformer? Wherein lies his claim to greatness?

The attempt to paint a complete – and balanced – picture of Morley is bedevilled by problematic documentation. There is an array of sources for Morley but, inevitably, research of this kind cannot escape problems, and these may partly explain neglect of his life and work. Documentation is sometimes completely missing. While there is a record of his baptism, nothing has been found to prove Morley's exact date of birth. This is also the case with his ordination: he must have been ordained to remain a 'student' (teaching fellow) at Christ Church (let alone his later career as dean and bishop), but no record of the event – where, when, and who performed it – has been found. The land for the building of Morley College, to take another example, was to be conveyed 'by lease' from the cathedral to the bishop but no trace of the transfer has come to light.

There are numerous occasions where the documents give some, but far from complete, information. Morley's BD and DD fall into this category; confusion still surrounds the reception of his sermon before the House of Commons in 1640/41; and his role in the religious settlement of 1660-62 is particularly frustrating. What looks, at first sight, like a torrent of 'original' paperwork – from Cardwell to Browning (acts and declarations) or from Cobbett (debates in Parliament) to Bray (proceedings in Convocation)[11] – turns out to be a flood carrying very little of substance. Contents of speeches, with the notable exception of the angry, if entertaining, reports by the Presbyterian Richard Baxter, are routinely missing with nothing to reveal what was actually said by Morley (and his colleagues) and this makes it much more difficult to gauge policies and motives. Most grievously, there appears to be no surviving evidence for the authorship of the Black Rubric[12] and, critically, Morley's role in the decision to include it in the Book of Common Prayer in 1662. Interpretation has to 'rule' in these cases: hence the numerous conflicting views of the motives of Charles, Clarendon[13] – and Morley – some more sensible than others.

Untangling the tangled is sometimes necessary. Surviving documents are confusing for want of proper headings and dates, together with lack of precision over the application of terms. This occurs with the various bills to implement comprehension or toleration in the late 1660s and another batch in the early 1670s. The bills of 1667/68 have to be read carefully to establish which concerned 'comprehension' and which concerned 'toleration'. The drafts of the bills of the mid-1670s have to be examined similarly to decide, amid overlapping terms and missing dates, exactly how many separate bills there were.

---

11 See bibliography for these compilers.
12 The Black Rubric asserts, in effect, that the bread and wine were reminders – symbols or tokens – of the flesh and blood of Christ.
13 Edward Hyde (1609-1674), Earl of Clarendon from 1661, was Lord Chancellor and, thus, Charles II's 'prime minister' 1660-1667.

Other sources are sound, some – particularly at diocesan level – are even plentiful and have proved *sine qua non* for this study. The entry on Morley by Anthony Wood, a contemporary, in his *Athenae* remains, for all the shortcomings and criticisms of his work, indispensable. Much of his information – about Morley's birth, education, and appointments, for example – has turned out, where it can be verified, to be right and, although much can be assembled from other, disparate sources, Wood's account is, within its terms of reference, an excellent summary and the best place to start.

For Morley's exile abroad during the Interregnum, we are saved by Morley himself. He wrote his *Several Treatises written upon Several Occasions* with a different purpose in mind but, in its course, he outlines his movements, sometimes tantalisingly omitting important information such as dates; but, once again, without it, it would be much more difficult to reconstruct his journeyings on the Continent in the 1650s.

Yield from documents concerning the church settlement may be disappointing for specific information about Morley, but they are plentiful and leave scope for interpretation. Large collections of documents, lodged mainly at the Record Offices of Hampshire and Worcester, make it possible, finally, to describe in some detail Morley's administration of his two dioceses. Episcopal registers cover ordinations, institutions, and visitations; consistory courts books contain the prosecutions of clergy and laymen; and lease books and a series of 'pipe rolls' reveal rent streams from estates. The subject matter of the lease books and pipe rolls is probably at a 'remove' from the personal oversight of Morley (or any other bishop at that time), even if he bore ultimate responsibility; but information will be drawn from them when they throw light on his activities.

Interpretation, the essence of assessment, is peril enough. Archives are the equivalent of straw for bricks or sand for glass, and flaws will inevitably affect the finished product. This presents researchers with a choice: to abandon the project or to make the most of what survives. The decision here has been to pursue the latter course. This account of the life and achievements of George Morley stands – or falls – on this basis.

CHAPTER 1: BIRTH, EDUCATION, AND EARLY CAREER

George Morley was baptised at the church of St Matthew, Friday Street, in the City of London, on 5 March 1598. This is the only certain event concerning the beginnings of Morley and, as the original register was destroyed in the Blitz of 1940, even this is based on a transcription of 1933.[1] There is somewhat less certainty about the date and place of his birth. Anthony Wood states that Morley was born at Cheapside, London, on 27 February 1597 (old style, 1598 new style)[2] and several comments by Morley himself appear to bear out the year, if not the month, when he was born. He wrote in a letter of 1674 that he was 'in the 77th yeare of (his) age' and in the Preface to his *Several Treatises*, 'An. Dom. 1682', he says he was eighty-four years and nine months old; but unfortunately neither comment is conclusive.[3] His will of July 1684 states that he was then in his eighty-seventh year and the inscription on his tomb, *'Anno Aetatis suae LXXXVIIo',* records his death in the eighty-seventh year of his age on 29 October 1684.[4] He was, thus, without much doubt, 86 when he made his will and when he died; and, while this does not rule out birth in November or December 1597, it makes it most likely that he was born in 1598. According to another of his letters, written on 13 February 1679, he was still 81:[5] the earliest he could have been born was therefore 14 February 1598 and, since his baptism took place on 5 March 1598, it is very likely that he was indeed born on 27 February 1598.

Wood provides a little more information about Morley's parents. His father, Francis Morley, belonged to the 'armiger' - gentry - class and was a man of some wealth; but his lending to others who failed to pay him back caused him to die in debt.[6] His mother, Sarah, had at least one important connection as her brother, Sir John Denham, was a Baron of the Exchequer.

---

1 *Register of St Matthew Friday Street London 1538-1812*, ed. and transc., A. M. Bruce Bannerman, Harleian Society Register, vol. 63 (London, 1933), p. 11.
2 Wood, *Athenae*, vol. 2, col. 768; Wood, writing '27th February 1597' in 1695, used old style dating which applied in England until 1752 before which date the new year began on 25 March and January, February, and most of March fell in the preceding year.
3 Longleat, Coventry MS, vol. 7, item 32; George Morley, *Several Treatises written upon Several Occasions* (London, 1683), p. xvi; but neither begins to provide a proper basis for a calculation as the month each document was written is either damaged or missing.
4 TNA, 1684 Prob 11/377; the 'o' after LXXXVII has determined my interpretation that it was his eighty-seventh year (an ordinal number) and not that he was eighty-seven (cardinal). George Morley's tomb lies in front of the screen, on the nave side and to the north, and the inscriptions are reproduced in Henry Earl of Clarendon and Samuel Gale (eds), *History and Antiquities of the Cathedral Church of Winchester,* (London, 1715), p. 67, and in T.D. Atkinson (ed.), *Winchester Cathedral Memorials,* typescript (1937), HRO, DC/K11/5/1, p. 114. My thanks are due to Mr Philip Ferris MA for providing me with an accurate translation.
5 Bod Tanner 39, f. 180.
6 Morley suffered arrest for debt - his own in the 1630s (J. Granger, *Biographical History of England*, vol. 3 [London, 1804], p. 236) or his father's *(DNB)*.

Both parents died in his childhood and Morley was, thus, by the age of 12, an orphan. Counter-balancing this, however, were his 'class' and connections, together with, presumably, a scholarly temperament, and he received a first rate education. He was sent, as a King's Scholar, to Westminster School[7] at the age of 13 in 1611 and, from there, he was able to proceed to Christ Church Oxford in 1615 where he gained successively his BA in 1618, his MA in 1621, and finally a DD in 1642. His early degrees - BA and MA - were gained while Calvinism was the prevailing theology at Oxford.[8] That is a generalisation, of course, making no allowance for independence of thought either by his teachers or by Morley himself or for change and development of his thinking in later life. It must therefore be at least questionable to conclude, on the basis of the timing of his degrees alone, that therein lay the origins of Morley's Calvinism. Wood, Burnet, and Kennett[9] all claim Morley was a Calvinist, however, and, if so, his time at university - his formative years - when Calvinism was so dominant, may have been its source. There appears to be no record of an 'intermediate' BD, and his DD is one of a number of 'creations' in 1642 which were bestowed after the battle of Edgehill for service or support for the king and, thus, would seem to have been honorific. Morley had, according to Wood, given his first year's 'profit' from his canonry to the royal cause.[10]

Morley remained part of the stipendiary studentship of Christ Church after taking his MA.[11] Christ Church, as a college and as distinct from the cathedral, lacked constitution and statutes until 1867[12], but the college developed, by custom and practice, conventions unique to itself that there should be a student body of one hundred, whose members would receive a stipend (or fixed payment) and who could

---

7   The custom at Westminster School is to name them King's or Queen's Scholars according to the gender of the monarch (no statute or order, merely custom and practice); Welch lists him mistakenly as a Queen's Scholar (J. Welch (ed.), *Alumni Westmonsterienses,* [London, 1852], pp. 83-84); but Russell Barker and Stenning do so correctly as King's Scholar (G. H. Russell Barker and A. N. Stenning, (eds), *Record of Old Westminsters* [London, 1928], pp. 666-67); I owe all this information to Ms Elizabeth Wells, Archivist, Westminster School.
8   M. H. Curtis, *Oxford and Cambridge in Transition 1558-1642* (Oxford, 1959), pp. 191-93; S. L. Greenslade, 'Faculty of Theology', in J. McConica (ed.), *History of the University of Oxford*, vol. 3 (Oxford, 1986), pp. 330-33; N. Tyacke, 'Religious Controversy', in N. Tyacke (ed.), *History of the University of Oxford*, vol. 4 (Oxford, 1997), pp. 569-71, 582, 585; N. Tyacke, A*nti-Calvinists: the Rise of English Arminianism* c.1590-1640 (Oxford, 1987), pp. 58-61, 72, 81.
9   Wood, *Athenae*, vol. 2, col. 768; O. Airy (ed.), *Burnet's History of my Own Time*, vol. 1 (Oxford, 1897), p. 314; W. Kennett, *Register and Chronicle Ecclesiastical and Civil,* (London, 1728), p. 666.
10 'created DD', Wood, *Athenae*, vol. 2, col. 29; *JF;* Wood includes Morley in a long list of such DDs for 1642 with a preceding note (Wood, *Athenae*, vol. 2; *Fasti*, col. 7) before the creations of 1642 stating 'the King retired to Oxon, and ... it was his pleasure that there should be a Creation in all Faculties of such that had either done him service in ... battel, or had retired to him at Oxon ... to avoid the barbarities of the Presbyterians ...'; for Morley's 'profit', Wood, *Athenae,* vol. 2, col. 768.
11 The late Canon Bussby mentions 'teaching' and the office of 'Regent' (F. Bussby, 'Early Life of George Morley', *Winchester Cathedral Record* [1970], pp. 19-20); the latter officer apparently acted as moderator in disputations (E. G. W. Bill, *Education at Christ Church Oxford 1660-1899* [Oxford, 1988], p. 195).
12 E. G. W. Bill and J. F. A. Mason, *Christ Church and Reform 1850-1867* (Oxford, 1970), *passim,* especially, pp. 180, and 241 onwards; J. F. A. Mason, 'A Brief History of Christ Church Oxford', in C. Hibbert (ed.), *Encyclopaedia of Oxford* (Oxford, 1988), pp. 79, 81.

be preparing for any of the degrees from BA to DD. Once they had reached MA level, they could continue, within the studentship, to teach in the college as long as they remained celibate, sought ordination, took further degrees within 'a reasonable time-scale', and declined any other post or work paying a living stipend or remuneration.[13] Morley was a bachelor all his life and, while there is no record of his ordination,[14] he must have sought it in the 1620s as he became chaplain, probably in 1628, to Lord Carnarvon.[15] Recompense for household chaplains was likely to have been modest, and a letter written by Morley in November 1659 implies he may have been receiving £20 *p.a.*[16] Money of this order would hardly have transgressed the 'living wage' rule or consumed much of his time, and he was able to combine the chaplaincy with his continuing duties at Oxford. Morley remained MA, omitting to proceed to BD and DD in the 1620s and 30s, the only transgression of which he may have been guilty; but this requirement does not seem, at least in his case, to have been rigorously enforced.

The conventions – and attractions – of Christ Church may explain, in part, his lack of advancement in the church; but there was another side to Morley. He may have upset William Laud,[17] Archbishop of Canterbury, with his infamous and often-retailed jibe when asked what the Arminians held to which he replied, 'all the best bishoprics and deaneries in England'. Edward Hyde, the source of this anecdote, comments, ominously, that Morley's religious views at this time were 'not yet grateful (pleasing) to the current churchmen with the greatest power'.[18] Among Morley's friends, to compound matters, were apparently John Hampden and Arthur Goodwin, both Buckinghamshire MPs and both 'resolute' opponents of the government of Charles I in the Short and Long Parliaments.[19]

---

13 Mason, 'Christ Church Oxford', pp. 79-83; J. Curthoys, *The Cardinal's College* (London, 2012), p. 45. I owe much of my understanding of the intricacies of Christ Church to Ms J. Curthoys, archivist of Christ Church.
14 e.g. the Bishop of Oxford's Episcopal Register 1599-1638 (Oxfordshire History Centre, MS Oxf. Dioc. Papers c. 265) has nothing on ordinations.
15 Wood implies 1628-1641 (Wood, *Athenae,* vol. 2, col. 769); Clarendon, writing about events of 1635, refers to the chaplaincy (*Life of Edward Earl of Clarendon ... in which is included a Continuation of the History of the Grand Rebellion,* vol. 1 [Oxford, 1827], p. 56).
16 C. R. Cheney (ed.), *Handbook of Dates* (Cambridge, 1945/1961/1996), p. 447; shillings rather than pounds p.a. were paid to two of the Lord Lieutenant of Surrey's chaplains in the 1660s and 1670s (LPL, FV/1/1, ff. 5v, 49v).
17 William Laud (1573-1645), Archbishop of Canterbury 1633-1645, stood for order, ceremony, and uniformity of worship in the Church of England – Arminianism – and his thorough and ruthless control of the Church led him to the block in 1645.
18 Clarendon, *Life and Continuation,* vol. 1, p. 56.
19 For these see e.g. *ODNB*; A. Thrush and J. P. Ferris (eds), *House of Commons 1604-1629,* vol. IV (Cambridge, 2010), pp. 526 (Hampden), 418 (Goodwin).

His fortunes had begun to change by 1640. He had become a regular member of the 'Tew circle' in the 1630s to which he was probably introduced by Lord Carnarvon. The role of Edmund Waller is less clear. Waller, 'a distant relation' of Morley according to one source, introduced Morley to the circle; but another claims they were 'friends' and it was Morley who introduced Waller.[20] The 'circle' was 'something of a ... Renaissance Court' of statesmen and divines who met at Great Tew, the home of Lord Falkland, which became a refuge of study, writing, and exchange of ideas.[21] This brought him into contact with, among others, Henry Hammond (a future canon, like Morley, at Christ Church), Robert Sanderson (a future Bishop of Lincoln), Gilbert Sheldon (a future Archbishop of Canterbury), and Edward Hyde (later Earl of Clarendon and future Lord Chancellor to Charles II).[22] It was through some of these people – most particularly Hyde and Sheldon – that Morley was eventually to gain advancement. Hyde, who seems in particular to have held him in the highest regard to judge from his later writings, was to describe him in 1653 as 'the best man alive';[23] and, when writing in retirement, as a man 'of very eminent parts in all polite learning; of great wit, and readiness, and subtilty (sic) in disputation...[24]

Politics took a fresh turn in 1640/41 with the summoning of the Short and Long Parliaments, and the subsequent political upheavals were probably decisive for Morley's early career. The arrest of Laud removed an obstacle to promotion, Morley's contacts were able to exert influence, and Morley acquired, in turn, livings at Hartfield in Sussex[25], Mildenhall in Wiltshire[26], and Pennant in Montgomeryshire[27]. Hartfield came in 1640, Mildenhall in 1641, and Pennant in 1644. Hartfield is said to have been a 'sinecure' and, whatever the status, it is far from clear that Morley ever resided in or even visited any of these parishes.[28] There appears to be nothing to show the income of Hartfield but a parliamentary survey from the 1650s records an annual value of £200 *p.a.* for the rectory of Mildenhall out of which income an absentee rector, like Morley, would have had to pay a vicar or curate.[29] How far the income from the rectory of Mildenhall was compatible with his studentship is not clear but he was soon to surrender the studentship for a canonry of the cathedral to which the rules about a living wage may not have applied.

---

20 See *ODNB*: the conflicting entries are by John Spurr on Morley and Warren Chernaik on Waller; Waller (1606-1687) was both poet and politician.
21 R. Ollard, *Clarendon and his Friends* (London, 1987), p. 31.
22 Clarendon, *Life and Continuation*, vol. 1, pp. 42, 48; for the lives and importance of these men see e.g. *ODNB*.
23 W. D. Macray (ed.), *Calendar of Clarendon State Papers*, vol. 2 (Oxford, 1869), p. 271.
24 Clarendon, *Life and Continuation*, vol. 1, pp. 55-56.
25 TNA: E 331 Chichester/9, day oblit. 8/1640 (institution); *Liber Institutionum,* Series A 1556-1660, vol. 5, 17/8/1640 (institution); TNA, E 334/20, 18/12/1640 (registration of composition/bond arrangements).
26 TNA, E 331 Canterbury/11, 8/9/1641; *LI*, ibid. and E 334/20, both 17/12/1641.
27 TNA, E 331 St Asaph/13, 6/4/1644; NLof W, SA-MB-15.
28 Wood, *Athenae,* vol. 2, col. 769 ('a sinecure').
29 Hartfield: e.g. LPL, MS 903, ff. 255-385 nil; Mildenhall: TNA, C/94/3, *Survey of Church Livings,* vol. 3, f. 36r, 16/1/1656; Pennant: TNA, E 331 St Asaph/13, £11-16-9 written beside the record of Morley's institution to Pennant and £5-16-3 for the vicar are the figures of 1535 and probably out of date by 1644 (*Valor Ecclesiaticus* vol. 4 [London, 1810-1834], p. 451).

It may not be clear at this length of time how Morley came into the service of Carnarvon as chaplain in the 1620s nor even when he was ordained, but from this starting point the social nexus seems to have come into play. Carnarvon had been a ward of Philip Herbert, Earl of Pembroke and Montgomery, and had later married Pembroke's daughter.[30] It is hardly surprising, in view of this relationship, that Carnarvon should seek to advance his chaplain and that Morley should receive in turn the three parishes of Hartfield, Mildenhall, and Pennant.[31] With Pembroke's wife a relation by marriage of the Tuftons, one of whom, Sir Humphrey, was patron of Hartfield in faraway Sussex,[32] and with Pembroke himself patron of Mildenhall in nearby Wiltshire, Morley's initial appointment to Hartfield and the transfer to Mildenhall - possibly wealthier and certainly somewhat nearer to Oxford - become more explicable. Mysteries surround Pennant: appointment was directly in the bishop's gift, not Pembroke's, and the bishop, John Owen, had apparently lost the bishopric in 1642, but it is clear, from the relevant document, that Owen was still directing affairs from Conway and it is further likely that Pembroke, also Earl of Montgomery, was able to influence the bishop's decisions.[33]

The 'puritan' revolutionaries seem to have thought Morley sympathetic to their reform programme up till this time, at least, since he was sought as one of the preachers before Members of the House of Commons at St Margaret's Westminster in November 1640.[34] It is not clear, from the surviving terse and fragmentary evidence, what he said or how it was received by his congregation; nor, indeed, whether this was the only occasion on which he preached to the Commons. Morley claims, according to his own account written years later, to have preached that 'the Constitutions of both Church and State as...by Law established...were both of them the best in their kind that were in the Christian World'. He urged avoidance of 'Popery, or Presbytery, or Independency' (sic), but acknowledged the need to correct 'the faults or frailties of some particular men'.[35] How far this is a true or full account of his preaching and how far it proved acceptable to the majority of MPs is not clear; and it may, in fact, have been delivered on a separate occasion. Morley recounts that he was given 'a Piece of Plate with this inscription, "Donum Populi Anglicani" ' but complains that, while the Commons

---

30 See *ODNB* (entry for Carnarvon); under the system of wardship, a magnate (such as Pembroke) could purchase from the Crown the right to custody of an heir, if a minor, until he or she came of age, together with the power to manage and to enjoy the profits of the ward's property.

31 Morley was chaplain to Pembroke according to the Pembroke's entry in *ODNB* but there appears to be no evidence for this.

32 Sir Humphrey Tufton was married to the daughter of a Morley of Glynde, West Sussex (Mr Anthony Paice, BA drew my attention to this), but whether she was a relation of George or the name is a remarkable coincidence is too difficult to say.

33 See *ODNB* (for Owen); the 'appointing' document does not name the bishop but clearly states (in Latin) 'collation' (appointment by the bishop) and its issue from Conway on 6/4/1644 in the 15th year of his consecration (1629) which would fit the dates of Owen's episcopate 1629-1651 (NLofW, SA-MB-15).

34 *Journals of the House of Commons*, vol. 2 (London, 1803), p. 24; W. Notestein (ed.), *Journal of Sir Simonds D'Ewes,* (Yale, 1923), p. 18.

35 *Bishop of Winchester's Vindication of Himself from divers False, Scandalous, and Injurious Reflexions made upon him by Mr Richard Baxter* (London, 1683), pp. 403-04.

ordered printing of the sermons of three other preachers at that time, they denied him that honour because they were 'displeased' with his preaching.[36] The Journals of the House of Commons and D'Ewes both record, however, that the MPs of 1640 resolved to thank him, and they issued an order, whether through appreciation or simply out of courtesy, to print that particular sermon.[37] There is no reference to plate and no mention of any other preaching by Morley in either of the Journals.[38]

Promotions and his own actions clearly identified Morley with the royal cause by 1642. He became a Canon of Christ Church, surrendering his studentship, early in 1642.[39] It was at this time, it is claimed, that he subsequently gave the first year's 'profit' from his canonry to help the Royalists, by then at war, and that he was honoured, together with many other loyalists, with the doctorate as a reward, no doubt, after Edgehill, in November of the same year.[40] He also became, according to Wood, a royal chaplain at this time.[41] He seems to have retained some standing and favour with the Commons, however, as in 1643 he was summoned as a delegate to the Westminster Assembly.[42] MPs, clergymen, academics, and a delegation of Presbyterians from Scotland sat from 1643 to review church government, beliefs, and worship and ultimately to produce a new national religious settlement. Their reform programme proved, hardly surprisingly in view of his sermon, too radical for Morley, while his canonry and chaplaincy tied him to church and king and he never took his seat in the assembly.[43]

Morley was apparently with the king at critical times in the war and almost to the end. He may have been with Charles during the fruitless attempt to achieve a treaty between king and Parliament at Uxbridge in 1645; and more certainly when Charles was in the hands of the New Model Army at Newmarket in 1647 and when imprisoned at Carisbrooke (Isle of Wight) during the final efforts of Parliament to come to terms with him in the Treaty of Newport of 1648. The army allowed the king access to his chaplains, including Morley, at Newmarket, according to Hyde and, although there is no evidence that Morley played a part in the talks between king and the parliamentary commissioners at Uxbridge and Newport, he was probably at those places also in his role as a royal chaplain.[44] Morley and his former patron, the Earl of Pembroke,

---

36 Ibid., p. 405.
37 *Commons Journal*, vol. 2, p. 40; *D'Ewes Journal*, p. 88.
38 This account appears necessarily incomplete and contradictory for want of fuller information; Morley's account of offence taken by the House of Commons is retailed by Wood (Wood, *Athenae*, vol. 2, col. 769) and followed by Bussby (Bussby, 'Early Life of Morley', p. 21), *DNB*, and *ODNB*; Wood and Bussby give the date as 1640, *DNB* and *ODNB* 1642, but Morley's reference to four preachers appears to fit the numbers of preachers in 1640 (*Commons Journal*, vol. 2, p. 24; *D'Ewes Journal*, p. 18).
39 J. Horn (ed.), *Fasti Ecclesiae Anglicanae*/Oxford (London, 1996), p. 105; the vagueness - 'early in 1642' - is because the only source is Disbursement Book, Christ Church, xii.b.85 (no folios) which shows the transfer from student to canon, with part payment of stipend for the canonry, during Term 2 (January to March) 1642.
40 Wood, *Athenae*, vol. 2, col. 768 (profit), *Fasti*, col. 29 (DD); *JF* (DD).
41 Wood, *Athenae*, vol. 2, col. 768 and *JF* (chaplaincy, no dates).
42 *Commons Journal*, vol. 3, p. 287 (order to attend 23/10/1643); but, confusingly, 'discharged', 11/10/1643, p. 273.
43 R. S. Paul, *Assembly of the Lord* (Edinburgh, 1985), pp. 105, 550.

found themselves on opposite sides during the conflict and, indeed, at Uxbridge, while Morley was there as a royal chaplain, Pembroke was a parliamentary commissioner. How their relationship fared at this time is not known.

These actions and his association with such prominent Royalists as Hyde were enough to condemn him, and he chose expulsion from his posts, the canonry at Oxford, and the rectory of Mildenhall, in 1647/48 rather than submit to the new regime. Anthony Wood gives full details in his own colourful way of the purge of Royalists from the University of Oxford: in particular, the arrival of the visitors in the Spring of 1647, the appointment of a university delegation to deal with them, the selection of Morley to instruct (legal) counsel, and the order from the visitors in April 1648 to 'the Souldiarie' to remove, 'by strength', if necessary, all opponents. Heads of House, fellows, canons, chaplains, and scholars were all expelled and, most infamously, the wife of John Fell, University Vice-Chancellor and Dean of Christ Church – Fell himself was already in prison – who was left on a chair in the quadrangle until rescued by Morley and colleagues. These last proceedings – the expulsions – were overseen by the new Chancellor of the university, the Earl of Pembroke, no less, and, once more, it would be fascinating to know how relations stood between the two men after a crisis of such controversy, bitterness, and loss.[45]

Morley's final 'error' was to minister to Lord Capel, who had been originally critical of the king but who turned to the Royalist cause in the 1640s and was a prime mover of the Second Civil War for which he paid the price of trial and execution at the hands of Parliament. Capel was an MP in 1640/41, a commissioner for the king at Uxbridge in 1645, and Morley may have known him at least since those times. Morley administered communion early in the morning and accompanied him to the foot of the scaffold on the day of his execution, two months after Charles I's, in March 1649.[46] Morley appears to have chosen at this point to exile himself. The House of Lords had already ordered a pass in January 1648 for him 'to go beyond the Seas'.[47] He wrote to the Duke of Beaufort from Gravesend on 27 March 1649, and it would seem that he took ship from there at that time for the Continent where he was to spend the next 11 years in exile.[48]

---

44 W. D. Macray (ed.), *The History of the Rebellion and Civil Wars in England,* vol. IV, (Oxford, 1888), p. 228 (Newmarket); Wood, *Athenae,* vol. 2, col. 769 (Newport); *ODNB* (Uxbridge, but with no contemporary source for this).

45 Wood offers a none too clear account (Wood, *Athenae,* vol. 2, col. 769) but see, primarily, A. Wood, *History of the Visitation of the University of Oxford by a Parliamentary Commission 1647-1648,* (Oxford, 1873), *passim;* M. Burrows (ed.), *Register of the Visitors of the University of Oxford 1647-1658,* (Camden Society, 1881), pp. lxiii, lxiv, lxxi, lxxxii, cxii, and 20 (which closely follows Wood but with more 'balance'); I. Walton, *Lives of Donne, Wotton, Hooker, Herbert, and Sanderson,* (London, 1825), pp. 390-92; *WR.*

46 *HMC, 12th Report,* Appendix, Part IX (London, 1891), pp. 34-38, (3/1649, Morley); Macray, *History of Rebellion and Civil Wars,* vol. IV, p. 509; *ODNB.*

47 *Journals of the House of Lords,* (London, 1767-1830), vol. 9, p. 677, 25/1/1648, without explanation; I owe the information (that there was a pass), if not the reference, to John Spurr *(ODNB).*

48 *WR,* p. 377; *HMC, 12th Report,* p. 38.

CHAPTER 2 : EXILE

As with his life at Oxford in the 1620s, much uncertainty and lack of detail surrounds Morley's exile abroad. Frederick Bussby offers the most complete version of events and Robert Beddard, among others, summarises and brings out the main points clearly enough.[1] It is Morley himself, however, who provides in his *Several Treatises written upon Several Occasions*[2] the most authoritative, though far from complete, detail of his activities in noble and royal households during his eleven years on the continent; and much of his 'itinerary' can be tracked through his surviving correspondence from that time.

It would seem that Morley crossed the North Sea from Gravesend to the Netherlands in March 1649. There he joined the king, Charles II, at The Hague. Charles, intent on recovering his kingdom, set his sights on Jersey, which was the only part of his inheritance still unoccupied by the rebels and still loyal to his cause. The royal household moved, according to Bussby, from The Hague, through Delft, Rotterdam, Breda, Antwerp, Brussels, and Bruges to St Germaine en Laye and Caen *en route*, ultimately, for Jersey. Morley himself mentions Paris and 'afterwards' to Caen, spending '6 weeks' at the latter, in the households of Sir Richard Brown, ambassador at Paris, and Lady Ormond respectively.[3]

He did not continue with the king to the Channel Islands. Instead he remained behind in Paris where he had, in his own words, 'a very little but very convenient lodging', dining 'allwais' with 'my Lady Moreton', one of 'the Queen's Maydes', and joined John Cosin (another exile, Master of Peterhouse, Cambridge, Dean of Peterborough before the Interregnum, among other posts, and Bishop of Durham after the Restoration) in ministering to the Protestant congregation of emigrés among the household of Queen Henrietta Maria, widow of Charles I, at the Louvre.[4] John Evelyn recalls one or two such occasions in the winter months of 1649/50.[5] Charles soon returned from Jersey, the venture having failed, and Morley re-joined him in the Netherlands.[6] Charles came to terms with the Scottish Presbyterians in May 1650, in spite of objections from Morley,[7] and sailed from Breda for Scotland in another attempt to regain his kingdoms, which was to end, disastrously from his point of view, with the Battles of Dunbar (1650) and Worcester (1651).

---

1 F. Bussby, 'An Anglican in Exile', in *Church Quarterly Review,* (1965), pp. 426-38; R. A. Beddard, 'Reward for Services Rendered: Charles II and the Restoration Bishops of Worcester 1660-1663', *Midland History,* vol. XXIX (2004), pp. 61-91; see also entries on Morley in *DNB, ODNB.*
2 George Morley, *Several Treatises written upon Several Occasions,* (London, 1683).
3 Ibid., p. viii; BL, Harleian MS 7190, f. 146 (20/1/1652?); the Duke of Ormond was Lord Lieutenant of Ireland under Charles I and Charles II.
4 BL, Harleian MS 7190, f. 146 (20/1/1652?).
5 E. S. de Beer (ed.), *The Diary of John Evelyn,* vol. 2 (Oxford, 2006), pp. 251 (5/12/1649), 252 (1/3/1650).
6 *HMC, Bath MSS,* vol. 2 (London, 1907), p. 92.
7 W. D. Macray (ed.), *Calendar of Clarendon State Papers,* vol. 2 (Oxford, 1869), p. 50.

Morley again did not accompany the king, possibly because of religious and political differences between himself and the Scots, as Bussby and Beddard suggest, or because he thought the expedition too hazardous. He moved briefly to The Hague and then to Antwerp, where he lodged in the household of Sir Charles Cottrell for 'one year or thereabouts'[8] before beginning his long association lasting, according to his own account, 'about three or four years' – from 1650 to 1654 – at Antwerp as chaplain within the household of Edward Hyde, who was then Charles II's Chancellor of the Exchequer and Ambassador to Spain.[9] Morley ministered particularly to Anne Hyde, Edward Hyde's daughter and herself the future wife of James Duke of York (James II, 1685-1688).

When Anne moved to the household of the Princess Royal (Mary, daughter of Charles I and wife of William II of Orange) at The Hague, Morley went with her to become chaplain to Elizabeth, sometime Queen of Bohemia (James I's daughter and aunt to Charles II and James, Duke of York).[10] He remained with her for the next two and a half years from 1654 to 1656 and then re-joined the king and the Hydes, by this time at Breda, according to Wood, for the last four years of his exile, from 1656 to 1660.[11]

Those were Morley's main lodgings – with the Cottrells for a year or so, with the Hydes for three or four years, with the Queen of Bohemia for a further two and a half years, and finally with the king and the Hydes for the remaining four years. He made several forays during these times. While in the service of the Queen, Morley mentions a visit to Heidelberg in July 1655, he wrote six letters to Cottrell from Cologne in September 1655, and other surviving correspondence shows he also travelled to Breda and Dusseldorf in the course of 1655.[12] Contemporary letters similarly reveal visits to Antwerp, Brussels, and Bruges while with the king and the Hydes during his last four years in Breda.[13]

---

8   Wood, *Athenae*, vol. 2, col. 769; Cottrell had been in the service of Philip Herbert, Earl of Pembroke and Morley's patron, in the 1630s, steward of Elizabeth of Bohemia in the 1650s, and in the 1660s and 1670s was MP, Master of Ceremonies, and Master of Requests.
9   *Several Treatises*, p. vi.
10 Ibid.
11 Ibid., p. ix; G. Morley, *Ad Cl. Virum Janum Ulitium Epistolae Duae* (printed in *Several Treatises*), pp. 6, 67; Wood, *Athenae*, vol. 2, col. 770; F. J. Routledge (ed.), *Calendar of Clarendon State Papers*, vol. 4, (Oxford, 1932), pp. 106-611, 19 letters 11/1658-4/1659; *Surtees Society*, vol. 52 (1868), p. 291, 2/1660.
12 For Heidelberg, BL, Harleian MS 6942, f. 149, 7/1655?; for Cologne, Cottrell MSS, private collection, see TNA, NRA 996 and typescript HRO, DC/K4/12/2, 9/1655; for Breda, *Calendar Clarendon SP*, vol. 2, pp. 333, 339, 4/1654; W. D. Macray (ed.), *Calendar of Clarendon State Papers*, vol. 3 (Oxford, 1876), p. 7, 1/1655; G. F. Warner (ed.), *Nicholas Papers*, vol. 2 (Camden Society, 1892), pp. 244, 251, 4/1655; for Dusseldorf, ibid., vol. 2, p. 156, 1/1655; Macray (ed.), *Calendar Clarendon SP*, vol. 3, p. 26, 3/1655.
13 For Antwerp, *Calendar Clarendon SP*, vol. 3, p. 146, 2/1659; vol. 4, p. 463, 12/1659, for Brussels, ibid., vol. 4, p. 106, 11/1658; for Brussels and Bruges, no dates, *Several Treatises*, p. ix; also Beddard, 'Reward for Services Rendered', p. 63.

Exile was a particularly formative time for Morley. He returned to England a widely travelled man, either visiting or living in some of the larger cities of the United Provinces, the Spanish Netherlands, France, and 'Germany'. These were major centres of religious, economic, and political activity. Religion was a particularly complex subject and highly relevant to Morley. War, caused in part by religious divergence, had raged over northern Europe, involving the numerous states within the Holy Roman Empire,[14] France, Spain, Sweden, the Netherlands, on and off, for thirty years by the time of his arrival on the continent and, while war continued between France and Spain into the 1650s, the Treaty of Westphalia (1648) brought peace within the Empire. All the minor rulers within the Empire had gained the right to choose between Catholicism and Lutheranism for their state since 1555[15] and their subjects were then required to conform. Westphalia extended this principle to Calvinists as well as Lutherans. This was the arrangement - a Catholic emperor with rulers of the numerous states within the Empire able to choose between Catholicism, Lutheranism, and Calvinism - when Morley was travelling through the Empire. This was far from 'pure' toleration, merely a step, with freedom for rulers, but not their subjects, to choose between the three religions; but an important step, nonetheless, towards the ideal of freedom of choice for everyone. A somewhat larger version of toleration was the position in France where Morley also spent time and where Catholicism was the prevailing religion but where the Huguenots (Calvinists) were allowed, by the Edict of Nantes (1598), to practise public worship in certain specified towns - two religions, thus, within one kingdom.

Morley was on the continent at a critical time and his acquaintance with such developments as these - matters of war and peace - was far closer than from England and Oxford. He witnessed wars of religion which, on top of his experiences in England, may have increased his fears of strife and devastation. He observed countries and communities with different religions living side by side which may have engendered thoughts of compromise, among Protestants at least, on matters of belief and practice.

Whether because Morley found the atmosphere stimulating, or because he came into contact with theologians whom he would probably never otherwise have met, or whether, more simply, his household duties were flexible enough to allow time for thinking and writing, exile proved a productive time. He engaged in controversies with theologians, and the 1650s saw the formulation and publication of important theological subjects. After re-joining the king in the late 1650s, he examined - and denounced - at Breda invocation of the saints[16] and, while at Bruges, he produced his first treatise, or pamphlet, attacking transubstantiation, with a further 'vindication'

---

14 The Holy Roman Empire was a conglomeration of several hundred principalities, kingdoms, duchies, cities, with Austria at its head, under the Holy Roman Emperor (who also ruled Hungary); Morley himself refers to 'Germany' at least twice in correspondence of the 1650s (BL, Harleian MS 6942, ff. 144, 150).
15 Treaty of Augsburg 1555 between the Emperor Charles V and his underling rulers which established the principle, *cuius regio eius religio* (whoever rules, his shall be the religion) with the choice at that time confined to Catholicism or Lutheranism.
16 G. Morley, *Ad Cl. Virum Janum Ulitium Epistolae Duae,* written in '1659' and printed in *Several Treatises* in 1683; my thanks are due to the late F. Bussby who acquired translations of the letters now lodged at HRO, DC/K4/11/3.

of this work somewhat later.¹⁷ These made clear his views on two central tenets of Catholic faith.

His rejection of invocation of saints came in his *Two Letters to Jan Ulitius,* in which he sets out to prove that neither in belief nor practice did St Augustine or any of the Early Fathers support the concept. In the first letter Morley challenges the authenticity of St Augustine's 'Meditations' which appears to support such intercession and dismisses the work as 'counterfeit'.¹⁸ In the second, much longer, letter, he denounces invocation because it implies worship of saints and demeans the role of Christ who was both 'Son of God' and 'Son of Man', and 'none can be found more powerful with God or more propitious to Mankind'.¹⁹ He next condemns various Catholic liturgical items – a Breviary, a Psalter, a Litany – together with engravings on walls of numerous 'edifices' in places such as Brussels. He proceeds, finally, in an apparently amazing display of learning, to dissect the writings of a string of Greek and Latin Fathers. The letter is laced, needless to say, with the usual censures – 'dunghill', 'idolatry', 'superstition' – which serve to enliven the text and underline his prejudice against 'popery'.

He condemned, in much the same way, the Catholic view of communion – transubstantiation – in his 'Argument drawn from Sense against Transubstantiation'. Morley asserts that Catholics employ faith to justify their claim that the bread became the flesh of Christ, the wine his blood, while Morley himself puts his trust in his senses – seeing, hearing, smelling, feeling, tasting – to insist that the bread and wine remain the same before and after consecration. His 'Argument' was challenged apparently and at some stage, 'a little while after the first', Morley produced a second pamphlet in much the same vein to rebut the challenge. There is nothing in the scriptures about transubstantiation. Miracles have to be evident to the senses – water changing into wine, for example – and the bread and wine undergo no such change: 'We taste in the Sacrament...as We by our taste find it to be and that is Bread and not flesh, Wine and not blood.'²⁰ Christ's body cannot be in more than one place at a time. The essence of his standpoint, that we must rely on our senses is, for all the convolution and imagery, clear – and blunt – enough, and verges on the simplistic when discussing the empty tomb in the first pamphlet, for example, as he writes 'if he (Christ) could not be seen, he was not there'.²¹ Nor can he resist the odd swipe against popery – as in so much of his writing – by remarking in the first pamphlet that 'Papists are as gros and grosse Idolators than ever any of the Heathens were'; and in the second, Catholics are dismissed as 'Idolatrous' and transubstantiation as 'one of...the mysteries of Satan'.²²

---

17 'An Argument Drawn from the Evidence and Certainty of Sense Against the Doctrine of Transubstantiation'; 'A Vindication of the Argument Drawn from Sense Against Transubstantiation'; the date of the first pamphlet is 1659, of the second 'a little while after the first', i.e. 1659 or thereabouts. (*Several Treatises,* p.ix, in which collection both pamphlets can be found).
18 First Letter to Ulitius, p. 4.
19 Second Letter to Ulitius, p. 23.
20 A Vindication of the Argument, p. 19.
21 An Argument Against Transubstantiation, p. 19.
22 Ibid., p. 22; A Vindication of the Argument, p. 16.

Morley came into contact with congregations and religious communities quite different from his own Church of England. He would have observed religious belief and practice, Catholic, Lutheran, and Calvinist, first hand, and most famously at Brussels with the Catholic Darcy and at Caen with the Protestant Bouchard.[23] Morley declined an invitation to participate in Bouchard's Calvinist congregation at Caen in 1649 because, the existence of his own 'congregation' and language problems apart, Calvinists had rejected episcopacy and supported regicide. He encountered Darcy in the Jesuit College at Brussels in 1649, and a 'debate' followed in which Darcy expressed willingness to compromise on such points as the Latin Service, the sacrament in one or two kinds, and clerical celibacy but not on matters of faith; while Morley challenged this by claiming that the Catholic Church had acknowledged error in the past and so should not refuse to compromise out of hand. Nothing was produced, needless to say, to bridge the gap. It was a case of debit and credit on both sides in assessing performance. Darcy was flexible with his practical concessions but obstinate over faith; Morley marshalled support from Pope Innocent and St Augustine to demonstrate his scholarship but, in what can only look like a moment of monumental tactlessness, he appeared to have likened the Catholic Church this time to 'a pesthouse'. The author of the account, anonymous but witnessed by Prince Neuburgh, one of Morley's party at the college, insists, nonetheless, that the meeting drew to a close 'with terms of great civility and respect, neither of them seeming to have taken any offence'!

Morley claims, not surprisingly in light of these events and comments, that he kept his distance from both religions, insisting that he 'never had any thing (sic) to do with the Classis...nor ever was so much as once present at a Mass, nor kneeled at the Exposition...of the Host'; proceeding to denounce (again) 'Popish Idolatries and Superstitions' and reject (again) 'novel Usages and Practices' of 'the Classis'.[24] Distancing himself from 'the Classis' also arose several times in his correspondence, presumably because he felt under suspicion as a recognised anti-Laudian and pro-Calvinist sympathiser, likely to have involved himself with Calvinist or 'Presbyterian' churches while on the continent. He claims in two letters of the 1650s that he led a congregation without 'subordination' to 'the Classis'. He insists in these letters that he followed the 'liturgy' and the 'rites' of the 'Church of England'[25] and he asserts he taught 'the fundamentals of the Protestant Religion as it is (sic)...professed in our Church'. He also proclaimed himself 'a true Son of the Church of England as it is Established by Law', though he never seems to have explained in detail exactly what he understood by these 'fundamentals' and 'the Church of England'.[26]

---

23 For Darcy, *Several Treatises* contains *The Summe of a Short Conference Betwixt Father Darcy and Doctour Morley at Bruxells* (1649); for Bouchard (or Bochart), LPL, MS 595, pp. 1-3 and, in the Preface to *Several Treatises*, Morley's summary of the exchange with Bouchard, p. viii.
24 *Several Treatises*, pp. vii, xii; the 'Classis' is a reference to Calvinist (and Presbyterian) church government by which each church was run by a council of elders (the minster and lay members), above them, regional councils and, overall, a national council; the term *classis* is Latin for 'a fleet' and should apply, strictly speaking, to the regional councils under which were the individual churches.
25 BL, Harleian MS 6942, ff. 149, 150 (dates obscured, 12/7 and 8/6/1653 or 1655?).
26 *Several Treatises*, pp. vi, xv.

Morley had held parishes in England and Wales in the 1640s but no evidence survives to show that he ever went to or performed duties at any of them and it may have been that while in the Netherlands he gained experience and insight into parochial ministry. Like any parish priest he conducted services, including baptisms and communion, and visited the sick. Morley is particularly detailed about his round of business at Antwerp - divine service twice a day, catechism once a week, eucharist once a month, as well as baptisms and funerals, according to 'our liturgy'.[27]

During all this time Morley suffered considerable poverty. He tells us he left England with £130, a substantial sum in the seventeenth century but not much when facing an uncertain and precarious future.[28] There is hardly any information about remuneration - no detailed 'accounts' - and the income on which he survived has to be surmised from comments, frequently vague and sometimes possibly contradictory, in his writings and letters. By 1650 he was writing, in the middle of recounting the misery Hyde's son had brought upon the family, that he himself had only £20 left and he never mentions any payment from, only the financial difficulties of, 'this family' - presumably the Hydes - in letters written in the early 1650s.[29] He did some tutoring while with them in Antwerp but he found such work abhorrent, 'enduring the vexatious employment of teaching little children' and concluding that 'nothing but pure Necesity shall make me turne Schoolmaster'. This went on 'for about a year' but he could then 'endure it no longer'. Morley remarks that his successor was paid £20 *p.a.* and that his own income during his time with 'this family' came to £30 *p.a.* but from what sources - teaching possibly, but apparently not the 'family' - he does not say.[30]

When he joined Elizabeth, Morley is quite specific in his treatise and correspondence that he received subsistence - 'diet and lodging' - but no stipend from Elizabeth, admitting that he would go with her to Heidelberg in 'Germany...because I know not otherwise how to subsist'; and he wrote letters begging free lodging from her, unsuccessfully at that time, to save himself 'the hire of my chamber'.[31] He also mentions, hardly surprisingly, a debt of £50 which was probably driving his efforts to secure support.[32] His finances may have looked up a little during this excursion with Elizabeth to Heidelberg and Dusseldorf in the Palatinate as the Elector had agreed to pay him £50 *p.a.* but for what service and for how long is, again, not clear.[33]

---

27 Ibid., p. v.
28 Ibid., p. vii.
29 BL, Harleian MS 6942, ff. 140 (26/11/1650), 148 (13/7/1652), 147 (23/11/1652), 149 (12/7/1653); see for 'misery', R. Ollard, *Clarendon and Friends,* (London, 1987), p. 142.
30 For dislike of teaching, BL, Harleian MS 6942, ff. 152 (25/5/1652), 150 (8/6/1653?), Harleian MS 7190, f. 147 (9/11/1652); for £20 and £30, Harleian MS 6942, ff. 149, 150.
31 *Several Treatises,* p. vii; BL, Harleian MS 6942, ff. 149, (12/7/1653?), 150 (8/6/1653?); Cottrell MSS, four letters, 9/1655.
32 BL, Harleian MS 6942, f. 149 (12/7/1653?).
33 BL, Harleian MS 6942, f. 150 (date obscured, 8/6/1653? 1655?), also possibly f. 144 (1/11/1655); the Palatinate was one of the three hundred or so states, now modern Germany, which, along with Austrian and Hungary, lay under the overlordship of the Holy Roman Emperor and whose ruler was entitled 'Elector' because he was one of the seven princes who 'elected' the Emperor.

All this information so far – irksome teaching duties, service for nothing, minute income, and debt – may justify the conclusion that these experiences made him more sympathetic to the plight of many of his diocesan clergy later in his career and may have encouraged him towards attempts to reform their income. He was, on the other hand and in spite of straitened circumstance, ever generous. He found £15 'out of mine little remainder of stock' (£20), to bail out the Hydes in their troubles;[34] and on at least one occasion he was involved in the purchase and dispatch of 'bookes of devotion' to someone, probably Sheldon's nephew, in England.[35] Both of these activities imply either means of some kind or incredible generosity. He claims, moreover, in a letter written in the 1650s to have received, over four years, 'from some friend or other', £550 (though £200 of this was a loan).[36] Money from friends such as these may help to explain how he survived this difficult time. In *Several Treatises,* written much later, he further claims to have lent more 'yearly' than the £130 he had originally brought with him and to have returned to England in 1660 with more than when he left.[37] This, if an accurate recollection, would confirm his generosity and imply excellent financial management.

Morley had shown loyalty to Church and Crown by sacrificing his career, suffering exile, and enduring poverty. He had sharpened his views on several theological issues. He had performed the daily duties and shared the mean existence of the humbler parish clergy and their curates. He was, thus, highly suitable for advancement in the English Church when the time came. He enjoyed repute and recognition in the households of leading figures such as the Ormonds, the Cottrells, the Hydes, and the Newcastles[38] and *entrée* into the counsels of the king himself before whom he preached, according to his own account, at Breda (before the Scottish venture), at Cologne (while chaplain to Elizabeth), and frequently after joining Charles and following him to Breda, Brussels, and Bruges.[39] This gave him insight, no doubt, into policy, both the thinking and the constraints, at the highest levels. He had been involved, moreover, in the talks at Breda in 1650. When the need arose – following surrender of the office of Lord Protector of England by Richard Cromwell (Oliver's son) in 1659 – for contact between Charles and Hyde on the one hand and Monck[40] and the Presbyterians in England on the other hand, not only was Morley known to the Royalists but he had also had opportunities to sharpen his skills in politics and diplomacy and so was a natural choice to act as emissary between the two sides.

---

34 BL, Harleian MS 6942, f. 140 (26/11/1650).
35 BL, Harleian MS 6942, ff. 145 (9/8/1655?), 147 (23/11/1652), 149 (12/7/1653?), 150 (8/6/165? date obscured); business stretched over four letters but the dates of three of them are obscured and it is difficult to tell whether there was one or several transactions.
36 BL, Harleian MS 6942, f. 150 (8/6/1653 or 1655?).
37 *Several Treatises,* p. vii.
38 The Duke of Newcastle was the Royalist commander of the Whitecoats at Marston Moor (1644); after this defeat he went into exile and, when he returned in 1660, he remained on the fringe of court and government.
39 *Several Treatises,* p. ix.
40 George Monck (1608-1670), Duke of Albemarle from 1660, originally a soldier with service under Cromwell, was central to the restoration of Charles II who made him Commander in Chief of the Forces 1660-1670 and First Lord of the Treasury 1667-1670.

CHAPTER 3 : MISSION TO ENGLAND

Political upheaval in England towards the end of the 1650s changed everything. Oliver Cromwell, the Lord Protector, died in September 1658 and Richard Cromwell, his heir and successor, proved utterly inadequate and resigned in May 1659. George Monck, military commander and governor in Scotland, took the initiative in January 1660. He marched south, dismissed Parliament, and approved the election of a new 'Convention Parliament'. Both of its houses passed a resolution on 1 May 1660 that 'the Government is, and ought to be, by king, Lords, and Commons' and on 8 May Charles II was proclaimed king.[1] Charles duly returned to Dover on 25 May and to London on the twenty-ninth. It was these events which were to propel Morley centre-stage in national politics from the Spring of 1660.

Cromwell had faced difficulties - Penruddock's Royalist rebellion in March 1655, for example, and at the other extreme, Venner's Fifth Monarchy Men in April 1657 - but the swift and steep descent of the Republic into oblivion began in September 1658 with his death and the succession of his son, Richard, as Lord Protector. Richard Cromwell was even less adroit than his father at managing Parliament and, fatally, could not command respect from the Army. Within months the army and Parliament were locked in conflict over pay and principles - republicanism and religion - and the expulsion of Parliaments twice over in 1659 forced Richard Cromwell's retirement from politics. A Royalist rebellion led by George Booth broke out in Cheshire during August 1659 in the midst of these struggles, and the City of London went on strike over taxation. With political paralysis prevailing, George Monck marched south from Scotland in January 1660 and, by February 1660, had established his base in the City of London. Monck ordered the return of all the original members of the Long Parliament of 1640 which, before dissolving itself, made the arrangements for the election of a new Parliament - the 'Convention Parliament'[2] - in March 1660.

---

1 For resolution, *Journals of the House of Commons,* vol. 8 (London, 1802), p. 8; *Journals of the House of Lords,* vol. 11 (London, 1767-1830), p. 8; for proclamation, *Commons Journal,* vol. 8, p. 16, *Lords Journal,* vol. 11, p. 18; A. Browning (ed.), *English Historical Documents, 1660-1714,* vol. 8 (London, 1953), p. 58.
2 It is known as the Convention Parliament because, although an elected body like all the other parliaments, it had not been summoned by the Crown.

Charles II and his advisers, still on the continent, had read the signs and early in April 1660 issued the Declaration of Breda which promised 'a free and general Pardon' for wrongdoers (ostentatiously 'upon the word of a King'), payment of army arrears, settlement of the land claims, and 'a Liberty to tender Consciences' in matters of religion – all carefully subject to the final verdict of Parliament.[3] The following month the new Convention Parliament welcomed the king's Declaration, passed the resolution about government by king, lords, and commons, issued the proclamation – trumpeted forth at the Palace of Westminster and, among other places, Whitehall, Temple Bar, and the Royal Exchange – and sent a commission with the official invitation to Charles II to return as King of England. Among the commissioners were, interestingly, the Earl of Pembroke, Morley's patron of the 1640s, Lord Fairfax, Commander in Chief of the New Model Army who had destroyed Charles I's remaining hopes at Naseby in 1645 and, perhaps a little less surprisingly, Sir George Booth who had led the abortive Royalist rebellion against the Protectorate in the summer of 1659.

The regime of Cromwell collapsed for many reasons. Most immediate were the succession of the inadequate and incompetent Richard Cromwell who lacked the confidence of the army; the debts of the regime; and the conflicts over pay and principle between the army and Parliament. The regime had seemed to do its best at times, more fundamentally, to frighten and antagonise conservative – influential conservative – opinion: the Parliament of the Saints[4] in 1653 with its radical reforming proposals concerning the courts and tithes, for example; and then the switch to rule by Major-Generals in 1655 1657[5] exercising arbitrary tax-collecting powers. All these were bound to disturb the propertied and professional classes – lawyers, clergy, and gentry in particular. The fundamental flaw became abundantly clear: that Cromwell could not rule without the army to suppress his enemies at home and abroad, and not without Parliament to give him legitimacy. The problem was that the two – army and Parliament – were simply not compatible. Even army figures like Monck came to see that rule with the consent of the powerful propertied classes was essential. It seemed that there was no alternative to 'government by king, lords, and commons' in a country where property spoke with a loud voice. The elections for the Convention Parliament in 1660 and, later in 1661, the Cavalier Parliament, both with their Royalist majorities, proved the point.[6] It was the army, ironically, which did the deed: it had brought down the last king in the first place and now it was the only body which, led by General Monck, was able to bring back a new king.

---

3 Breda can be found in e.g. *Lords Journal*, vol. 11, p. 7; *Commons Journal*, vol. 8, p. 5; W. Cobbett (ed.), *Parliamentary History of England*, vol. IV (London, 1808), col. 16; Browning, *English Historical Documents, 1660-1714*, p. 57.
4 This Parliament, known variously as 'the Parliament of the Saints', 'The Nominated Parliament', and 'the Barebone's Parliament' (1653), was a truly experimental and revolutionary assembly called by Cromwell in his search for a settlement of the constitution.
5 A phase from August 1655 to January 1657 of direct military government under which England and Wales were divided into ten regions each governed by a major-general who answered to the Lord Protector.
6 R. Hutton, *The Restoration: A Political and Religious History of England and Wales 1658-1667* (Oxford, 1985), pp. 111-13; 153.

From this train of events, climaxing in the return of Charles II, it may seem that the restoration of monarchy was inevitable. The collapse of the Protectorate probably was inevitable; the restoration of the monarchy, however, was not entirely so. For one thing, luck, good and bad, played its usual part in politics: bad luck for the Republic that Richard Cromwell, a man with no military or political skills, became head of state through inheritance; good luck for royalism that Monck for whatever motive, principle or personal gain, assumed control of affairs. Insofar as luck would determine events, there could be no certainty that the revival of monarchy and the return of Charles II would be the outcome.

A decade and more of civil wars had thrown up, moreover, a kaleidoscope of issues and groupings conflicting with each other, dividing communities, friends, and even families, and bequeathing a legacy of strife and bitterness. There were still adherents of Church and king but there were also plenty of natural opponents of monarchy: regicides, republicans, military generals, rank and file soldiers and a host of religious groups from the more 'moderate' Presbyterians, Congregationalists, and Independents to an array of extremist sects – Ranters, Seekers, Quakers, and Fifth Monarchy Men – who really did seek to turn the world of the seventeenth century upside down in the 1650s and who, with the overthrow of the monarchy, had enjoyed the freedom to experiment with new forms of government and worship.[7]

It was from these groups that ex-army officers, Lambert and Ludlow, were able to raise forces in another rebellion in the Spring of 1660. The Convention Parliament was well on with its plans by this time to restore Charles II and monarchy, and this was the last chance of opponents to stop the whole process. The restoration plans of the conservatives seemed momentarily threatened and, though the main centres of resistance, the Midlands, Yorkshire, and Wiltshire, were easily crushed by Monck in April 1660,[8] many of these revolutionaries survived into the 1660s and 1670s as an underclass, 'a cultural matrix...aflame with enormities and enmities...which had lost the habit of church attendance, had abandoned the regime of episcopal discipline, or fallen prey to apathy and cynicism';[9] and they occasionally broke to the surface as in the Venner Rising of January 1661 and the Yorkshire revolt of 1663. Events such as these served as occasional reminders of the fragility of 'government by king, lords, and commons' in the 1660s and 1670s.

The restorers could count on 'the fervent' – Royalists and Anglicans – but these alone would not be enough. What was required was a coalition of broader support.

---

7   C. Hill, *The World Turned Upside Down* (London, 1972), *passim;* D. Cressy, *Birth, Marriage and Death: Ritual Religion and the Life Cycle in Tudor and Stuart England* (Oxford, 1997), *passim.*
8   Hutton, *The Restoration,* pp. 113-16.
9   Cressy, *Birth, Marriage and Death,* p. 12.

Memories of the 1630s still coloured thinking in the 1660s: certainly among moderate Protestants who feared another dose of Laudian worship and even among the propertied classes with their memories of arbitrary taxation under Royalist government in the 1630s. These groups had to be won over. They sought safeguards and, before the return of the king could be assured, a host of issues remained to be settled: the army, its pay and the constitutional controls over it; Parliament, its meetings and powers; the boroughs, their composition and powers; finance, the royal income and taxes to pay for it; land, the ownership of Crown, church, and private estates nationalised by Cromwell; and religion, the search for agreement on a new national church to bring the diverse and warring groups together. Even if the restoration of the monarchy was the most likely outcome of the crisis of 1658-1660, the exact nature of the settlement between monarch and subjects remained far from clear. With so many groups and so many issues, a thorough and lasting settlement must have seemed a remote prospect. There would always be objectors to proposals, always obstacles to agreement, and it is a wonder - and therefore far from inevitable - that any agreement or settlement emerged at all; and in fact, concerning religion, compromise was never able to overcome division in the end.

This was the stage on to which Morley ventured in March 1660. Littered with complex issues and numerous hostile groups, it was a stage extremely difficult to navigate. There are many actors on the stage - not least Hyde (Clarendon) and the king himself among them - and most matters, though contentious enough, were settled, with reforms and safeguards, in the first two or three years of the Restoration. The part offered to Morley - contact with religious opponents and an interim agreement, if not yet a long term settlement, of religious divisions - was the most challenging of all and must have looked well-nigh impossible to play. There was certainly nothing inevitable about a happy outcome for all concerned.

Monck had opened contact with the royal party, still at Breda, in March 1660. The decision was made by the Royalists to send Morley to England to meet the Presbyterians[10] and he was in London by the end of March or beginning of April 1660.[11] Morley was presumably seen as their best hope, the acceptable face of the

---

10   The fullest modern accounts of the mission are G. R. Abernathy, 'English Presbyterians and the Stuart Restoration 1648-1663', *TAPS*, vol. 55, part 2 (1965), pp. 46-66; R. S. Bosher, *Making of the Restoration Settlement*, (London, 1951), pp. 108-14, 126-27, 134-35.
11   Contemporary correspondence gives an indication but not a precise date: Morley was in England by the '30th March 1660' according to Broderick (R. Scrope and T. Monkhouse (eds), *State Papers Collected by Edward Earl of Clarendon*, vol. 3 [Oxford, 1786], p. 714); Ross in a letter of the '11th/21st March 1660' says Morley was leaving for London 'next' week (*HMC, Bath MSS*, vol. 2 [London, 1907], p. 144); another letter, written by Cottrell at Breda on the '30th March 1660' (Bod Clarendon MS 70, f. 207; also F. J. Routledge (ed.), *Calendar of Clarendon State Papers*, vol. 4, [Oxford, 1932], p. 610) states Morley would not be leaving for England 'till Thursday'; all depends, for precise dating, on which system - old style or new - is applied but in either case he must have begun his journey towards the end of March and the beginning of April; this also leaves uncertain how long the journey took.

Royalists, with his Calvinist sympathies and his former friendships with Hampden and Goodwin. Some contemporaries thought him highly suitable. Hyde, who would not otherwise have chosen him, of course, described Morley in successive letters as 'a right worthy person as well of habit as integrity' and 'a very worthy and discreet Person'; while one of Hyde's agents, Alan Broderick, acclaimed Morley as worth 'ten Lord Mordaunts ...A worthier person is no where of his profession...'[12] The Mordaunts themselves, moreover, both wrote warmly about him.[13]

Morley's remit, over and above 'frequent Conferences with those of the Presbyterian party', was by no means clear either to himself or to later researchers.[14] No such statement – no official document – survives and, in fact, there may never have been a set of specific instructions. A letter from Morley to Hyde during the mission, asking for guidance, appears to confirm this.[15] It is more likely that Hyde, not really knowing what to expect by way of conditions and attitudes, outlined some general suggestions which he clarified in later letters or which became clearer in Morley's mind during the mission: to check temptation among his own side, Anglicans and Royalists, to talk – with 'heat', 'passion', and 'distemper' – of triumph and revenge;[16] to allay Presbyterians' suspicions about Charles II's Catholicism;[17] to generate a spirit of goodwill and co-operation on both sides – the right 'Temper' – 'by a freindly (sic) and familiar manner...to gayne upon them and to get an interest in them';[18] and, ultimately, no doubt, to explore the possibilities for any putative settlement.

Whether there was anything more – ulterior or devious – is debateable. The Royalists, led by Charles II himself and Edward Hyde, may have been determined from the start to deceive the Presbyterians and to restore the Church of England in its entirety, without any reforms or concessions, with Morley, wittingly or unwittingly, their agent at this time.[19] The Declaration of Breda, issued by Charles II in April 1660, while Morley was in England, promised 'liberty of conscience' and 'indulgence'.[20] How far this was a reflection of sincere commitment to the principle of toleration, how far a smokescreen to hide his views and to please as many people as possible, is difficult to say. Clarendon's letters at this time, one aspiring to 'this grande affayre of the Church', another expressing his hope, referring to the Presbyterians, to 'reduce them to such a

---

12 Bod Clarendon MS 70, f. 61r (12/3/1660); P. Barwick, *Life of John Barwick*, (London, 1724), p. 517 (16/4/1660); Scrope and Monkhouse, *State Papers*, vol. 3, p. 714 (30/3/1660); Mordaunt was a peer and, in exile in the 1650s, an abortive Royalist conspirator who held honorific posts in the Restoration.
13 Bod Clarendon MS 72, ff. 63r (26/4/1660), 63Br (26/4/1660); Scrope and Monkhouse, *State Papers*, vol. 3, pp. 720-21 and *Calendar Clarendon SP*, vol. 4, p. 666 (19/4/1660).
14 Barwick, *Life of John Barwick*, p. 525 (22/4/1660).
15 Scrope and Monkhouse, *State Papers*, vol. 3, p. 722 (5/4/1660).
16 Bod Clarendon MS 71, ff. 151v (n.d., written by Hyde?); Barwick, *Life of John Barwick*, pp. 520 (16/4/1660), p. 526 (22/4/1660); *Calendar Clarendon SP*, vol. 4, p. 636 (Morley, 5/4/1660).
17 Bod Clarendon MS 72, f. 117v; Scrope and Monkhouse, *State Papers*, vol. 3, p. 735; F. J. Routledge (ed.), *Calendar of Clarendon State Papers*, vol. 5, (Oxford, 1970), p. 3 (all the same, all 1/5/1660); also ibid., p. 635 (24/1/1671).
18 Barwick, *Life of John Barwick*, p. 525 ('Temper', 22/4/1660); Bod Clarendon MS 72, f. 199v ('to gayne' etc. 4/5/1660).
19 For discussions of motives e.g. Bosher, *Making of the Restoration Settlement*, e.g. pp. 89, 123, 136-39; Abernathy, 'English Presbyterians', p. 47; I. M. Green, *Re-establishment of the Church of England*, (London, 1978), p. 22; A. H. Wood, *Church Unity without Uniformity*, (London, 1963), pp. 120-21.
20 e.g. Browning, *English Historical Documents, 1660-1714*, p. 57.

Temper, as is consistent with the good of the Church', are hooks too weak on which to hang a conspiracy. Another expressing the hope that 'no Arts or Artifices are omitted to dispose them...to repair the ruins they have made' may be more revealing;[21] and Charles, in an open meeting at The Hague with a delegation of Presbyterian ministers (who accompanied the Commissioners bearing the invitation for the king's return) in the middle of May, perhaps betrayed, if true, his real, conservative feelings when he said he thought the Book of Common Prayer 'the best in the world' and the surplice 'had been still retained by him' during his exile.[22] Morley himself, writing to Hyde at this same time – the middle of May – to offer his views on some of the delegates praised those who sought 'to defend (the Church of England) from... Heretics (?) and Schismatics', strong vocabulary but not necessarily condemning the Presbyterians.[23] Morley's tactics do not exactly exonerate him from bad faith, however. The French ambassador wrote of Morley in May 1660 that 'Il promet tout à tout le monde'; and Morley, in one of his own earlier letters written in early April when consultations were in full swing, wrote that 'if anything shalbe (sic) determined...With which I cannot... comply I will ...passively submit to it...*Ego cedam, atque abibo, et si bona Republica (sic) frui non possum carebo mala*' ('I will concede and retreat and if I cannot advance the public good I will avoid a bad outcome')[24].

These sentiments are hardly ringing endorsements of sincerity, but there would seem to be nothing more explicit and, while such worldly wise operators would hardly commit deceit to print, it is just as possible to conclude that Charles, Hyde, and Morley saw the opportunity to restore church and king but were sensible and moderate men, desperate to avoid antagonism, determined to navigate fragilities, and keen to build a consensus at this critical juncture in their search for a lasting settlement. Two of Morley's letters to Hyde, while offering concessions to the Presbyterians, make abundantly clear his commitment to episcopal government of the Church. On 13 April 1660 he wrote that 'Those that are the chief...amongst them, are content to admit of the name Bishop, but not with the power, which we think to be inseparable from his office...though not without the advice, yet without the consent of his clergy, if he cannot have it.'[25] This comment is open to interpretation depending on which phrase the reader considers more significant: 'without the consent of his clergy, if he cannot have it', implying Morley's innate conservatism; 'not without the advice...of his clergy' suggesting his willingness to compromise. On 4 May he wrote of his hope that the Presbyterians would 'admit of and submit to Episcopall government and the Practise (sic) of the Liturgy' and went on to make two proposals: that 'before and after theyr sermons' the Presbyterians be allowed to use 'such arbitrary forms as they themselves shall think fit'; and that they should all consider 'Hypothetical re-ordination' as a

---

21 Bod Clarendon MS 70, f. 61r (12/3/1660); Barwick, *Life of John Barwick*, pp. 525 (22/4/1660), 512 (2/4/1660).
22 W. D. Macray (ed.), *The History of the Rebellion and Civil Wars in England*, vol. IV (Oxford, 1888), p. 232; Bosher casts doubt on Hyde's recollections written much later and possibly coloured by 'his animus against the Puritans' (Bosher, *Making of the Restoration Settlement*, p. 130).
23 Bod Clarendon MS 72, f. 357r (11/5/1660); Bosher gives the wrong reference and lays the worst interpretation upon it (Bosher, *Making of the Restoration Settlement*, p. 135).
24 TNA, PRO Transcript 31/3/107 (3/5/1660); Bod Carte MS 30, f. 566r (16/4/1660).
25 Scrope and Monkhouse, *State Papers*, vol. 3, p. 727 (13/4/1660).

solution for Presbyterian ministers, presumably avoiding admission of the 'nullity' of their original ordination, and merely providing a regularising ceremony within a newly unified church.[26] Both these proposals can be seen either as empty gestures, even sleight of hand, or as signs of his willingness to compromise.

The Morley mission, whatever the motives or thinking behind it, achieved a measure of success. He certainly met the Council of State within the first few days of April 1660,[27] likewise subsequently leading Presbyterians (Baxter, Calamy, Reynolds),[28] and he felt able to assert by the 4 May in a letter to Hyde that he was 'as little unwellcome... as any of our party' to the Presbyterians.[29] It is difficult to be sure how far he had managed to limit the extremists on his own side – he said he had – and how far, likewise, to convince the Presbyterians to accept episcopacy – even he had doubts about that – and he remained silent about their attitude to 'Hypothetical re-ordination'. All this, with the notable exception of ordination, can be found in his letter to Hyde of 13 April 1660; but it must be said, on the one hand, that the letter was rather early in the proceedings and, on the other, that, as a party involved, he may not have been the best judge of his own success.[30] Lord Mordaunt, in a later letter of 9 May, written on Morley's behalf but still relying on Morley's own estimate, claims that he had won over Reynolds and Calamy, if not 'their brethren', to 'Episcopacy and the Liturgy with little alteration'.[31] Morley himself implies in an earlier letter to Hyde of 1 May that he had allayed concerns of one leading figure, Matthew Hale, about Charles II's Catholicism[32] and, writing about the same matter in a letter to the Duchess of York eleven years after the event in 1671, he claimed 'neither were... my indeavours...altogether unsuccessfull' (sic) with 'the Leaders of the Presbyterian and Independ't parties'.[33] It should be said as well, however, that, cautions about personal assessment of achievement apart, other letters written in May 1660, dwelling more on the problems, are less optimistic.[34]

---

26 Bod Clarendon MS 72, ff. 199r-200v; Scrope and Monkhouse, *State Papers*, vol. 3, p. 738 (both 4/5/1660).
27 Bod Clarendon MS 71, f. 138 (also Scrope and Monkhouse, *State Papers*, vol. 3, p. 722 and *Calendar Clarendon SP*, vol. 4, p. 636), written 5/4/1660, a Thursday, if old style, and referring to Morley's meeting with the Council of State 'Tuesday last' i.e. 3/4/1660; if new style, a Monday and 'Tuesday last' would have been 30/3/1660 - see C. R. Cheney (ed.), *Handbook of Dates* (Cambridge, 1996), Tables 32 and 7, and note *HMC, 7th Report*, (London, 1879), p. 484 (records, on the 4th April, the meeting but does not say when exactly it took place).
28 M. Sylvester (ed.), *Reliquiae Baxterianae*, (London, 1696), part 2, p. 218; Bod Clarendon MS 72, ff. 199r (4/5/1660), 284r (9/5/1660); Edward Reynolds was originally a Presbyterian sympathiser within the Church of England, a member of the Westminster Assembly (1643), one of the deputation to Charles II at Breda (1660), and Bishop of Norwich (1660-1676); Edward Calamy was, like Reynolds, a Presbyterian and a participant in the Westminster Assembly who, like Baxter, refused a bishopric in 1660 and who was expelled from his living in 1662.
29 Bod Clarendon MS 72, f. 199 (4/5/1660).
30 Bod Clarendon MS 71, f. 233; Scrope and Monkhouse, *State Papers*, vol. 3, pp. 727-28; *Calendar Clarendon SP*, vol. 4, p. 654 (all 13/4/1660).
31 Bod Clarendon MS 72, f. 284r; Scrope and Monkhouse, *State Papers*, vol. 3, p. 744 (both 9/5/1660).
32 Concerns about Catholicism - Bod Clarendon MS 72, ff. 118v (1/5/1660, concerns of Hale), Clarendon MS 87, ff. 74-87 (written 1671 but referring to 1660 and claiming he had allayed concerns more generally); Matthew Hale was a lawyer and holder of high legal office - Common Pleas in the 1650s, Chief Baron of the Exchequer and Chief Justice of King's Bench under Charles II.
33 Bod Clarendon MS 87, f. 75v (24/1/1671).
34 Bod Clarendon MS 72, f. 316r (10/5/1660), f. 357r - not f. 352 as in Bosher, *Making of the Restoration Settlement*, p. 128 (11/5/1660).

The final outcome was, nonetheless, as he had hoped. He had certainly managed to generate enough goodwill to allow the return of the king and he had managed to postpone discussion of a permanent settlement until after the restoration. These were his most important achievements since they allowed Charles to return to his kingdom and to return without any religious, or other, conditions. It must be said, however, that lack of a settlement left open the prospect of conflict in the future.

These achievements reflect considerable diplomatic skill on the part of Morley, and his role in the relatively smooth process of transition was important. How far his tactics ran to dividing the opposition is questionable. Such a tactic, sowing seeds of 'Schism', was certainly entertained by Hyde;[35] and Morley, even without wishing to foment conflict, would certainly have aimed to attract the more moderate Presbyterians.[36] Offer of preferment was another tactic certainly entertained by Hyde, and Morley himself wrote to Hyde suggesting promotion at a more modest level than bishop such as 'Mastership of the Savoy, the Provostship of Eaton, or... Prebends of Paul's or Westminster'; and at an even lower level, promotion of leading figures in Yorkshire and Lancashire who would 'gain...all the Presbyterians, both lay and Clergy, of the North'.[37] Morley was also encouraging the king, by early May, to enlist the support of 'Foreign Divines' for episcopal government to impress the Presbyterians.[38] He further advised the king, two days running apparently, in the middle of May, to issue a declaration against 'Atheism, Blasphemy, and Profanes' (sic) to forestall the Presbyterians – they losing credit for the initiative and the king telling them of his own free will what they wished to hear and at no cost to himself.[39] How far these measures – preferment, foreign support, and the declaration against blasphemy – were effective is, again, difficult to say.[40] Morley appears, otherwise, to have relied on evasion and postponement. Evasion is most evident when he advised, as an alternative to 'Hypothetical ordination', that the issue should be ignored and allowed to drift.[41] Postponement until 'a national Synod and free Parliament' was his advice to Hyde and the king as early as 5 April 1660 and, while the distinction between 'a conference', sought by the Presbyterians, and his 'synod' is none too clear, his faith in elections for a new parliament proved well-judged in terms of the Convention and Cavalier Parliaments.[42]

---

35 Barwick, *Life of John Barwick*, pp. 514-15 (2/4/1660), 525 (22/4/1660).
36 Barwick, *Life of John Barwick*, p. 525 (22/4/1660); Bod Clarendon MS 72 f. 199v (4/5/1660).
37 Barwick, *Life of John Barwick*, p. 525 (Hyde, 22/4/1660); Bod Clarendon MS 72, f. 199r/v, Scrope and Monkhouse, *State Papers*, vol. 3, p. 738, *Calendar Clarendon SP*, vol. 5, p. 13 (Morley, Mastership of the Savoy etc., all 4/5/1660); Clarendon MS 72, f. 357r (mistakenly 'f. 352', again, in Bosher, *Making of the Restoration Settlement,* p. 135), *Calendar Clarendon SP,* vol. 5, p. 30 (Morley, North of England, both 11/5/1660).
38 Bod Clarendon MS 72, ff. 284r (9/5/1660), 357r (11/5/1660).
39 Bod Clarendon MS 72, ff. 316r (10/5/1660), 357r (11/5/1660), *Calendar Clarendon SP,* vol. 5, p. 27 (10/5/1660).
40 For foreign support see Bosher, *Making of the Restoration Settlement,* pp. 129-34.
41 Bod Clarendon MS 72, ff. 199r-200v (4/5/1660); Scrope and Monkhouse, *State Papers,* vol. 3, p. 738 (4/5/1660).
42 Scrope and Monkhouse, *State Papers,* vol. 3, p. 722 (5/4/1660); *Calendar Clarendon SP,* vol. 4, p. 636 (5/4/1660); Hutton, *The Restoration,* pp. 111-13; 153.

The actions and success of Morley must be placed in context. The role of other royal agents such as Barwick, Mordaunt, and Broderick should not be overlooked; nor the manoeuvres of Monck and the co-operation of at least some of the Presbyterians. Credit should be given, above all, to Charles and Hyde themselves for recognising the difficulties in the way of harmonising religious differences and accepting the need for compromise. There were, then, many people involved in managing the return of the monarch, and Morley was not the only actor on the stage.

Explosiveness was another aspect of the 'context' in which the restorers were working. There were, above all, the severe pressures of a fractious army, murmurings from 'Fanaticks' and 'Sectaries' in the west and in such places as Leicestershire and Northamptonshire, and a total lack of authority at the centre. Restoration was, thus, far from inevitable. Morley and others – Barwick and Hatton, for example – were fully aware of the pressures[43] and of the need to resolve the political *impasse* by careful manoeuvring and skilful navigating among the more moderate politicians and clergy to ensure the return of the king. Morley in particular appears, by a combination of tactics – division possibly, preferment, 'foreign' pressure, reassuring pronouncement, evasion, postponement, anticipation, and sleight of hand more certainly – to have played a vital part in avoiding confrontation, at the very least, and, on the positive side, to have conveyed an attitude of accommodation which smoothed the way for the Restoration.

The main point is that conflict over the most explosive issue of the time – religion – had been put to one side for the moment, at least; and Charles II entered in upon his kingdom in May 1660 peacefully, without any conditions or commitments other than those, like the Declaration of Breda, he himself chose to make; and Morley had played a crucial part in the outcome.

---

43 Morley to Hyde 13/4/1660, Bod Clarendon MS 71, f. 233r-234r (also Scrope and Monkhouse, *State Papers*, vol. 3, p. 727 and *Calendar Clarendon SP*, vol. 4, p. 654); Morley to Hyde 16/4/1660, Clarendon MS 71, f. 272r (also *Calendar Clarendon SP*, vol. 4, p. 662); Barwick to Hyde 16/4/1660, Clarendon MS 71, f. 281r (also Scrope and Monkhouse, *State Papers*, vol. 3, p. 729 and *Calendar Clarendon SP*, vol. 4, p. 663); Hatton to Hyde 19/4/1660, Clarendon MS 71, f. 301r (also *Calendar Clarendon SP*, vol. 4, p. 665).

CHAPTER 4 : THE SEARCH FOR A SETTLEMENT: PART 1 THE 1660s: RESTORATION RAPPROCHEMENT AND UNIFORMITY

Before the Restoration and while still in exile, Morley had declared in a letter to Hyde, modestly or otherwise, that 'my Canonry and my Sine Cura would please me better than any addition or exchange whatsoever'.[1] The exact sequence of his appointments is, for want of detailed documentation, sometimes difficult to establish. A petition, one of many from returning expellees, shows that Morley tried to recover Mildenhall in June 1660 but, whether successful or not, other surviving documents record his 'resignation' from that rectory and his institution in July 1660 as rector of Great Haseley in the Diocese of Oxford.[2] He was restored to his canonry at Christ Church, possibly in June and certainly by July 1660, and he acquired another canonry, at Wells, in September 1660.[3] By this time, in spite of his earlier protestations, he had been raised to the deanery of Christ Church and so had to relinquish his canonry there.[4] Deanery, rectory, and the canonry at Wells were soon gone as, within a matter of months, in October 1660, he was raised to the Bishopric of Worcester.[5]

Morley received what were probably the traditional warm welcomes in turn from the inhabitants of Oxford and Worcester. Morley himself, in a letter of 26 July 1660 to John Nicholas describes his welcome at Oxford the same day, with 'above 80 horsemen', mainly 'students' of Christ Church (i.e. fellows of the college), crowds lining the streets from Magdalen Bridge to Christ Church, amid 'loud acclamations and ringing of bells'.[6] He was promptly installed as Dean and then he installed four of his 'brethren' to vacant canonries at the cathedral. Even grander was the greeting at Worcester in September 1661 by the Lord Lieutenant, gentry, soldiers and clergy, ten trumpeters, and volleys of shot; to be followed by the ceremony of enthronement in the cathedral.[7]

National politics would not go away, however, and, at this time, while Dean of Christ Church and Bishop of Worcester, he was much preoccupied with national affairs, so much so that he signed deeds naming officials and devolving powers first at Oxford and later at Worcester.[8] Charles II and Hyde faced a full and complex agenda in the

---

1   Bod Clarendon MS 62, f. 86 (24/7/1659).
2   For petition, *HMC, 7th Report,* (London, 1879), pp. 101, 107; for resignation, WSHC, D1/18/6a (no precise date); for Great Haseley, OHC, MS Oxf. Dioc. Papers, d. 106, f. 9r (episcopal register); ibid., c. 78 (bond); *Forty-Sixth Annual Report of the Deputy Keeper of the Public Records,* (London, 1886), Appendix 1, p. 86.
3   For Christ Church, J. Horn (ed.), *Fasti Ecclesiae Anglicanae*/Oxford, (London, 1996), p. 106; W. Kennett, *Register and Chronicle Ecclesiastical and Civil,* (London, 1728), p. 213 (Kennett does not give a precise date for Morley's recovery of the canonry); for Wells, Horn (ed.), *Fasti*/Wells (1979), p. 26.
4   26/7/1660, TNA SP 29/8, f. 77 (*CSPD 1660-1661,* p. 132).
5   OHC, MS Oxf. Dioc. Papers, c. 70 (rectory); Horn (ed.), *Fasti*/Oxford, p. 106 (deanery); *Fasti*/Wells, p. 26 (canonry); *Fasti*/Worcester, p. 107 (bishopric).
6   TNA, SP 29/8, f. 77 - the recipient of the letter is not clear and authority for 'John' Nicholas rests on *CSPD 1660-1661,* p. 132 who, if right, may have been the son of Edward Nicholas, Secretary of State to Charles I and Charles II (see *ODNB*).
7   S. Porter, S. K. Roberts, and I. Roy (eds), *Diary and Papers of Henry Townshend 1640-1663,* (Worcestershire Historical Society, 2014), p. 303; Kennett, *Register,* pp. 534-36.
8   Christ Church Oxford, Dean and Chapter Act Book, i.b.3, p. 101 (31/7/1660); Worcester, WRO, 716 093 2648 10 iii, p. 22 (16/11/1661).

first months – and years – after their return to England and religion was probably the most controversial of all. The immediate issue outstanding was the 'manpower' of the Church. There were huge gaps in the ranks of deans, canons, and bishops; while, at the parish level, there were, over and above the usual vacancies, problems with 'intruders' and returning dispossessed clergymen. Intruders held parochial appointments but all lacked episcopal institution and some lacked episcopal ordination as well. Surviving original incumbents who had been dispossessed during the Wars and Interregnum were, at the same time, now returning and petitioning the Crown for recovery of their former clergy livings. Even more complex was the issue of the future system of church government. 'Anglicans', Presbyterians, and, possibly, Independents, if not the plethora of sects which had grown up in the Commonwealth and Protectorate, all hoped for a settlement in their own favour.

This chapter will therefore examine the role of Morley in these matters: It will describe in turn his particular contributions to the problems of manpower and the religious settlement – what were they and were they successful? – and then attempt to assess his motives.

MANPOWER

Morley was still at the heart of royal counsels and was centrally involved in both these matters – ecclesiastical appointments and the search for a settlement – over the summer of 1660 in spite of his own newly acquired duties at Great Haseley and Christ Church. Ultimately the rules for contentious appointments were laid down in September 1660 by the Act for Confirming and Restoring Ministers which, essentially, allowed a dispossessed minister to return to his parish and otherwise confirmed the 'new' intruder incumbent as rector or vicar.[9] Parishes standing vacant, clergy disputing ownership to the point, as at Andover (Winchester),[10] of forcibly ejecting rivals, patrons

---

9   12 CII c.17.
10 The dramatic stir at morning service caused by the returning sufferer Robert Clarke at Andover is well known *(WR)*.

missing or warring among themselves – these problems arose from the time of the return of the monarch and could not wait for legislation. Decisions at this time (May to September 1660) fell to Hyde, now Chancellor, who resumed control of Crown appointments, both those traditionally in the name of the king and a much wider number of parishes for want of a legal patron to nominate and a bishop to institute. He faced a flood of petitions for recovery[11] and apparently chose to delegate approval or rejection of at least some of them to Sheldon, Morley, and Earle.[12] State Papers show numerous recommendations of parochial appointments signed by permutations of Hyde's three confidants from June to September 1660.[13]

This activity is, in the eyes of Robert Bosher, all evidence of a 'Laudian' conspiracy: the establishment of a 'committee' to guarantee, 'obviously', a parochial ministry, 'orthodox' in theology and loyal to the Crown.[14] Ian Green contests this on several grounds.[15] He may or may not be right about lack of a doctrinal or liturgical test. On the face of it there was no 'test', but who can say for sure through what mental process petitions passed? Who can see through the opaque phrasing of testimonials with such phrases as 'well affected', 'principled in matters touching church government', and even 'conformable to the ancient doctrine and discipline of the Church of England'? Certainly, faced with gaps in the usual, or proper, appointing 'machinery' and an avalanche of petitions, it must have seemed sensible to turn, in an 'innocent' way, for help, as Green says, to three knowledgeable churchmen. The scale of the 'committee's' involvement, moreover, was relatively small, though not insignificant: of 800 presentations or so, the committee dealt with just under 100, of which at least 59 were parochial incumbencies and the remaining 37 were higher clergy. Many of the decisions concerning the rest – some 700 – were made by Hyde or the king.

The concern of this study is Morley's specific involvement in these presentations. Examination of the surviving relevant state papers shows that, in terms of scale, Morley was involved in at least 50 presentations – more than Green identified and about 6 per cent of the 800 – either recommending them on his own or together with Sheldon and Earle.[16] At least 12 of the 50 had been intruders: for example, William Harby of Hambledon and Barnaby Love of Wonston, both in the Winchester Diocese.[17]

---

11 *HMC, 7th Report,* Part VII (London, 1879), Appendix, 'House of Lords', e.g. pp. 104-08 (*Journals of the House of Lords*, vol. 11 (London, 1767-1830), p. 73 is only a general instruction to the 'Clerk of the Parliament' without details of petitions).
12 John Earle was an academic and clergyman before the Wars, in exile in the 1650s, and at the Restoration successively Dean of Westminster, Bishop of Worcester, and Bishop of Salisbury.
13 TNA, 66/2916-19; I. M. Green, *Re-establishment of the Church of England* (Oxford, 1978), pp. 52-60, 238-45.
14 R. S. Bosher, *Making of the Restoration Settlement,* (London, 1951), pp. 159-60.
15 Green, *Re-establishment,* pp. 52-60.
16 *CSPD 1660-1661.*
17 Harby, rector of Hambledon 1658-1701 (LPL, 9 or 10/1658, Comm II and Comm III/7), 'Dr Morley's recommendation' 8/1660 *(CSPD 1660-1661),* institution 2/1661 (TNA, E 331/Winchester/1), with an even earlier intruder history on the Isle of Wight (LPL, Comm XII A 7, Comm III/3, BL, Lansdowne MS 459); Love, rector of Wonston 1649-1689, there by 12/1649 (HRO, DC/J10/2/1, f. 249), recommendation by the 'committee' 7/1660 *(CSPD 1660-1661),* institution 7/1661 (TNA, E 331/Winchester/1).

Men with intruder origins must have satisfied Cromwell's Triers and Ejectors in the 1650s[18] and their churchmanship was likely - deceit apart - to have been Calvinist or Presbyterian. Some of the 800 clergy newly installed in 1660 subsequently fell foul of the Act of Uniformity in 1662 but none of Morley's 50 was among them. While practical factors such as a scarcity of suitable candidates and the political need for a peaceful and lasting settlement should not be overlooked, the existence of intruders of the 1650s (some of them expellees in 1662) may indicate a generosity of spirit and a willingness to compromise on the part of the Charles, Hyde, and even Bosher's 'committee' of three, including Morley, in the rush of presentations in 1660.

THE SEARCH FOR A SETTLEMENT 1660-1662

'Manpower', though a considerable matter in itself, comes somewhat lower on the scale of complexity in comparison with the truly major issue of the time - the overall church settlement - and George Morley played a vital part in the attempts to come to terms with the more moderate Protestants outside the Church in the early 1660s. Morley's attempts, like everyone else's at this time, must continue to be seen against a background of always changing political developments. It remains as difficult as ever to be certain about his real views and the motivation of his masters, Charles and Clarendon.[19] There were many thorny issues and many contending parties - Anglicans, Presbyterians, Independents, and a host of sects - and, whatever the ultimate intentions of Charles, Clarendon, and Morley, one thing was clear: they would have to move with caution in the early days, and the two Declarations of 1660, Breda just before, and Worcester House soon after, the Restoration of May 1660 appear to reflect this approach.[20]

The Declaration of Breda of April 1660 had proposed 'a liberty to tender consciences' but did not attempt to outline a specific scheme or settlement. The king made his next move in September 1660 with another Declaration which turned out to be a preliminary 'discussion' draft of proposals for a settlement between Anglicans and Presbyterians. Morley was a leading figure at the conference which followed and which was held at Worcester House, one of Clarendon's homes, on 22 October

---

18 Cromwell's system for 'policing' appointments and behaviour of parish clergy in the 1650s.
19 For the main modern interpretations: a 'Laudian' conspiracy, Bosher, *Making of the Restoration Settlement*, pp. 176, 184; N. Sykes, *From Sheldon to Secker: Aspects of English Church History, 1660-1768* (Cambridge, 1959), pp. 3, 68-70; A. H. Wood, *Church Unity without Uniformity*, (London, 1963), p. 149; the government stood for toleration: G. R. Abernathy, 'English Presbyterians and the Stuart Restoration 1648-1663', *TAPS*, vol. 55, part 2 (1965), p. 93; the government was for *realpolitik*: Green, *Re-establishment*, p. 25 (Charles II), pp. 203-15 (Hyde), pp. 20-23 (Morley); A. Whiteman, 'Restoration of the Church of England', in G. F. Nuttall and O. Chadwick (eds), *From Uniformity to Unity*, (London, 1962), pp. 55-57, 60-61; see also P. Seaward, *Cavalier Parliament and the Reconstruction of the Old Regime 1661-1667* (Cambridge, 1985), pp. 26-34.
20 For the relevant documents: Breda, April 1660 e.g. A. Browning (ed.), *English Historical Documents, 1660-1714*, vol. 8 (London, 1953), p. 57; Worcester House (preliminary version September 1660), M. Sylvester (ed.), *Reliquiae Baxterianae*, (London, 1696), part 2, pp. 259-64, seemingly the only surviving draft of the original declaration; Worcester House (final version October 1660), e.g. Browning, *English Historical Documents, 1660-1714*, p. 365; G. Gould (ed.), *Documents Relating to the Settlement of the Church of England by the Act of Uniformity 1662*, (London, 1862), pp. 63-78.

1660, in the presence of the king himself, and reminiscent of his grandfather's role at Hampton Court in 1604.

The original intention was an orderly proceeding – the Declaration to be read out point by point, both sides commenting, and Charles 'disposing'.[21] The accounts of two chief participants – Morley and Baxter – though quite different from each other, between them paint a vivid picture of actual events. Richard Baxter, a leading figure in the Presbyterian delegation, thought Morley a 'moderate' before the conference but, according to his account, as debate turned into conflict, the two soon clashed over prelacy – bishops acting with or without presbyters – and ordination – whether or not to accept Presbyterian orders in the ministry of the new Church. Morley's account is both more systematic and optimistic about the same conference. Both sides had agreed, according to Morley, that bishops should act with presbyters and that liturgical ceremonies should be optional, at least in the interim, until settled by another conference.[22]

The one issue outstanding, as Morley saw it, was the acceptability of Presbyterian ordinations in the new united Church. Presbyterian ministers had been ordained by elders in the 1640s and 1650s and the question concerned the validity of these orders if these men were to be absorbed into the ministry of the Church of England from 1660. He asserts in his letter that he had proposed at the conference 'hypotheticall or conditionall ordination'.[23] While his intention is clear enough – to remove doubts surrounding the validity of Presbyterian orders – his solution, 'hypotheticall or conditionall ordination', is much less so. There would be no provocative declarations of the illegality or 'nullity' of the Presbyterian ordinations, though both he and Clarendon seem, from the letter, to have thought of them in that way; and precisely what form the new ordinations should take they did not specify – presumably some form of 'regularising' ceremony, largely a formality but which would involve the bishop.[24]

The conference was cut short after four hours or so of debate, when Anne Hyde, Duchess of York, went into labour. Charles (prospective uncle) and Clarendon (prospective grandfather) were both personally involved. They may or may not have rushed to her bedside but, as Charles was still without a legitimate heir, there were implications for the succession, so the birth momentarily overrode the debate, and the conference came to an abrupt end.[25]

21 Baxter, *Reliquiae*, part 2, p. 276.
22 Contemporaneous accounts with any detail are Baxter, *Reliquiae*, part. 2, pp. 276-79; NLofS, Wodrow MS, Folio XXXII, no. 9 (Morley's Letter); *HMC, 5th Report*, (London, 1876), p. 157 (letter from Newport to Leveson); later detailed – and representative – accounts include Bosher, *Making of the Restoration Settlement*, pp. 184-99; J. Stoughton, *History of Religion in England*, vol. 3 (London, 1901), pp. 113-26; B. D. Till, 'Worcester House Declaration and the Restoration of the Church of England', *Historical Research*, vol. 70 (1997), *passim;* Whiteman, 'Restoration of the Church of England', pp. 66-75.
23 NLofS, Wodrow MS Folio XXXII, no. 9 (23/10/1660).
24 *Life of Edward Earl of Clarendon... in which is included a Continuation of the History of the Grand Rebellion*, vol. 2 (Oxford, 1827), pp. 130-32; the issue of incorporation of Presbyterians into the Anglican ministry appears to have been revived by Tillotson (Archbishop of Canterbury 1691-1694) who proposed to preface such an ordination with the words 'If thou art not ordained.....' LPL, MS 1743, pp. 151-54, no date but he is entitled 'Archbishop'.
25 Clarendon, *Life and Continuation*, vol. 1, p. 389; *HMC, 5th Report*, p. 157 (the former mentions Morley specifically, the latter only the presence of bishops and not Morley specifically); Bosher, *Making of the Restoration Settlement*, p. 187.

The Worcester House Declaration, the revised version of the king's original draft, was issued, three days later, on 25 October 1660. A comparison of the September and October drafts[26] shows that the two documents were much the same but with a few important differences. Over episcopacy and the Book of Common Prayer, the two documents struck a conservative note by declaring in both cases – and echoing the king's earlier comment – that they were 'the best'. The principle of oversight of bishops' powers by presbyters remained a key feature of both documents; likewise, optionality over the surplice, bowing at the name of Jesus, the cross in baptism, and kneeling for communion.[27] The revisers made a few important concessions, mainly to do with the prayer book, in this later version of the Declaration. The reform process of the book was made a little more precise – to be done not, vaguely, by 'some learned divines' but in 'equal numbers' from both sides – and, more importantly, there was a specific promise that no minister would be punished for failing to use the current prayer book until it had been revised. Bishops' powers, including future ordinations, were to be exercised with the 'advice and assistance', but not the 'consent', of presbyters.[28] Over the integration of ministers already ordained only by presbyters, however, both the original and the final declaration remained silent.[29]

The concessions concerning presbyters, the surplice, ceremonies, and the reform process of the prayer book went some considerable way towards meeting Presbyterian demands; and silence over the contentious issue of ministers ordained by Presbyterian elders during the Commonwealth and Protectorate was probably a wiser course than 'hypotheticall or conditionall ordination'. An episcopal ceremony for these ministers, however much a formality, would have been provocative and, if all future ordinations were performed by bishops (in conjunction with presbyters), the presence of ministers ordained by elders in the 1640s and 50s would have 'died out' in the course of time. It was Morley who had proposed, six months earlier in a letter to Clarendon during his mission to England, this very course in the first place: that an alternative to 'hypotheticall...ordination' could be to ignore the problem and to allow ministers ordained by elders to serve in the new church.[30] Baxter's verdict, written in 1665, some years after the conference, was damningly critical about the meeting itself but he welcomed the subsequent Declaration. Morley's mood, the day after the conference, was optimistic overall, and Clarendon concludes, though his mind may have been

---

26 Gould, *Documents 1662*, p. 63; Wood, *Church Unity without Uniformity,* p. 153.
27 There is no mention of the ring in marriage in either Declaration.
28 'Consent' was not in the first draft, but requested by the Presbyterians, and disallowed by the king because, in his eyes, consent gave the presbyters 'a negative voice' (Baxter, *Reliquiae,* part 2, pp. 262, 275); see also Morley Wodrow MS, Folio XXXII, no. 9; Gould, *Documents 1662,* p. 70.
29 Gould claims that acceptability of Presbyterian orders was in the original Declaration but there is nothing specific about the matter in either version and he appears to have confused the original document with Baxter's request for recognition of these ordinations (Gould, *Documents 1662,* p. 77; Baxter, *Reliquiae,* part 2, p. 276).
30 For the first occasion, Bod Clarendon MS 72, f. 199 (4/5/1660), reproduced in part in R. Scrope and T. Monkhouse (eds), *State Papers collected by Edward Earl of Clarendon* vol. 3 (Oxford, 1767-1786), p. 738; and see Chapter 3.

obscured, like Baxter's, by time and the need for justification, that both sides seemed 'well content' by the outcome.[31] All came to nought, however, when attempts to enact the concessions failed in the House of Commons in December 1660.[32]

Failure should not be allowed to obscure the importance of Worcester House. It is true that the Declaration proposed a future 'review' of the Book of Common Prayer and that an ambivalence – whether its proposals were to be seen as permanent or merely interim – surrounds the document.[33] It is also true that Worcester House set in train important concessions, signalled compromise, and raised hopes, at least, of unity among the more moderate, both Anglican and Presbyterian. Its promise to protect 'private consciences...by indulging...their omitting those ceremonies' would have stood if the bill had passed and might have tempered – or 'cautioned' – the acrimonious debaters at Savoy and the compulsory requirements in the revised version of the prayer book. Roger Thomas declares it 'the most effective attempt at comprehension between the Restoration (1660) and the Revolution (1689)'; while Barry Till considers the 'communique', 'a remarkably irenic document' and 'the high water mark of plans for comprehension...between the Reformation and the present day'.[34] The Hampton Court Conference of 1604 should not be overlooked but Worcester House was certainly the first such move since the Restoration, showing a practical route and laying the ground for future bills in the 1660s, 70s, and 80s, with similar proposals.

Questions persist about the authorship of the Declarations – both the first draft and the final version – and about the motives of their authors, the king and the episcopal contributors. It is highly likely that Clarendon was the mastermind of the first draft and there must have been consultation with leading figures such as Morley, but, for want of evidence, it is difficult to be specific. Anne Whiteman claims Clarendon was the author of the second version as well and, while he must have played a crucial role, Seaward stresses the 'intervention' of Presbyterians Holles and Anglesey. Both Baxter and Morley state quite specifically that the same four men – Morley himself, Henchman, Calamy, and Reynolds – together with the two lay assessors (Holles and Anglesey) were the drafters. It remains difficult, for want of detail and at this distance in time, to determine their respective roles and who, if anyone, was decisive.[35]

---

31 Clarendon, *Life and Continuation,* vol. 1, p. 481.
32 W. Cobbett (ed.), *Parliamentary History of England,* vol. IV (London, 1808), col. 154.
33 See Bosher, *Making of the Restoration Settlement,* p. 189.
34 R. Thomas, 'Comprehension and Indulgence', in G. F. Nuttall and O. Chadwick (eds), *From Uniformity to Unity,* (London, 1962), p. 193; Till, 'Worcester House Declaration', pp. 218, 230.
35 Whiteman, 'Restoration of the Church of England', p. 67, whose sources include Burnet who is imprecise (O. Airy (ed.), *Burnet's History of my Own Time,* vol. 1, [Oxford, 1897], p. 315); P. Seaward, 'Circumstantial Temporary Concessions: Clarendon, Comprehension, and Uniformity', in N. H. Keeble (ed.), *Settling the Peace of the Church: 1662 Revisited,* (Oxford, 2014), p. 76; NLofS, Wodrow MS, Folio XXXII, no. 9; Baxter, *Reliquiae,* part 2, p. 278.

Motives for this scheme for union of Anglicans and Presbyterians – and, for that matter, Clarendon's proposal of freedom of worship for 'others' (whether Protestant sects or Catholics was not clear) at one point during the meeting[36] – are equally problematic. The establishment – the king, the chancellor, and the bishops – stands condemned as a group: by Stoughton for the 'hollowness' of the whole exercise; by Bosher as participants in the continuing conspiracy – 'promises, promises' by the king, the chancellor, and the bishops in the certainty that concessions to the Presbyterians, let alone freedom of worship for 'others', would never pass the Commons. Echoing these views, Sutch sees the September Declaration as a 'maneuver' by Hyde and Sheldon and the whole episode characterised, he remarks more fairly, by 'subterfuge' and 'trickery' on both sides.[37] Abernathy, at the other end of the scale, imagines king and chancellor, if not the bishops, seeking toleration or comprehension, for political, if not visionary, reasons.[38] More likely were considerations of *realpolitik* expressed *mutatis mutandis* by Green, Seaward, and Whiteman.[39] Charles may have preferred the Catholics, Clarendon may have been a traditionalist, but faced with the need to contain passions, to reconcile opposing camps, and, above all, to snatch peace from the flames of turbulence and fanaticism, they sought peace by compromise – concessions to the Presbyterians in the final version of the Declaration and the more fleeting suggestion of freedom for 'others'.

More important for this study of Worcester House are the actions and motives of Morley. He was a central figure in the conference, one of the authors of the final version of the Declaration, and a source of important initiatives to do with the divisive problems of ordination. For Bosher, Morley was one, albeit important, figure among the conspirators; Green, while momentarily entertaining 'a slight suspicion' about his integrity, sees him as a pragmatist but a staunch supporter of uniformity after its enactment;[40] and Fincham and Taylor place Morley, in the end, among the 'hardliners'.[41] His original Calvinism[42] or a natural pragmatism may have inclined him to a compromise settlement but which camp he belonged to for certain – conspirator to deceive and subvert, sincere striver for unity, or advocate of *realpolitik* – must be left, for want of decisive evidence, to interpretation.[43]

---

36 Baxter, *Reliquiae,* part 2, p. 277.
37 Stoughton, *History of Religion,* vol. 3, p. 116; Bosher, *Making of the Restoration Settlement,* pp. 184, 188, 190-92; V. D. Sutch, *Gilbert Sheldon, Architect of Anglican Survival 1640-1675* (The Hague, 1973), pp. 75-77.
38 Abernathy, 'English Presbyterians', p. 93.
39 Green, *Re-establishment,* pp. 208-10; Seaward, *Cavalier Parliament,* pp. 28-31, 32-34; id. 'Circumstantial Temporary Concessions', pp. 80-81; Whiteman, 'Restoration of the Church of England', pp. 55-57.
40 Bosher, *Making of the Restoration Settlement,* e.g. p. 138; Green, *Re-establishment,* pp. 21, 23.
41 K. C. Fincham and S. Taylor, 'Restoration of the Church of England 1660-1662: Ordination, Reordination, and Conformity', in S. Taylor and G. Tapsell (eds), *The Nature of the English Revolution Revisited,* (Woodbridge, 2013), p. 226.
42 Wood, *Athenae,* vol. 2, col. 768; Airy (ed.), *Burnet's History,* vol. 1, p. 314; Kennett, *Register,* p. 666.
43 Analysis will return to this issue later in this chapter and in the next chapter.

Doomed though Worcester House turned out to be, religion continued to dominate the agenda but the mood – certainly of Parliament and of the bishops – was changing since the early days of the Restoration, from caution, compromise, and accommodation to royalism, Anglicanism, and suppression of difference. MPs and bishops may have been more confident; more likely they were more fearful. The Venner Rising of Fifth Monarchy Men in January 1661 provoked memories of the sects of the 1650s with the accompanying horrors of fanaticism and rebellion; and, just when these fears might have been subsiding, the Yorkshire Plot of April 1663 revived them again; hence the prevailing concern with security in the 1660s, 70s and 80s.[44] Consistent themes in Parliament over the next twenty years and more were law and order; a religious settlement with full episcopacy, surplice, prayer book; and suppression of Catholics and the sects with their dangerous religious and social views.

Charles II was apparently determined, nonetheless, on a settlement rather than suppression and, in March 1661, sticking to his proposal in the Worcester House Declaration, announced a conference of bishops and Presbyterians – twelve a side – to review the liturgy at the Savoy under the presidency of Gilbert Sheldon, now Bishop of London.[45] At the same time (April/May 1661) there was a general election and Parliament, together with the concomitant Convocation, assembled thereafter. There were also regular meetings of the Privy Council. This meant there were four overlapping institutional bodies concerned with the new prayer book in 1661/62: Savoy, Convocation, Parliament, and the Privy Council; then, after the failure of Savoy, Parliament and Convocation, together with meetings of the Privy Council throughout. Morley, now Bishop of Worcester, was potentially in all four.

Savoy was a disaster for the Presbyterians and for church unity.[46] Baxter condemns the proceedings as a mockery.[47] He was, as chief advocate of the Presbyterians, a participant and provides the most detailed account, written apparently in 1665, which was sometime after the event. He is quick to record collisions between himself and Morley over the nature of human sinfulness and *ex tempore* prayer; and quick also to produce caricatures of many of the bishops: Cosin for possessing 'so little logic', Gauden for 'no logic', Sanderson for 'peevishness', Sheldon for absence; while venting his full frustration on Morley, complaining of his interruptions and 'vehemency'.[48]

---

44 See e.g. R. L. Greaves, *Deliver Us from Evil* (Oxford, 1986), Preface, where he lists a large number of rebellions and conspiracies 1660-63.
45 For the warrant for the conference, e.g. E. Cardwell, *History of Conferences* (Oxford, 1841), pp. 298; for Sheldon as bishop, Horn, *Fasti*/St Paul's, p. 3; Sheldon was also Master of the Savoy Hospital (*ODNB*).
46 For the main contemporaneous sources see subsequent footnotes; for the main later accounts, e.g. Bosher, *Making of the Restoration Settlement*, pp. 226-30; Cardwell, *History of Conferences*, pp. 238-68; E. C. Ratcliffe, 'Savoy Conference', in G. F. Nuttall and O. Chadwick (eds), *From Uniformity to Unity*, (London, 1962), pp. 92-128; Stoughton, *History of Religion*, vol. 3, pp. 161-64; 176-88.
47 Baxter, *Reliquiae*, part 2, pp. 335, 339, 363; 'mockery' is Stoughton's verdict (Stoughton, *History of Religion*, vol. 3, p. 185).
48 Baxter, *Reliquiae*, part 2, pp. 363-64.
49 Baxter, *Reliquiae*, part 2, p. 336
50 BL, Addit. MS 28053, ff. 1-2; Henry Fearne was Bishop of Chester for five weeks before death in 1662.
51 Airy (ed.), *Burnet's History*, vol. 1, pp. 318-22; Gilbert Burnet was Bishop of Salisbury 1689-1715.
52 See Cardwell, *History of Conferences*, p. 254.

He paints a picture of confrontation – bishops haughty and angry on the one side, Presbyterians, frustrated and divided on the other – and his damning comment, 'we spoke to the deaf', succinctly sums up his view of episcopal attitudes.[49] Fearne's account, written in 1661, was closer to events than Baxter's, but offers little more than an outline. It makes no criticism of his fellow bishops but does, to some extent, balance Baxter's strictures of the bishops by commenting on Baxter's own approach – 'more boldness and ignorance then (sic) reason' – and criticising his voluminous documentation which involved one set of answers over twenty-nine sheets and a liturgy of 'extraordinary length'.[50] Burnet, the only other seventeenth-century recorder, is more balanced but brief.[51] It is clear from all three accounts, however, that Savoy was nothing more than a confrontation between complainants (the Presbyterians) and defendants (the bishops) with the latter acting as both judge and jury and extinguishing all hope of progress.[52]

Consideration of the new liturgy moved between Savoy and Convocation in the course of 1661.[53] Scrutiny lay from March to July with the bishops and Presbyterians at Savoy and, although Convocation made a start on the new prayer book, it was at first constrained to await the outcome of Savoy. When both sides locked horns and the remit for Savoy expired, however, Convocation assumed control. It dealt with complex issues of liturgy with remarkable speed – just a few weeks in November and December 1661 – which may imply much preliminary preparation between July and November but which also implies, with more certainty, 'superficial' consideration since the upper house appears to have covered 1500 words in five two-hour sittings, for example, during November and December.[54] The bodies of bishops and clergy were evidently steered by a committee of eight bishops[55] set up in November on the resumption of Convocation. Morley was one of the eight and according to Burnet 'everything... was directed by Sheldon and Morley' but Kennett, while admitting that he 'cannot say', awards most credit – 'more than any single Man at the Convocation' – to Robert Sanderson; and Cuming makes a convincing if somewhat circumstantial case for the dominant roles of Cosin, Wren, and, in particular, Sanderson.[56] The fact remains, however, that no documents have come to light to show exactly what was said and by whom, either in the committee or on the floor of both Houses of Convocation.

---

53 The main contemporary sources for Savoy and Convocation are: Fearne BL, Addit. MS 28053, ff. 1-2; Airy (ed.), *Burnet's History*, vol. 1, pp. 318-26; Kennett, *Register*, pp. 398, 503, 568, 585, 633; for the main later accounts, Bosher, *Making of the Restoration Settlement*, pp. 213-16, 230-31, 244-49; Cardwell, *History of Conferences*, pp. 369-89; Ratcliffe, 'Savoy Conference', pp. 129-39; Stoughton, *History of Religion*, vol. 3, pp. 166-77, 215; for the main documents, E. Cardwell (ed.), *Synodalia*, (Oxford, 1842), pp. 631-60 (May to December 1661); Bray (ed.), *Records of Convocation*, vol. VIII (Woodbridge, 2006), pp. 269-303 (May to December 1661).

54 G. J. Cuming, 'The Prayer Book in Convocation November 1661', in *JEH*, vol. 8 (1957), p. 182; Mr Anthony Paice, BA drew my attention to this article.

55 For composition and meeting place of the committee see e.g. Bray (ed.), *Records of Convocation*, p. 288; Clarendon appears to be the only authority for preparations over the summer and autumn by 'the bishops' (Clarendon, *Life and Continuation*, vol. 2, p. 118); notes of changes are apparently in Sancroft's hand (Cardwell, *History of Conferences*, p. 389).

56 Airy (ed.), *Burnet's History*, vol. 1, 326; Kennett, *Register*, p. 633; Cuming, 'Prayer Book', pp. 183-87, 190, 192; John Cosin was Bishop of Durham 1660-1672; Matthew Wren was bishop three times over, lastly Bishop of Ely 1638-1667; and Robert Sanderson was Regius Professor of Divinity at Oxford 1642-1648, 1660-1661, and Bishop of Lincoln 1660-1663.

The revisions of the committee were then largely approved in December 1661 by full sessions of both Upper and Lower Houses of Convocation.[57] The new Book of Common Prayer made some 600 changes to the Prayer Book of Elizabeth I but most were minor in nature, with few concessions to the Presbyterians, still less to the other sects.[58] It retained the sign of the cross at baptism and the ring in the marriage ceremony, both of which were strongly opposed by the Presbyterians.' It also restored, however and most interestingly, the famous Black Rubric which had been part of the Edwardian prayer book of 1552 but cut from the Elizabethan book of 1559, and which strongly implied that the bread and wine were symbols only and not the flesh and blood of Christ.[59]

The Black Rubric was the most striking concession to the Presbyterians, Baxter among them, and, in the absence of fuller records, there can only be speculation about the source for this insertion.[60] Burnet and the Duke of York attribute the Black Rubric to John Gauden (Bishop of Exeter at the time);[61] while, among later writers, Ratcliffe considers Gauden and Morley as possibilities; and Seaward asserts either Gauden and Morley or Clarendon himself. Except for Burnet, relevant contemporary sources - the Privy Council, House of Lords, and Kennett's *Register* - offer no information about its authorship or about the body responsible.[63] A case can be made for Morley: he was an active member of Convocation, attending on seventeen separate occasions in the summer and eighteen in the autumn, and, with his readiness to intervene in discussion, his rejection of transubstantiation, and his Calvinist sympathies, it is possible that he was the proposer, or at least a supporter, of the Black Rubric during the sittings of 1661; but there is nothing 'clinching' about such a claim and he and Baxter clashed at Savoy over kneeling - Morley for, Baxter against - to receive communion.[64]

The Book of Common Prayer - the new text - passed next for approval to the Privy Council and then to Parliament for enforcement in 1662. The Privy Council appears to have endorsed their deliberations in a single session in February 1662. Morley was not a member of this body at that time, though he did attend with four other bishops, in an 'exceptional' capacity, on this one occasion.[65] The new prayer book was then annexed

---

57 Bray (ed.), *Records of Convocation,* pp. 289, 302.
58 HL/PO/LB/1/36/1 and HL/PO/LB/1/36/2; see Bosher, *Making of the Restoration Settlement,* p. 247 (and for references, p. 245, footnote 1), and Cardwell, *History of Conferences,* p. 386 for a summary of the changes to the BCP.
59 e.g. HL/PO/LB/1/36/2, pp. 250 (communion), 256 (baptism), 286 (marriage); other contentious issues were bowing at the name of Jesus (canon 18, 1604) and the surplice (canon 58, 1604).
60 Cuming does not deal with the Black Rubric (Cuming, 'Prayer Book').
61 Airy (ed.), *Burnet's History,* vol. 1, p. 324; J. Macpherson (ed.), *Original Papers Containing the Secret History of Great Britain,* (London, 1775), p. 25.
62 Ratcliffe, 'Savoy Conference', p. 139-40; Seaward, *Cavalier Parliament,* p. 174.
63 Several historians claim it was inserted by the Privy Council (Ratcliffe, 'Savoy Conference', pp. 139-40; Seaward, *Cavalier Parliament,* p. 174) or Parliament (Wood, *Church Unity without Uniformity,* p. 230) but Seaward in particular is in error - his reference to the Privy Council is wrong and should be TNA, PC2/55, pp. 552, 554, 634; Kennett's *Register* (p. 585) gives no body, while the Privy Council Register and Burnet imply the body was Convocation (Airy (ed.), *Burnet's History,* vol. 1, p. 324-26), and Cardwell, *History of Conferences,* p. 373 rules out amendment by the Lords.
64 Baxter, *Reliquiae,* e.g. part 2, pp. 363-64 (debating); George Morley, 'An Argument Drawn from the Evidence and Sense Against the Doctrine of Transubstantiation', in id., *Several Treatises written upon Several Occasions,* (London, 1683) (transubstantiation); Wood, *Athenae,* vol. 2, col. 768; Airy (ed.), *Burnet's History,* vol. 1, p. 314; Kennett, *Register,* p. 666 (Calvinism); Baxter, *Reliquiae,* part 2, p. 347 (kneeling).
65 TNA, PC2/55 Privy Council Register, p. 554; see also Ratcliffe, 'Savoy Conference', p. 139.

to the Act of Uniformity. Parliament, which had begun work with repressive legislation the so called Clarendon Code - passed the Bill of Uniformity by the summer of 1662 which required all incumbents to undergo episcopal ordination, to take oaths giving 'assent and consent' to the new prayer book - making its use compulsory in all churches - and to renounce the Covenant and the use of arms against the king.[66]

The Journal of the House of Lords shows that Morley was present for twenty-seven of the thirty-one days the Bill of Uniformity spent there.[67] Proceedings in both the Privy Council and the House of Lords are mostly 'anonymised', as with Convocation, and who steered the book through the Privy Council and the bill through the House of Lords - and more particularly what Morley said or did in these bodies to secure its passage - must remain largely in question. Clarendon made several attempts to soften the impact of uniformity both during the passage of the bill and after its enactment but before its enforcement,[68] and surviving documents link Morley to all three of the moves. One was an exemption of ministers from wearing the surplice or using the sign of the cross in baptism.[69] Another was apparently relaxation of the requirement on clergy to declare against the Covenant.[70] Yet another was a proposal that clergy likely to be expelled under the terms of the Act of Uniformity should receive one fifth of the income from their former living (parish).[71] All these proposals were lost before the royal assent to the final version of the Act,[72] and when Clarendon proposed a royal power to dispense from the Act - to make exceptions for particular ministers - Sheldon stood in his way and, to judge from a letter written by Morley to Clarendon, Morley took Sheldon's side - no change or retreat now that the Bill had been passed.[73] These developments show that Morley was still doing his best to accommodate the moderate Presbyterians but that there were limits and, once the bill had become law, he saw it as his duty to respect the will of Parliament and to enforce it.

The new Book of Common Prayer, for all its concessions, was just not acceptable to the Presbyterians. Savoy deadlocked, Convocation 'economical' in its concessions, Parliament bent on conformity - not only was all this a disaster for a host of clergymen

---

66 14 CII c.4; the Solemn League and Covenant was originally a treaty between the English and Scottish Parliaments signed in 1643 - a Scottish army to fight the king in return for the establishment of Presbyterianism in England - and, theoretically, all men were required to take an oath committing themselves to the deal.
67 *Lords Journal,* vol. 11, pp. 351-477.
68 See e.g. Bosher, *Making of the Restoration Settlement,* pp. 250-51, 253, 263.
69 *Lords Journal,* vol. 11, p. 409; *HMC, Hastings MSS,* vol. 4 (London, 1928-1947), pp. 129-30; *HMC, 15th Report,* Appendix, Part VII (London, 1898), p. 94; the 15th Report merely asserts support from 'the chancellor and four of the bishops' but the Hastings MS links Morley specifically, *inter alios,* to the proposal.
70 *Lords Journal,* vol. 11, pp. 422, 424; *HMC, 10th Report,* Appendix, Part VI (London, 1885), p. 177; the issue is discussed by Clarendon but without mention of Morley (Clarendon, *Life and Continuation,* vol. 2, pp. 134-39).
71 *Lords Journal,* vol. 11, pp. 424-25; Morley sat on the committee and, though the terse report does not reveal what was said and by whom, it came out in support of the proposal.
72 Modification of the Covenant was 'laid aside' by the Lords (*Lords Journal,* vol. 11, p. 424); exemption from the surplice and the cross in baptism, together with sustentation for dissenting clergy were lost when the Lords accepted amendments from the House of Commons (*Lords Journal,* vol. 11, p. 450).
73 Bod Clarendon MS 77, f. 307, 28/8/1662; f. 340, 3/9/1662; Bosher points out that the first of Morley's letters was written on the very day of the confrontation between Clarendon and Sheldon (Bosher, *Making of the Restoration Settlement,* p. 263); but Morley was not as bold as Bosher implies and the letter ends with Morley's promise of a prebend to a 'kinsman' of Clarendon!

who had to vacate livings and endure the 'Bartholomew Massacre' on and after 24 August 1662;[74] by embittering relations and entrenching division it left the Protestant religion more fractured and splintered than ever and proved a disaster to this day for the cause of church unity.

THE LATER 1660s: COMPLETION OF THE 'CLARENDON CODE'

The drive for uniformity continued with the rest of the so-called Clarendon Code. A key measure was the Five Mile Act which banned all dissenting ministers - men who refused to accept the terms of uniformity and, in particular, the Book of Common Prayer - from coming within five miles of a town, city, or parliamentary borough and, if once beneficed, likewise from his former parish.[75] Morley was certainly involved in the passage of the bill through the Lords in October 1665, present at all its stages, even serving on the committee.[76] Among the eight or nine speakers in one of the few debates on record, Lord Wharton spoke against it and Gilbert Sheldon (by then Archbishop of Canterbury) and George Morley (by then Bishop of Winchester) for it.[77] Morley spoke at length (Wharton was a close second) and with passion - 'There are no Persons dangerous if these persons are not dangerous' - and his speech was enlivened with details of the unruly behaviour of the Quakers in his diocese and reminders of the 1640s ('murtherers' of the king and expulsion of the bishops from Parliament). The speech reached a climax with the resounding assertion that 'If there bee noe Lawes there can bee noe Society.'

Three years later Morley's mood appears to have changed again. Two bills for comprehension and one for toleration were apparently 'in the air' between October 1667 and February 1668.[78] The chief source of the comprehension bill of 1667 was Sir Robert Atkins, of the comprehension and toleration bills of 1668 Sir Matthew Hale, John Wilkins, and Hezekiah Burton;[79] but a note at the end of a scheme for comprehension at that time states that Morley and three other bishops, were 'favourers of this Comprehension'.[80]

---

74 See section 'Dissenting Clergy 1662', in Chapter 7.
75 17 CII c.2.
76 *Lords Journal,* vol. 11, pp. 694-701.
77 Bod Carte MS 80, ff. 757-59; see Caroline Robbins, 'The Oxford Session of the Long Parliament of Charles II 9th to the 31st October 1665', *BIHR,* 21 (1948), pp. 214-24.
78 'in the air' because none appears in the Journals of either of the Houses of Parliament or in W. Cobbett's *Parliamentary History.*
79 For Atkins, Bod MS B. 14. 15. Linc, pp. 4-5; for Hale, ibid., pp. 8-9, 11 and BL, Addit. MS 19526, f. 157v; for Wilkins and Burton, Baxter, *Reliquiae,* part 3, pp. 23-36 (NB faulty page numbering); also R. Latham and W. Matthews (eds), *Diary of Samuel Pepys,* vol. 9, (London, 1983), pp. 31, 51, 60; Atkins was an MP in the Cavalier Parliament and Chief Baron of the Exchequer under William III; Hale was Chief Baron of the Exchequer and Chief Justice of King's Bench under Charles II; Wilkins was vicar of St Lawrence Jewry 1662-1668 and Bishop of Chester 1668-1672; Burton was rector of St George Southwark 1668-1680 - see *ODNB* for all of these.
80 Corpus Christi College, Oxford, MS 298, f. 84v, 2/1668 - dismissed by Spurr as 'of little weight' (J. Spurr, 'The Church of England: Comprehension and the Toleration Act of 1689', *EHR,* CIV, No. 413 (10/1989), p. 941).

The repressive policies of the majority continued, however, with the passage of the Second Conventicle Act in 1670, which renewed the powers of magistrates to arrest and punish participants of illegal religious assemblies.[81] The role of Morley is, again, the question. Archbishop Sheldon, Morley's colleague and ally, was actively organising his fellow bishops to attend Convocation and Parliament in 1667-69.[82] For which bills and for what vote neither his correspondence nor surviving parliamentary activity reveals. Numbers of bishops present during the passage of the conventicle bill through the Lords in March and April 1670 averaged fifteen a day and Morley was there for all eighteen days; this suggesting that Sheldon's urgings had some effect this time as their average attendance for the Five Mile Bill in 1665 had been only ten or eleven a day.[83] There are, frustratingly, no records of actual debates but most likely he and Morley were, at this stage, against comprehension and toleration and for the new conventicle bill.

Morley appears to have wavered when fresh attempts were made to achieve a comprehension in the late 1660s; if so, showing his willingness to consider such a scheme if it would bring a settlement at last and, with it, peace and security. He seems otherwise, in the 1660s and early 1670s, to have thrown his shoulder behind the wheel of repression either because he recognised the reality - Royalist/Anglican dominance and plots and rumours of plots - or because, by this time, this was his true and natural inclination.

CONCLUSION

There can be no doubt that Morley was at the centre of religious affairs throughout the 1660s: as a member of the 'committee', filling parochial vacancies; and, as a vital figure in the debates at Worcester House, Savoy, House of Lords, Convocation, and Privy Council, attempting to achieve a settlement. There can be no doubt, either, that the eventual settlement was unquestionably 'Anglican'. Most of the new incumbents conformed in 1662 and there was no compromise - no comprehension or toleration - with other faiths and sects.

---

81 22 CII c.1.
82 Bod Addit. MS c.308, ff. 98v, 101; BL, Harleian MS 7377, f. 6r, v;Note, many of the references on this subject are wrong in W. G. Simon, *Restoration Episcopate* (New York, 1965), p. 73; he also attempts, pp. 69-70, 'sessional averages' of bishops' parliamentary attendance but how trustworthy remains the question.
83 *Lords Journal,* vol. 11, pp. 694-701 (Five Mile Bill), vol. 12, pp. 305-51 (Conventicle Bill).

Morley's contributions were substantial: fifty incumbents for the manpower of the Church who all conformed at the critical moment in 1662; and initiatives - chiefly 'Hypotheticall ordination' and possibly the Black Rubric - in the various debates and conferences about a future settlement. His performance is easy to assess superficially: vacancies were filled - success - and the initiatives failed. Whether these new men were the type he wished for and whether the eventual settlement was the type he aimed at depends on motive - Morley's inner thinking.

There is no record of discussion in the committee concerned with appointments. Accounts, seen in the case of Savoy mainly through the eyes and pen of Richard Baxter, are strongly *parti pris* and, crucially, what was said in the key deliberating bodies, Convocation, Privy Council, and the House of Lords, which actually produced the BCP and the Act of Uniformity, is in the main either missing or 'anonymised'. Motives, without speeches or writings - usually a matter of interpretation in any case - are extremely difficult to establish at this remove from events. It has therefore proved too difficult to be certain about the true thoughts - the personal religion - of Charles II, of Hyde, or, more relevant to this study, of Morley himself; difficult to be certain also about public policy and political considerations of peace, security, and stability; and difficult to be certain of the interplay between the two - the personal and the political.

Interpretations of the motives underlying the appointments of 1660 and, more particularly, Savoy and its aftermath range, as with Worcester House, from conspiracy to sincere attempts at toleration and comprehension with *realpolitik* considerations somewhere in between.[84] To the 'conspiracists', it was deception and betrayal throughout by the 'Laudians', who were determined on a straight course to Anglican uniformity. Honest attempts at comprehension, in the interests of unity, with the more moderate Presbyterians and toleration for the extremer sects (and, in the case of Charles II, deceitfully or otherwise, for Catholics), is the directly opposing view. A third interpretation suggests that *realpolitik* - avoidance of religious (or any other) strife to guarantee security of the throne and government - was the chief consideration in the 1660s (and subsequently).

---

84 Modern interpretations of the motives behind Savoy in particular are: conspiracy, e.g. Bosher, *Making of the Restoration Settlement*, p. 216; a sincere attempt at compromise, e.g. Abernathy, 'English Presbyterians', p. 93; *realpolitik*, e.g. Green, *Re-establishment*, pp. 20-21; Whiteman, 'Restoration of the Church of England', p. 76.

It is possible to see Morley as part of a conspiracy, temporising with the Presbyterians, embarking on endless debates, hiding behind the ranks of the Cavaliers, and finally supporting the settlement – the 'Clarendon Code' – he had aimed at from the start. It is just possible to imagine him, at the other extreme, as some kind of ecumenist visionary, advancing comprehension or toleration freely from his heart. He was, more likely, a practical man of affairs or *realpolitik:* a moderate churchman who strove for *rapprochement* in the interests of peace in church and state: by filling vacancies with a balance of clergymen; and by producing important initiatives – most notably 'Hypotheticall ordination' and, less certainly, the Black Rubric – in the various forums or meetings of 1660 and 1662.

Morley may still have been willing to consider schemes for comprehension in the late 1660s but, essentially a pragmatist and always at the mercy of political reality, he acknowledged the Cavalier-Anglican majority in Parliament and was fully aware of the dangers of revolts and conspiracies. His initiatives failed to produce an effective compromise and he fell back on uniformity and into line with the prevailing political majority as the best hope for peace and stability above all else.[85]

---

85 A full assessment of motives, ranging over the whole of Morley's episcopal career, will be attempted in Chapter 5.

CHAPTER 5 : THE SEARCH FOR A SETTLEMENT: PART 2
THE 1670s: MORLEY'S LAST ATTEMPTS AT A SETTLEMENT

Politics intervened and church unity came to the fore again in the middle and later years of the 1670s. Charles II announced a Declaration of Indulgence in February 1672, suspending enforcement of the penal statutes, permitting freedom of conscience to Protestant dissenters and Catholic recusants alike, and allowing private worship for Catholics and public worship, by licence, for the Protestants.[1] The Declaration, combined with the disclosure of the conversion of James Duke of York to Catholicism and rumours of a secret treaty between Charles II and the Catholic Louis XIV, destroyed the relative calm of the preceding three or four years and provoked an outcry when Parliament assembled in February 1673, climaxing in rejection of the Declaration by the Commons and its subsequent retraction by the king.[2]

The Royalist/Anglican Parliament proceeded to pass the first Test Act,[3] excluding Catholics from public office, and to consider bills to comprehend or to tolerate Protestant dissenters. A bill for toleration made its appearance when Parliament assembled early in 1673.[4] It passed all stages in both Commons and Lords, to reach a joint conference of the two Houses, but was then killed by prorogation of Parliament.[5] Morley was certainly hostile to this bill, saying twice in a letter to Sheldon in April 1673 that he was 'very glad' it had failed and suggesting 'a Proclamation... or some such authoritative notice' to strengthen the resolve of magistrates against 'the Sectaries';[6] but his own actions would have been weakened as he was ill and thus absent from the Lords during all readings of the bill.[7]

A comprehension bill was produced by 'some great Men of the House of Commons', apparently later in the year, according to Baxter.[8] There is no sign of its appearance in the Commons,[9] however, and Baxter pins responsibility for its death on Morley but supplies no evidence for his claim.[10] Morley subsequently introduced to the House of Lords, moreover, in February 1674, a bill[11] - 'moved by the Bishop of Winchester'[12] - in which he sought to establish his form of comprehension. His bill would have removed the requirement on incumbents to renounce the Solemn League and Covenant, which had involved an oath taken by many clergy in the 1640s and 50s

---

1 e.g. A. Browning (ed.), *English Historical Documents, 1660-1714,* vol. 8 (London, 1953), p. 387.
2 W. Cobbett (ed.), *Parliamentary History of England,* vol. IV (London, 1808), cols 517-526 (debate); col. 561 (retraction).
3 25 CII c.2.
4 e.g. Bod Tanner 43, ff. 189, 191-94; *Journals of the House of Lords,* (London, 1767-1830), vol. 12, pp. 561-85.
5 *Journals of the House of Commons,* vol. 9 (London, 1803), pp. 263-81; *Lords Journal,* vol. 12, pp. 561-85.
6 Bod Tanner 42, f. 7 (or f. 5? because of confusing numbering of the original); 'sectaries' are not defined (as usual) and could have meant Protestants and Catholics(?).
7 *Lords Journal,* vol. 12, pp. 528-30 ('not well', 13 February 1673); ibid., pp. 521-85 (absence for the entire session).
8 M. Sylvester (ed.), *Reliquiae Baxterianae,* (London, 1696), part 3, p. 140 (comprehension bill).
9 *Commons Journal,* vol. 9, pp. 281-314 (sessions from 20/10/1673 to 24/2/1674).
10 Baxter, *Reliquiae,* part 3, p. 140.
11 HL/PO/JO/10/135 - 70 (Bill); *HMC, 9th Report,* (London, 1884), p. 44 (Bill); *Lords Journal,* vol. 12, pp. 635, 643 (1st and 2nd Readings then apparently lost at prorogation of Parliament); Bod Tanner 44, f. 249 (link to Morley), Baxter, *Reliquiae,* part 3, p. 140.
12 Bod Tanner 44, f. 249 signed by a John Lowland with the right month (February) and no year.

to support Presbyterianism.[13] It would also, more surprisingly and more importantly, have removed the requirement on incumbents to declare 'assent and consent' to the Book of Common Prayer. Removal of this declaration was common to both Baxter's and Morley's bill and, if Morley opposed Baxter's efforts, it might have been either because Baxter's bill, unlike his own, narrowed clergy support from all to just the doctrinal of the Thirty Nine Articles; or, more likely, he feared a bill coming from Baxter and 'some great Men' might gain momentum, become a Trojan horse, and encourage Baxter and his friends to press for further reforms foreshadowed in Baxter's 'background papers' such as acceptance of ministers ordained by Presbyters and optionality over ceremonies and vestments.[14] He would take charge of his bill, control events, and kept reform within limits.

Debates – what was actually said – in Parliament and the Privy Council, which would illuminate much more fully the views of Morley and his fellow bishops, are missing from the crucial documents. Sheldon (the Archbishop) certainly resumed marshalling bishops and arranging votes in the Lords just when the Declaration of Indulgence, the Test Bill, and the comprehension and toleration bills were to be considered. His letters of 1672/73 survive, urging attendance by bishops in Convocation and Parliament 'at so criticall a time'.[15] Morley, however, never appeared in the Lords in February or March 1673, it will be recalled, when the Test and the comprehension bills were progressing through the Lords.[16] Sheldon himself was not always there; and fourteen bishops – not twenty-one, as claimed by Simon[17] – were present at the second reading of the Test bill – facts which may explain Sheldon's anxiety about attendance but which must, at the same time, cast doubt on the effectiveness of his control and discipline as well as on Baxter's accusation of sabotage of the comprehension bill by Morley. One contemporary commentator considered the majority of bishops were for enforcement of the penal statutes against 'papists' and (presumably Protestant) 'Phanatics' alike[18] but, if so, on this showing, at least, they were not very active.

---

13 A proposal less radical than it looks since, according to the terms of the Act of Uniformity, the requirement was due for repeal in 1682.
14 Baxter, *Reliquiae,* part 3, pp. 109-13, 156-60.
15 BL, Harleian MS 7377, ff. 39r, 39v, 48v, 49v; see also V. D. Sutch, *Gilbert Sheldon: Architect of Anglican Survival 1640-1675* (The Hague, 1973), p. 135.
16 *Lords Journal,* vol. 12, pp. 553-85 for both bills and for episcopal attendance.
17 Simon claims that 21 bishops attended the Test Bill's second reading and that Morley was a 'principal speaker' but gives no source (W. G. Simon, *Restoration Episcopate* [New York, 1965], pp. 83-84).
18 Bod Clarendon MS 72, f. 253.

After the failure of Morley's bill - it drifts out of sight - there were yet more contacts in 1674/75 between the two sides.[19] Morley encouraged John Tillotson and Edward Stillingfleet (then Dean of Canterbury and a prebendary - or canon - at St Paul's respectively) to hold discussions with Baxter.[20] Baxter had high hopes of Tillotson and Stillingfleet and had written as early as December 1673 that, if discussion could be confined to the Presbyterians and those latter two Anglicans, they would have reached agreement 'in a Week's time'.[21] By 1674 he was writing that there was 'none so forward' - showing eagerness for comprehension - as Morley and Ward (Bishop of Salisbury), none more sincere than Tillotson and Stillingfleet.[22] A scheme for comprehension was apparently agreed between them but nothing seems to have come of it.[23] More letters from Sheldon to bishops about attendance at Parliament survive for 1675 but their tantalising phrases - for example, 'there is more than ordinary occasion for your Lorships attendance' and 'Religion... shall have the priority' - do not tell us what the business was or what view Sheldon was taking.[24] In the end the initiative seems to have led nowhere and the whole thing died down after another toleration bill - the Duke of Buckingham's - had failed by November 1675;[25] though it should be said that Tillotson's reform programme, including revision of the prayer book and optionality over ceremonies, together with his ordination proposals, though without date, echoes Morley's initiatives.[26]

The following January 1676 Archbishop Sheldon issued his Three Questions which launched the Compton Census to discover the extent of 'dissent' in the Northern and Southern Provinces; and Morley's involvement - his last in the national politics of religion - was, in common with all the other bishops, inevitable. The scale of 'dissent' was miniscule according to the census returns and questions arise about the accuracy of these figures and the motives of the compilers.

Archbishop Sheldon's instructions to the bishops of the Southern Province were, Anne Whiteman considers, 'remarkably straightforward'.[27] There are numerous survivals of the instructions, however, and one set has additional paragraphs. The first paragraph downplays in advance the numbers of 'dissenters' as 'groundless and untrue' and the second concludes 'the just numbers of dissenters being known...their suppression will be a work very practical'.[28] A letter from Morley in June 1676 to Lord Treasurer Danby[29] underscores both these points - minimisation of the numbers

---

19 Baxter, *Reliquiae*, part 3, p. 156.
20 Stillingfleet was Dean of St Paul's 1678-1689 and Bishop of Worcester 1689-1699; Tillotson was Dean of Canterbury 1672-1689, Dean of St Paul's 1689-1691, and Archbishop of Canterbury 1691-1694.
21 N. H. Keeble and G. F. Nuttall (eds), *Calendar of the Correspondence of Richard Baxter*, (Oxford, 1991), letter 937.
22 Baxter, *Reliquiae*, part 3, p. 156.
23 Baxter, *Reliquiae*, part 3, pp. 158-60; LPL, MS 1743, pp. 145-48 (a reproduction of Baxter).
24 BL, Harleian MS 7377, f. 58r.
25 *HMC, 9th Report*, p. 68, *HMC, 10th Report*, Appendix Part VI (London, 1887), p. 183.
26 LPL, MS 1743, pp. 151-54, without date.
27 A Whiteman (ed.), *Compton Census of 1676: a Critical Edition*, (Oxford, 1986), p. xxviii.
28 Bod Tanner 282, ff. 66r,v.
29 Thomas Osborne, Earl of Danby and Duke of Leeds, was Lord Treasurer 1673-1679, advocate of the marriage between Mary, daughter of James Duke of York (the future James II), and William of Orange in 1677, and a signatory of the Invitation to William to replace James in 1688.

and suppression – by referring to Charles II's reluctance to suppress 'Conventicles' and by proceeding to 'hope the King' will note the smaller numbers of dissenters and see 'there is neither danger in attempting nor...difficulty in effecting this great work'.[30] Sheldon's parallel instructions to the Archbishop of York contain the phrase 'if your Grace...shall...returne any reasonable accompt... I shall improve it to the best advantage I can.'[31]

Anne Whiteman pins the policy (suppression) and the strategy (minimising numbers to suggest, in the event of suppression, small risk of rebellion) on Danby.[32] She absolves the bishops of any sinister activity and insists on their innocence. She relies, for this, on the version of Sheldon's letter as apparently dispatched to the bishops, but questions linger over the other two 'surrounding' paragraphs. Anne Whiteman's 'detective work' concerning the original plan – their order and their evident subsequent discarding – is convincing; but then to ignore them is more questionable. It is these paragraphs which posit minimisation of numbers and mention the ease of suppression; and, though laid aside in the end, they had had 'a life' among official documents. The very same notions – minimisation and suppression – are, moreover, quite explicit in Morley's private letter to Danby written shortly afterwards and these sentiments are likely to have coloured, intentionally or subconsciously, his thinking. There is also the matter of interpreting 'improve it to the best advantage I can' in Sheldon's letter to the Archbishop of York: merely improving the appearance of the document or improving – adjusting – the figures to strengthen them and to justify Sheldon's thinking?

The phrase was removed and replaced by an instruction to one of his archdeacons the same day and to a dean round about the same time with the less provocative phrase – in order to 'make use' (of the figures) – which may suggest that Sheldon was now trying to conceal his real motives. Much would depend on which came first – the letter to the Archbishop (with 'improve') or the ones to the archdeacon and dean (with 'make use') but, again, this is none too clear.[33]

Resolution of these problems is full of difficulty – even interpreting words like 'improve', let alone deciding which letter was written first, or delving into the subconscious thoughts of Sheldon and Morley – and, in the end, all turns on which document (or parts thereof) is considered more truthful, the included or the discarded, the public or private? Even if Danby was the prime mover, it looks very much as if

---

30 BL, Egerton MS 3329 f. 119; *HMC, 11th Report, (London,* 1888), part VII, p. 14.
31 BL, Harleian MS 7737, f. 62r.
32 Whiteman, *Compton Census,* p. xxiv; but there is much evidence of Sheldon's concern about dissenters and disorder before 1676, e.g. Bod Addit. MS c. 308, ff. 31v; 142r; BL, Harleian MS 7377, ff. 38r, 55v; see also other contemporary concerns about emboldened conventiclers *(CSPD 1673-1675,* pp. 424, 581 and Sparrow of Exeter's comment that 'the factions grow bold' (Bod Tanner 42, f. 112, no date), though he paints a more obliging picture of Devon and Cornwall in 1671 (Bod Clarendon c. 305, f. 231); also Thomas attributes to Sheldon in 1669 the opposite tacit of conducting a census to exaggerate the numbers of dissenters in 1669 to impress on Parliament the need for another Conventicle Act (R. Thomas, 'Comprehension and Indulgence', in G. F. Nuttall and O. Chadwick (eds), *From Uniformity to Unity,* [London, 1962], p. 216).
33 BL, Harleian MS 7377, f. 61v, 63v (letters to an archdeacon, 22/1/1676, and to a dean, no date unless 2/3/1676 applies to both letters on the folio – and neither identifies the intended recipient by name); f. 62r (letter to the Archbishop of York, 22/1/1676).

Sheldon and Morley were colluding with him over policy (suppression) and strategy (minimising numbers) by 1676; though actual manipulation of the figures is more speculative. It would seem that the bishops, including Morley, were ready and willing at this time to embark on prosecutions of 'dissenters' (Catholic and Protestant). The prime target of the bishops was Catholicism but their overtures, through Tillotson and Stillingfleet to Baxter and the Presbyterians, had failed by 1676 and, if preventing Catholicism meant suppressing Protestant dissenters as well, the bishops, including Morley, may have been ready to do so by 1676.

There remains one other puzzle. The level of prosecutions in the episcopal consistory court at Winchester - for example, seven specific, fifteen 'putative' in 1675/76 - was very much smaller than the numbers of 'dissenters' in his census return and infinitesimal in archdeaconry populations of 68,000 (Winchester) and 75,000 (Surrey).[34] There would have been prosecutions in the archdeacons' and in the secular courts, of course, but Morley knew the figures - 9,000 or so dissenters and recusants altogether - and could have enforced more prosecutions in his own court - the choice was his; lack of prosecutions suggests that he did not wish to do so and that his real motive was peace within his diocese. If there was any deceit, moreover, it may therefore have lain in a wish, when writing to Danby, to convince Danby of his loyalty. In one of the discarded paragraphs Sheldon states that he hopes to 'justify the diligence Zeal and Integrity of both my Self and Brethren'.[35] This seems to have been their central concern and, while Sheldon may have meant to act, Morley's response seems to have been more ambivalent.

Politics underwent yet more upheaval with the outburst of the Popish Plot and Exclusion in the late 1670s. This triggered another 'turnaround', with further attempts to make common cause with the Protestant dissenters against Catholicism;[36] but Morley was, by this time, too old, sick, and blind, to take his seat in the Lords and join the fight.[37]

CONCLUSION

Religion had continued to be a major - divisive - issue in the national politics of the 1670s and, while Morley was centrally involved, his record is by no means clear or straightforward. He changed tack - or appeared to do so - several times in his approach towards the Protestant dissenters and there is even some ambivalence in his treatment of Catholics at this time.

---

34 For prosecutions, see Chapter 7; for population, see Whiteman, *Compton Census,* pp. xcvii, 72-74, 96.
35 Bod Tanner 282, f. 62v.
36 See, for a thorough account, H. Horwitz, 'Protestant Reconciliation in the Exclusion Crisis', *JEH,* XV, No. 2 (10/1964); also E. Polhill, *Samaritan,* (London, 1682), pp. 120-29; LPL, MS 1743, p. 149 (which has notes for a bill involving comprehension and toleration).
37 *Lords Journal,* vol. 13, *passim* (showing Morley's absence); for his afflictions e.g. Bod Tanner 40, f. 87 (faulty numbers again) 1/3/1677, 'a great cold in my head.... the loss of the sight of one of mine eyes wholy and the decaying of the other.... the growing of the scivy and the dropsy...the akeing of my legs and shinns.... shortage of breath.... the swelling of my feet and ankles.... reading and writing as little as possible.... Cataract....'

It is important, at this point, to recall the prevailing context of the times. The 1670s and 1680s continued, like the decades before them, to be as disconcerting and dislocating as ever: the king imposing and then withdrawing his Declaration of Indulgence; James Duke of York, his heir and brother, converting from Protestantism to Catholicism; rumours of a secret treaty between Charles II and the Catholic Louis XIV; peace, war, and peace again with the Netherlands; climaxing in the occurrence of plots - Popish and Rye House - in the late 1670s and early 1680s; and the campaign to exclude the Catholic James from the throne. Change, confusion, suspicion, fear - conditions were uncertain and unstable - this was the background against which Morley was operating and it is hardly surprising that his actions and the thinking behind them appear to be ever changing as well.

Morley's motives and, in particular, his sincerity, during this crucial period have been assailed just as in the 1660s. Norman Sykes, writing about the 1670s, relies on Baxter - all 'snares' (Baxter's favourite word) - and, concurring with earlier detractors, concludes that the purpose of Morley's initiatives was to divide and weaken the dissenters. Of the most recent writers, John Spurr declares him guilty of 'machinations' and ends his account, with apparent endorsement from Ruth Paley and Beverly Adams, on a similarly depressing note.[38] Morley appears in their eyes as a cynical calculator and a far from a sincere reformer.

One definite and consistent theme was Morley's hostility to Catholicism. Morley's hatred (not too strong a word) of 'Popery' was a consistent theme of his letters and writings from the 1650s to the 1670s,[39] and he never ceased to denounce and condemn Catholicism and all its works. Some of his most striking attacks were written in the 1670s and were addressed directly and openly to the king once he had marshalled support from the body of the clergy. In January 1675, for example, he was a signatory of the reply to the king's paper in which the bishops thundered against 'the superstition and idolatrous practices and usurpation of Rome'. In 1678 or 1679 he was again involved, together with the Dean and Chapter and the clergy of Winchester, in an address to the king, which stressed 'the Darkness and Chains of Popery' and the need to 'guard against the Evils of Faithless Popery and relentless Bigottry'.[40]

All the more surprising and puzzling, therefore, is the lack of concrete action - as distinct from writing - by Morley against the Catholics. There is no evidence of his involvement in the Test Acts of the 1670s and there were few prosecutions of Catholic recusants in his declining consistory court. Illness in 1673 appears to explain his absence from the Lords during the passage of the first Test Act and his physical

---

38 Baxter dwells on Morley's 'snares' (Baxter, *Reliquiae,* part 3, pp. 101, 109, 140) and 'vehemence' (ibid., part 2, pp. 337, 343, 363; part 3, p. 101); N. Sykes, *From Sheldon to Secker: Aspects of Church History 1660-1768,* (Cambridge, 1959), p. 79; John Spurr, 'Church of England: Comprehension and the Toleration Act of 1689', *EHR,* CIV, no. 413 (10/1989), p. 936; R. Paley (ed.), *The House of Lords 1660-1715,* vol. 5 (Cambridge, 2016), entry on Morley, B. Adams and R. Paley, pp. 316-29.
39 The prevailing mood according to e.g. J. P. Kenyon, *The Popish Plot,* (London, 1972), pp. 2-5.
40 *CSPD 1673-1675,* p. 549; HRO, 7M49/3, paper 19 (no date).

ailments and decline similarly ruled him out of action by the time of the second Test Act in the late 1670s. Lack of prosecutions at Winchester over the twenty years of his reign are more difficult to explain. There were other courts, ecclesiastical (archdeacon's courts) and secular (magistrates' courts and quarter sessions) but it is astonishing that such a stout defender of the Church of England, such a loud opponent of the church of Rome, did not tackle the problem with greater vigour with his own judicial machinery in his own territory. A host of other matters - though not, apparently, debates on the Test Acts - was always pressing to distract him from diocesan business.[41] Otherwise, practical considerations - pragmatism - the wish for peace within the diocese - may have prevailed.

Establishing Morley's approach towards the Protestant dissenters is even more complex. Morley was certainly no 'irenic' visionary. He was no advocate of toleration. He consistently urged 'Execution' of the laws against dissenters. This had been so when he declared in his famous tirade on the floor of the House in 1665: 'If there bee noe Lawes there can bee noe Society...All must Live under a Rule or none must...'[42] It was so when he urged a greater degree of conformity on the Huguenots of Southampton in 1668 and Wandsworth in 1683;[43] it was so when he pressed Sheldon in 1673 for a 'Proclamation' or 'some such authoritative notice' to restate the law and so encourage its 'Execution';[44] and it was so when he expressed to Danby in 1676 his 'hope' that the king would note the smaller numbers of dissenters and see 'there is neither danger in attempting nor...difficulty in effecting' execution of the law against 'dissenters' (Catholic and Protestant in his use of the term).[45]

Morley's record towards comprehension, as distinct from toleration, is much less clear. He uttered damning comments on comprehension more than once in his correspondence. In July 1672 he told the Earl of Anglesey that the solution was 'not a comprehension'; and in April 1673 he wrote to Sheldon that 'I never would... nor ever will consent to that which they call a Comprehension.'[46] The phrase 'that which they call a comprehension' - does not rule out *all* - just *some* - schemes for comprehension, however; while the letter to Anglesey proceeds to mention the possibility of 'a Coalition or Incorporation' of the Presbyterians.[47] His Bill of 1674 and the contacts with Baxter may well reflect such an approach - comprehension with limits. Removal of 'assent and consent' to the Book of Common Prayer was a substantial concession to the dissenting clergy but was not nearly as wide as Baxter and his Presbyterian colleagues sought.[48]

---

41 See, for a summary of his other activities, Chapter 9.
42 Bod Carte MS 80, ff. 757-59 (reprinted in Caroline Robbins, 'The Oxford Session of the Long Parliament of Charles II 9th to the 31st October 1665', *BIHR*, 21 (1948), 214-24).
43 R. Gwynn, 'Strains of Worship: the Huguenots and Non-Conformity', in D. J. B. Trim (ed.), *The Huguenots: History and Memory in Transnational Context*, (Leiden, 2011), pp. 134, 138.
44 Bod Tanner 42 f. 7 (7/4/1673) comments on unsettling of magistrates by the Declaration of Indulgence (1672).
45 BL, Egerton MS 3329 f. 119; *HMC, 11th Report, (London,* 1888), part VII, p. 14.
46 Bod Carte MS 69, f. 446; Bod Tanner 42, f. 7 (or 5? - confusing numbering) - in the latter Morley manages to provoke suspicion by appearing to endorse the benefits of dividing 'the Presbyterians' from 'the Sectaries'; (see I. M. Green, *Re-establishment of the Church of England* [Oxford, 1978], p. 22).
47 Bod Tanner 42, f. 7 (Sheldon); Bod Carte MS 69, f. 446v-447v (Anglesey).
48 Baxter, *Reliquiae*, part 2, pp. 109-13 (Baxter's scheme 1673); 158-60 (Baxter's scheme after talks with Stillingfleet *et aliis* 1674/75); Keeble and Nuttall, *Baxter Correspondence,* item 937 (reproduces the scheme of 1673).

Assessing the extent of his comprehension is problematic enough, assessing his motives even more so. Sympathy for the plight of the dissenters is a possibility. Contemporaries - Wood, Burnet, and Kennett[49] - considered Morley a Calvinist and this, together with a possible bond of feeling for the 'ejectees' of 1662, arising from his own years of exile and suffering, may explain his attempts at *rapprochement*.

There is no specific evidence for this, however, and hard - pragmatic - calculation may have lain at the root of his comprehension proposals. This sits well with his views on Popery. Security from superstitious, treacherous, and dictatorial Catholics (in his eyes) and security also from the king and his Catholic heir (James Duke of York) are likely to have been the prime considerations which drove Morley further in the direction of *rapprochement*. 'Wee only desire Security' is a memorable phrase in his speech of 1665, and his anxieties about 'Sectaries' in his letter to Sheldon of 1674 underline Morley's concerns.[50] Union or alliance of Anglicans with the more moderate Protestant dissenters would strengthen the cause of Protestantism and deprive the king and the duke of their stance as supporters of a general toleration under which cloak they hoped to improve the lot of Catholics. Morley was quite open about his tactic. He wrote in January 1674 of 'a Coalition or Incorporation of the Presbyterian Party into the Church'...as 'the only way to hinder the growth of Popery...'; and Baxter believed this when he wrote that in 'the last Sessions of Parliament [1674/1675], bishop Morley had on all occasions...cryded out...the danger of Popery, and talked much of abatements, and taking in the Nonconformists ...'[51] Morley was, undoubtedly, conservative at heart wanting really to retain bishops, surplice, and ceremonies, for example.[52] He opposed Catholicism - 'Popery' - from start to finish, likewise toleration - he was a man of his age - but his attitude to comprehension is more complex. He seems to have made a distinction between his private - conservative - views and his public policy, and on several occasions he took steps to reach a measure of *rapprochement* with the moderate Protestant dissenters. His own comment - 'I am no more a Presbyterian than I am a Popish Bishop, tho' I have been said to be both the one and the other and indeed as much one as the other'[53] - is a typical 'Morleyian' convolution which may capture something of his ambivalence and the reputation he had gained, accidentally or otherwise, for himself.

It is more convincing to see Morley less as an idealist, conspirator, or hardliner and more as a pragmatist - a practical director - who recognised the need for change

---

49 Wood, *Athenae*, vol. 2, col. 768; O. Airy (ed.), *Burnet's History of My Own Time*, vol. 1 (Oxford, 1897), p. 314; W. Kennett, *Register and Chronicle Ecclesiastical and Civil*, (London, 1728), p. 666.
50 Bod Carte MS 80, ff. 757-9; Bod Tanner 42, f. 7 (or f. 5 - number problem).
51 Bod Carte MS 69, f. 447, 7/1672; Baxter, *Reliquiae*, part 3, p. 156.
52 See, e.g. his letter to Sheldon denouncing Herbert Croft (Bishop of Hereford 1661-1691) for his willingness to abandon ceremonies (Bod Tanner 42, f. 7).
53 Bod Tanner 43, f. 33.

at national level, whatever his private feelings. He saw the need for *rapprochement* in the interests of peace and was the source of several initiatives, doomed, as it turned out, to achieve it in the early and mid-1670s. It is apparently true that, by the later 1670s, disappointed, disillusioned, and in a state of exhaustion, he fell back on calls for suppression but, for whatever reason, there does not seem to have been much persecution of Catholics and Dissenters in his own consistory court; while the Huguenot communities at Southampton and Wandsworth more than survived his regime.[54]

If Morley had hopes of some form of comprehension, they failed. It should be remembered, however, that, if he failed, so did everyone else during his time as bishop: his two Archbishops, Sheldon and Sancroft;[55] the colleagues to his 'right', Cosin and Wren; the colleagues to his 'left', Wilkins, Reynolds, and Croft; even the future bishop, Stillingfleet, and the future archbishop, Tillotson;[56] as well as Presbyterians such as Calamy and Baxter; Atkins the MP; and Hale the judge.[57] When Morley died in 1684 there seemed no hope for comprehension or for toleration. None of the schemes for comprehension came to pass in the seventeenth century – or later – and, when toleration came in 1689,[58] it came with limits – no freedom for Catholics or Unitarians, and no civil rights for Protestant dissenters – and it came after the Revolution of 1689, the overthrow of James II, the arrival of William III, a Calvinist, and the political need to reward Protestant dissenters for their loyalty and to retain their support for the new regime. Few strove harder than Morley for some form of *rapprochement* or unity among the more moderate religious groups and, if he failed, so did all the others in his time.

---

54 For 'restraint' of the court towards dissenters, see the above section on Compton Census; towards the Huguenots, see Gwynn, 'Strains of Worship', pp. 133, 139.
55 Bod Addit. MS c. 308, f. 114r (Sheldon); Tanner 300, f. 143 (Sancroft); see Sykes, *Sheldon to Secker*, pp. 188-89; M. D. W. Jones, 'Ecclesiastical Courts before and after the English Civil War: Office Jurisdiction at Oxford and Peterborough 1630-1675' unpub. B.Litt. thesis (Oxford, 1977), p. 247; Sheldon was Archbishop of Canterbury 1663-1677, Sancroft was Archbishop 1677-1690.
56 LPL. MS 1743, pp. 111-18 (Stillingfleet); ibid., pp. 151-54 (Tillotson) is evidence of the continuing interest of Stillingfleet and Tillotson in reforms which would have met at least some of the objections of the Presbyterians; neither document has a date but styling (Stillingfleet as 'Bishop' and Tillotson as 'Archbishop') means they must be of the 1690s.
57 These men have all been identified in earlier or later footnotes and can be found in e.g. *ODNB*.
58 1 W+M c. 18.

CHAPTER 6 : MORLEY AND WORCESTER: HIS STEWARDSHIP OF THE DIOCESE[1]

CONSECRATION AND ENTHRONEMENT

The elevation of Morley to the Bishopric of Worcester took place in the autumn of 1660. The process began towards the end of September with the order from the Crown to the Dean and Chapter of Worcester to elect a bishop (the *congé d'élire*) and then a second royal order (by letter missive) to nominate Morley for the bishopric. The formalities of election by the Dean and Chapter, royal assent, and archbishop's confirmation followed; and the procedures climaxed with the consecration of Morley in October 1660.[2]

Morley swore the oath of allegiance in a preliminary ceremony at St Mary le Bow on 9 October and the consecration itself took place at Westminster Abbey on the twenty-eighth.[3] Four others became bishops at the same time: Griffith to St Asaph, Henderson to Salisbury, Sanderson to Lincoln, and Sheldon to London. Brian Duppa, Bishop of Winchester, one of the eight bishops from the reign of Charles I who lived to see the Restoration, conducted the ceremony, assisted by Accepted Frewen, Archbishop of York, and Matthew Wren, Bishop of Ely, newly released from his eighteen-year stint in the Tower.[4]

Enthronement was the final stage in the process. Two ceremonies took place, in fact, for Morley at Worcester: the first by proxy, shortly after his consecration, on 10 November 1660; and the 'real thing' ten months later on 12 September 1661.[5]

Morley arrived in person at Broadway in the diocese on 11 September 1661. The next day he passed through Pershore, among other Worcester parishes, accompanied by some of 'the good and the great', bells ringing, crowds waving as he dispensed blessings and money to the poor (until it ran out). He was met at various stages by the archdeacon and canons, by Sir John Pakington and other gentry, and finally by the lord lieutenant, his deputies, and the high sheriff, gentry, and clergy who brought him into the city in a grand procession with troops on horse and foot, ten trumpeters, and 'divers' volleys of shot.[6]

---

1 A version of this chapter is due to appear, with appropriate modifications, in *Midland History* during 2019.
2 J. Horn (ed.), *Fasti Ecclesiae Anglicanae*/Worcester, (London, 1992), p. 107; LPL, Juxon's Register, ff. 182r, 183r, 186v, 208v; WRO, Episcopal Register, 716.093 2648 10 iii, f. 3r-4r/p. 5-7;Notea discrepancy over the date of the election - 9 October (Juxon), 6 October (Worcester); see also R. Latham and W. Matthews (eds), *Diary of Samuel Pepys*, vol. 1 (London, 1971), p. 276.
3 S. Porter, S. K. Roberts, and I. Roy (eds), *Diary and Papers of Henry Townshend 1640-1663*, (Worcestershire Historical Society, 2014), p. 293; W. Kennett, *Register and Chronicle Ecclesiastical and Civil*, (London, 1728), p. 296.
4 The eight were Duppa (Salisbury), Frewen (York), Juxon (London), King (Chichester), Peirs (Wells), Skinner (Oxford), Warner (Rochester), Wren (Ely); see relevant *Fasti Ecclesiae Anglicanae*; for Wren's eighteen years in the Tower, see his will TNA, Prob 11, 1667, 324.
5 WRO, 716 093 2648 10 iii, ff. 3r-5v/pp. 5-10.
6 Kennett, *Register*, p. 535 (apparently an anonymous letter); Townshend, *Diary*, p. 303.

The enthronement ceremony began apparently 'within half an hour' of his arrival at the bishop's palace.[7] Giles Thornborough, the acting dean, and eight other canons accompanied Morley, having put on his 'Rochet', from his palace to the north door of the cathedral; and, joined there by the choir, they processed, while singing the *Benedicite,* into the cathedral and up to the altar where Morley prostrated himself in prayer. One of the canons, William Dowdeswell, tendered the oaths of loyalty to the cathedral and of respect for its statutes and customs, which Morley then swore on the Gospels. The notary public produced the commission from the Archdeacon of Canterbury to the Dean and Chapter authorising the enthronement, and the Dean and Chapter led him first to the throne in the Choir and then to his customary place in the Chapter House. Morley, sitting on the throne, then received oaths of obedience from the Dean and Chapter.[8]

All then accompanied him in procession, bells ringing and trumpets sounding, back to the palace 'for a very noble entertainment...of all Sorts of Meats and Wines' which, according to a witness, was 'not like the Dulness of these divided Times' but worthy of the reception 'Alexandria and Constantinople gave to... Athanasius and Chrysostome at their Return from Banishment.'[9]

These events are vividly recorded in the episcopal register. They bring to life some of *the dramatis personae* of Worcester in the early 1660s and place the account of their work which follows in a more human context.

THE ROLE OF THE BISHOP

Bishops were central to the life and well-being of the Church and, although Gilbert Sheldon, archbishop and administrator in chief, was always sending out instructions,[10] no definitive list of their duties appears to exist, not in Gibson's Codex for example, nor in the canons of the Church.[11] The duties were clear enough from custom and practice if nothing else. General oversight and management of the diocese lay with him: ordinations and confirmations were specifically his – only he could perform those ceremonies – and institutions of clergy to livings, together with regular visitations of the diocese and the operation of the consistory court, though subject to varying degrees of delegation, were ultimately his responsibility; likewise the administration of his estates which really was a matter for delegation. His role, beyond all this 'routine' business, was to ensure the well-being of his flock – both clergy and lay men and women – and to advance the interests of the Church; and there was, on top of all this, a political expectation that he would attend the House of Lords; not to overlook commitments arising from other posts such as membership of the Privy Council.

---

7   Kennett, *Register,* p. 535; Townshend, *Diary,* p. 303.
8   WRO, 716 093 2648 10 iii, ff. 3r-5v/pp. 5-10.
9   Kennett, *Register,* p. 536.
10 e.g. Bod Tanner 240, f. 184, Tanner 282, f. 66.
11 E. Gibson (ed.), *Codex Juris Ecclesiastici Anglicani,* (Oxford, 1761); G. Bray (ed.), *Anglican Canons 1529-1947,* (Woodridge, 1998).

To turn specifically to Worcester and Morley, the dispatch of business in 1660 was even more urgent than usual: in particular, the recovery of ecclesiastical property, together with a repair programme, and the overhaul of manpower in the form of rectors, vicars, and curates were two huge items overwhelming the agenda at Worcester no less than elsewhere. This survey lies, as always, at the mercy of document survival and must inevitably appear uneven. Much can be said about manpower and some aspects of property; something about the revival of diocesan machinery and visitations; hardly anything about ordinations and nothing about confirmations for want of documents and perhaps also because there would not have been much to report within the timescale.[12] That leaves the consistory court where the fortunate survival of the relevant court book allows a glimpse of episcopal discipline under Morley's regime.

OFFICIALDOM

Morley was Bishop of Worcester from October 1660 to April 1662 but parallel commitments at national level, religious, political, and social, either kept him in London or forced his return there for most of his time as bishop. He was, as we have seen, a central figure at Worcester House in October 1660.[13] This was brought to an abrupt end when the Duchess of York went into labour, affecting the succession as her husband, the Duke, was presumptive heir to the throne, and Morley was one of the figures required to confirm the legitimacy of the child.[14] Revision of the Book of Common Prayer could not wait: two bodies, the Savoy Conference from March to July 1661 and Convocation from May 1661 onwards, were commissioned to consider the matter, and Morley was a member of both assemblies. The coronation, at which Morley was preacher, took place in the middle of all this in April 1661;[15] and, as if this was not enough, Morley, *en route* for Worcester in early September, delayed at Oxford to accompany his friend, Clarendon, Lord Chancellor of England and prospective Chancellor of the University, during a lengthy degree ceremony.[16]

---

12   There would appear to be nothing in the records at WRO or the cathedral about any of these aspects of business: there is no trace of confirmations, the relevant visitation book is confined to names of clergy and churchwardens (WRO, 802 2951 1 i, 1661), and a search through ordination originals (WRO, 7322 2049), the calendar of ordinations (778 7322 2448), and clerical subscriptions (116 051 2697) revealed nothing definitive
13   See Chapter 4.
14   *Life of Edward Earl of Clarendon... in which is included a Continuation of his History of the Grand Rebellion,* vol. 1 (Oxford, 1827), p. 389; *HMC, 5th Report,* (London, 1876), p. 157 (this source mentions the presence of bishops but not Morley specifically); R. S. Bosher, *Making of the Restoration Settlement,* (London, 1951), p. 187.
15   *A Sermon Preached at the Magnificent Coronation of Charles II,* (London, 1661); Clarendon, *Life and Continuation,* vol. 2, p. 12; E. S. de Beer (ed.), *The Diary of John Evelyn,* vol. 3 (Oxford, 1955), p. 282.
16   A. Clarke (ed.), *Life and Times of Anthony Wood,* vol. 1 (Oxford, 1891), p. 411.

Morley would seem to have spent, not surprisingly, only one short spell in person in Worcester. The episcopal register records an 'institution' (or appointment) of a rector to a parish on 13 December 1660 and mentions a 'commission' with an authorised substitute acting on his behalf.[17] This shows he was not present in Worcester at the beginning of his episcopate. He must have been in Worcester for his second, proper, enthronement ceremony on 12 September 1661, and his register records his conduct in person of nine institutions in the palace over the following weeks from September to November 1661.[18] He signed a 'deed of delegation', devolving stewardship of the diocese to others on 16 November,[19] and he must have left Worcester for London at that point, never to return during the remainder of his term as bishop.[20] This strongly implies a stay of nine or so weeks; after which he was required back in London for more work on the prayer book in Convocation from mid November 1661 and then on the floor of the House of Lords and in committee to steer the Bill of Uniformity to completion from January to May 1662.

Surviving evidence - mainly the episcopal register, a consistory court book, and the writings of Baxter and Morley - shows that the flow of business continued whether the bishop was present or not. Morley took personal charge of diocesan business, certainly institutions, when he was present at Worcester; but bishops were often absent, and it was customary to leave much of the routine business of the diocese to others. Revival of diocesan machinery - personnel if not a restructure - to ensure the conduct of business with or without the bishop's personal intervention was Morley's prime task. Episcopal and cathedral documents at Worcester record the appointment of key officials in 1660: in particular, Timothy Baldwyn as chancellor in charge of as much of the general diocesan administration (institutions, licences, dispensations and the like) as the bishop thought fit to delegate to him, together with the more specific legal business of the diocese; and Thomas Streete as the overseer of the bishop's 'property portfolio'.[21] Under these leading figures was a host of subordinates attached to the estate and diocesan offices: surrogates, notaries public, apparitors, and advocates running the consistory court; together with stewards, bailiffs, and surveyors managing the estates. It would be fascinating to know how these officials gained their posts in the first place but there the record falls silent.

---

17 WRO, 716 093 2648 10 iii, p. 12/f. 6v; R. A. Beddard, 'Restoration Oxford and the Remaking of the Protestant Establishment', in N. Tyacke (ed.), *History of the University of Oxford*, vol. 4 (Oxford, 1997), p. 817.
18 WRO, 716 093 2648 10 iii, ff. 4v-5v/pp. 8-10 (enthronement); ff. 9r-10r/pp. 17-19 (institutions); 'Idem Reverendus Pater Epus Wigorn... in palatio suo' prefaces the nine institutions; the phrase 'Idem Reverendus Pater' is applied to nineteen others, implying his personal involvement, but these do not include 'in palatio' and fall outside the known dates (9/1661 - 11/1661) when he was definitely at Worcester; a further twelve make it clear that delegates were acting on his behalf; one (entry) is uncertain.
19 WRO, 716 093 2648 10 iii, f. 11/p. 22 (16/11/1661).
20 WRO, 716 093 2648 10 iii, f. 11/p. 22; subsequent institutions show two acting alone (p. 20), three (p. 21), and also Chancellor Baldwyn (p. 21), who was strangely omitted from the deed but who would have been the most likely figure to conduct such business - presumably his involvement was taken for granted by Morley and Co. when they were setting up the delegation arrangement.
21 WRO, 716 093 2648 10 iii, f. 5v/p. 10 (Baldwyn); Worcester CL, Chapter Act Book A76, f. 7r (confirmations of appointments of Baldwyn and Streete *inter alios*); other appointments, ff. 9r, 18v.

Revival of officialdom after a gap of at least fourteen years was necessary in every diocese, and other bishops had, like Morley, to make a host of appointments at this time. Survival of a patent book shows that Duppa, newly translated from Salisbury to Winchester and to be succeeded by Morley himself in 1662, raised 25 people to 27 secular posts in his first few months at Winchester - auditors, receivers, bailiffs, woodwards, treasurers, constables, and apparitors - after which the pace of such appointments slackened noticeably.[22] Sanderson, meanwhile, was engaged on a similar operation within Lincoln Diocese and, presumably because it took time to find officials who could ensure efficiency and command trust, Ward took several of his men with him on his translation from Exeter to Salisbury.[23]

These officials ensured the day-to-day running of the diocese, as was standard practice before the upheavals of the 1640s, whether the bishop was there or not. The evidence of his register shows that Morley made specific arrangements to strengthen the episcopal bureaucracy of Worcester and to leave no doubt about authority during his inevitable absences. No details of the 'commission' mentioned in one of the institutions before his arrival survive - when it was set up, who were its members, and what were their powers - but the 'deed of delegation' signed by Morley on 16 November 1661 specifically devolved power, as mentioned earlier and as he had done similarly when Dean of Christ Church Oxford, to a group of officials to act on his behalf in his absence.[24] The deed named four cathedral officials - the dean, the archdeacon, and two prebendaries (cathedral canons) - together with his domestic chaplain, and gave powers to any two to institute (fill parochial vacancies) in his absence.[25] The document does not mention permanent officials such as Baldwyn or Streete. The assumption was, no doubt, that they would continue to exercise their normal functions, and the record shows Baldwyn in particular instituting clergy to parishes and presiding in court.[26] He was often absent, however, and, while the 'deed of delegation' did not apparently impede the regular officials, it ensured an additional mechanism for filling vacancies. There were limits, by convention, to the powers of a diocesan chancellor, however, and he could not confirm prospective communicants, nor ordain, nor deprive errant clergy.[27] Nothing was said in the deed, moreover, about these other aspects of episcopal activity. It would seem that the immediate or most likely duty (institutions) was supplied by the deed, but matters such as visitations, ordinations, and confirmations were left unresolved.

---

22 HRO, A1/32.
23 A. Whiteman, 'Re-establishment of the Church of England 1660-1663', *TRHS*, 5th series, vol. 5 (1955), p. 115; A. Whiteman, 'Episcopate of Seth Ward, Bishop of Exeter 1662-1667 and Salisbury 1667-1689', unpub. D.Phil. thesis (Oxford, 1951), p. 164.
24 Christ Church Oxford, Dean and Chapter Act Book, i.b.3, p. 101 (31/7/1660); Worcester, WRO, 716 093 2648 10 iii, f. 11/p. 22 (16/11/1661).
25 There are the usual problems with documents of this kind, e.g. (Latin) endings missing, writing into the binding, etc., together with the possibility of a clerking error, but the import is clear and borne out by subsequent institution entries.
26 See infra, sections in this chapter on institutions and on consistory court.
27 There appears to be no precise blueprint, with nothing on deprivations and only the presumption of reservation of powers to the bishop over ordinations, e.g. Canons 31 to 36, 1604; and confirmations, e.g. Canon 60, 1604; Gibson, *Codex,* vol. 1, pp. 169, 375; vol. 2, pp. 958, 962.

Morley had thus guaranteed that the episcopal machinery would run, with or without him, at least in the short term. This enquiry will examine next, and in so far as the documents allow, the recovery of episcopal property, repairs to the cathedral and other buildings, the supply of clergy to parishes, the proceedings of the consistory court, and the case of Richard Baxter. It will conclude by attempting to assess overall Morley's record as Bishop of Worcester.

BISHOP'S INCOME AND CATHEDRAL REPAIRS

Two of Morley's early concerns were the income of the bishopric and the fabric of the cathedral and its houses after twenty years of war and neglect. The cathedral was in a terrible condition overall, according to an early entry in the Chapter Act Book, 'very ruinous and some parts thereof in verie greate danger of fallinge...'; and Morley adds that 'severall houses of the Diocese... are demolished (or) very much defaced and ruined...'[28] Nor was Worcester the worst place to have suffered damage and neglect in the Wars and Interregnum. Heavy damage of cathedrals and their properties was widespread. One had become a stable, another a prison, and Lichfield in particular was all but destroyed in two sieges and was standing without a roof by 1660.[29] The sources of the bishop's income – mainly his estates – had, like all the others, been dispersed, moreover, by the sequestration of episcopal lands and revenues in the Interregnum.[30]

The two issues came together over the recovery of a lease in December 1660. Morley petitioned the king – or at least there is a petition in his name – for the recovery of one of the leases lost in the upheavals which, with the return of the king, apparently lay at the Crown's disposal.[31] There appear to be no records to show how other episcopal and cathedral properties were recovered. The petition for this particular deed involved a group of tenements at 'White Friars' which produced an income of £80 *p.a.* and this, together with 'occasional' entry fines for re-leasing, would have helped to restore the bishop's income and would have enabled Morley to fulfil his intention, declared in the petition, to make contributions toward the repair of the cathedral and several of its houses. The matter was referred to the Lord Treasurer, so the outcome is not clear; but Morley's altruism and concern for the physical plant of the diocese are clear enough.

---

28 Worcester CL, Chapter Act Book 1660-1702, A76, f. 1v, 13/9/1660; TNA, SP 29/23 no. 47 (calendared in *CSPD 1660-1661*, p. 406); see also S. E. Lehmberg, *Cathedrals under Siege 1600-1700* (Exeter, 1996), pp. 63-64.
29 See e.g. Lehmberg, *Cathedrals under Siege*, pp. 58-68; I. M. Green, *Re-establishment of the Church of England* (Oxford, 1978), pp. 107-09; R. Hutton, *The Restoration: A Political and Religious History of England and Wales 1658-1667* (Oxford, 1985), pp. 143, 172.
30 C. H. Firth and R. S. Rait (eds), *Acts and Ordinances of the Interregnum 1641-1660*, vol. 2 (London, 1911), pp. 81-82, 200-01.
31 TNA, SP 29-23, no. 47; I owe my awareness of this petition to Robert Beddard (R. A. Beddard, 'A Reward for Services Rendered: Charles II and the Restoration Bishopric of Worcester, 1660-1663' *Midland History*, vol. XXIX (2004), p. 65).

It is possible to gain a fairly clear idea of repairs and costs for the cathedral and the houses in the close in spite of documents which sometimes lack dates and which are far from complete. The contemporaneous Henry Townshend put costs of repairing the cathedral in 1660 at £10,000.[32] A sheet of somewhat scrappy jottings among the cathedral archives appears to be another estimate made in November 1660 of individual costs from spire to sewers with numerous other important items – timber, glazing, and lead for the roof, together with repair of vestry, chapter house, cloisters, choir stalls, and organ – amounting to a total of £16,350 or so.[33] Actual spending on the cathedral, according to a 'Brief of the accounts', from August 1660 to November 1661, the first fifteen months of the return of the dean and chapter, came to some £1,500.[34] A more 'official-looking' book of accounts does not give spending figures for 1660–62, Morley's years, but does provide figures for 1639/40, the last year before the upheavals, and 1663/64, after the high emergency spending of the first years of the Restoration: on the cathedral, £140 (1639/40) and £335 (1663/64) respectively; on the deanery and prebendal houses £63 (1639/40) and £24 (1663/64).[35]

These figures put matters in some kind of perspective and show just how exceptional was the spending (£1,500) on the cathedral in 1660/61 and just how quick was the return to normality at Worcester. Most repairs were achieved, likewise, in other dioceses – Winchester, Morley's future diocese, for example – in the early 1660s through the energies of bishops, deans, and chapters and essentially because of the bonanza – with large entry fines in particular – which flowed to their treasuries with the 'releasing' of recovered lands and properties.[36]

At Worcester the cathedral's own resources, mainly the fines and rents arising from its property transactions, would have paid for much of this expenditure but a note, listing one or two gifts, including a donation of £50 from Morley, is attached to one set of cathedral accounts.[37] Morley appears to have given £200 altogether from his episcopal revenues, although over what timescale is not clear, to contribute to the needs of the cathedral, helped no doubt by the recovery of at least one of his own leases; and he spent another £950 on the palace at Worcester – £150 to remove an interloper and a further £800 on the repairs themselves.[38]

32 Townshend, *Diary*, p. 291.
33 Worcester CL, D 197.
34 Worcester CL, A73, p. 60.
35 Worcester CL, A26, ff. 132r-133v (cathedral 1639); ff. 134v-135r (houses 1639); ff. 209r-210v (cathedral 1663); f. 211r (houses 1663).
36 For the scale of leasing by the Bishop of Winchester, HRO, 11M59/D1/2, Bod Tanner 140, ff. 33-34; for his rents and fines, HRO,11M59/F/BP/E/B4, points 6, 7; for Winchester Cathedral leasing, HRO, DC/B5/9; its fines and repairs, HRO, DC/C15/1, Bod Tanner 140, ff. 118, 123; see also e.g. A. Thomson, 'The Diocese of Winchester before and after the English Civil Wars: a Study of the Character and Performance of its Clergy', unpub. Ph.D. thesis (London, 2004), pp. 217, 223; Green, *Re-establishment*, p. 10.
37 Worcester CL, A73, p. 60.
38 HRO, DC/H4/1, p. 19; LPL, MS 943 p. 805; Portsmouth HC, 179/1/9/1/4; BL, Stowe MS 541, f. 135r; this subject is discussed more fully in Chapter 9.

INSTITUTIONS OF CLERGY

'Manpower' was the other outstanding issue when Morley took charge of the diocese. After some twenty years of political and religious upheaval, 'intruder' incumbents – men imposed in the absence of king and bishops in the 1640s and 1650s and whose religious outlook was, by definition, 'questionable' – occupied large numbers of parishes in the Diocese of Worcester. It is clear, if we trust Edmund Calamy,[39] that at least twenty-one incumbents, intruders all of them, left their livings in 1660 and 1661, some before Morley's arrival, others during his tenure,[40] and all before the exodus of 1662. Twenty one represents a proportion of eight to ten per cent of the total body of parish clergy.[41] This nearly conforms with Calamy's national tally of expulsions in 1660/61 – 10 per cent or so of the total body of clergy in England and Wales.[42] The scale of departures inevitably varied from diocese to diocese. The proportion of departures at Winchester was, like Worcester's, a little below the national average; but both contrast with an estimate of 25 per cent for Leicestershire (Diocese of Lincoln).[43] Some departures were accompanied, moreover, by some difficult, not to say explosive, scenes: most graphically illustrated in the Diocese of Worcester at Tredington where issues of livelihood and rival theologies climaxed with Richard Durham, the intruder, and Joseph Crowther, the new incumbent, preaching sermons at opposite ends of the church for three Sundays in a row; and there were similar incidents elsewhere.[44]

The episcopal register survives, containing all appointments of rectors and vicars, including details of numbers, qualifications, and patrons, during Morley's tenure as bishop.[45] The register shows there were 41 institutions of rectors and vicars, involving 38 men to 40 parishes, while Morley was bishop,[46] and it is possible to draw conclusions which are fairly definite about the extent, though more tentative about the nature, of Morley's impact on the ministry of the Diocese of Worcester in the early 1660s. One

---

39 *CR;* Baxter seems to corroborate (without precise dates) seven of the twenty-one, (M. Sylvester (ed.), *Reliquiae Baxterianae,* [London, 1696], part 3, pp. 90-93).

40 Episcopal register WRO, 716 093 2648 10 iii, f. 3v/p. 5. - f. 11r/p. 21, e.g. Bromsgrove 20/8/1660 (before); Tredington 20/11/1660 (during Morley's tenure); information in *CR* and Morley's register never corresponds exactly – mainly because of missing names of intruder/predecessors in the register (and it looks as if the authorities in 1660 chose to ignore intruders and record only the fate of the last 'legal' predecessor).

41 The total numbers of clergy are based on entries for 1661 and 1679 in visitation books (WRO, 802 2951 1 i and 2 ii).

42 *Calamy Revised,* pp. xii-xiii; endorsed by e.g. R. A. Beddard, 'Restoration Church', in J. R. Jones (ed.), *Restored Monarchy 1660-89,* (Basingstoke, 1979), p. 164; Green, *Re-establishment,* p. 49; J. Spurr, *Restoration Church of England 1646-1689* (Yale, 1991), p. 34.

43 For Winchester 29 expulsions of rectors, vicars, and curates 1660-61 out of about 390 clergymen (*CR;* Thomson, 'The Diocese of Winchester before and after the English Civil Wars', p. 23; J. H. Pruett, *Parish Clergy under the Later Stuarts: the Leicestershire Experience* [Urbana, 1978], p. 17); these should all be seen as estimates bedevilled by missing information, types of clergy counted (rectors, vicars, curates), inclusion or not of peculiars and the like.

44 For Tredington and Andover (Diocese of Winchester) see *CR;* also Witherley (Lincoln) (Pruett, *Parish Clergy* p. 18)

45 WRO, 716 093 2648 10 iii, ff. 6v-11r/pp. 12-21.

46 There were forty-one institutions but only thirty-eight men because three – Joseph Crowther, Edward Phillips, and William Thornburgh – were apparently pluralists; and only forty parishes because one – White Ladies Aston – had two institutions under Morley; entries in the register are confined to rectors and vicars and do not include e.g. perpetual curates.

or two comparisons are instructive about the extent of Morley's impact on the body of parish clergy in his new diocese. Comparison of the 41 with a possible total of 230 parish clergy implies a considerable impact - nearly 20 per cent - on the diocesan ministry by Morley.[47] Comparison of the 41 over 18 months with 21 institutions by an immediate predecessor and with 9 by one of his successors, over three years in both cases, shows again the scale of his impact. His impact on numbers was undoubtedly large, but not unique, at this time. At Winchester, for example, whereas institutions were 17 or 18 a year - between one and two a month - before and after the Wars and Interregnum, Bishop Duppa or his officials (Duppa was by then in his 70s) had to institute 87 times - 5 or so a month - in the 18 months of his rule from October 1660 to March 1662.[48] Morley's scale of operations - two or three a month - was somewhat smaller than Duppa's but, then, so was his diocese.

Departing intruders - 21 in 1660/61 according to Calamy - did not cause most of the vacancies Morley had to fill because either the original incumbent, a sufferer under the military regime of the 1650s, returned to his parish under the terms of the legislation of 1660;[49] or Clarendon (chancellor) with the help of the national committee (of which Morley, with Sheldon and Earle, had, of course, been a leading member)[50] had been filling vacancies after the Restoration of May 1660 but before the appointment of Morley to Worcester in October (1660). There were, even so, more vacancies than usual at Worcester and, no doubt, elsewhere. Analysis of his institutions within his own diocese at this time reveals 12 were caused by resignations and one by a deprivation but, without further detail, it is not possible to say how far the resignations were voluntary or forced or on what grounds - principle or otherwise - these men left their parish.[51] The death of 23 predecessors was by far the largest cause of vacancies and it would seem that the natural cycle of life and death more than any other reason was responsible for the volume of institutions under Morley.

The quality of the replacements can be measured quite easily in academic terms. Ten of the 38 'appointees' were MA, 3 were BA, 2 were STB (BD), and 1 was STP (DD). That leaves 22 who were merely 'clerks'. The choice of so many 'clerks' casts doubt on the academic ability of the new men and on their standing in the communities; and these must, in turn, reflect on the quality of the ministry as a whole at the end of Morley's tenure. The explanation lies, very likely, in a scarcity of candidates to fill so many vacancies rather than negligence or slipping standards on the part of the ecclesiastical authorities.

---

47 WRO, 802 2951 1 i and 2 ii (lists of clergy for 1661 and 1679 averaged and is the total body - rectors, vicars, perpetual curates, sequestrators, 'ministers').
48 The calculations per month are based on analyses of episcopal registers HRO, A1/31, A1/33; Duppa's, in the absence of his register, from a range of sources but mainly TNA, E 331/Winchester 1.
49 12 CII c. 17 (Act for Confirming and Restoring Ministers).
50 See Chapter 4, section on Manpower.
51 WRO, 716 093 2648 10 iii; in addition to twenty-three deaths, twelve resignations, and one deprivation, there were two promotions and the reason for three more vacancies is not stated; there were also discrepancies between it and *CR* e.g. the fate of John Read of Great Witley - death by 1662 according to the scribes, active nonconformist activity to 1712 according to Calamy - is only one example; this and other discrepancies were probably caused by a likely policy decision in 1660 to exclude the name of an intruder.

It is possible to comment on academic levels quite easily, their political and religious outlook rather less so. Critically, loyalty to Church and State in the shape of uniformity was yet to be put to the test after Morley's time at Worcester and, in any case, it was not until after the passage of Uniformity in May 1662 that Morley seems to have arrived at a view about the issues involved - the prayer book, ceremonies, and episcopacy.[52] The register gives nothing away about such matters but at least 2 of the 38 new incumbents - Cornelius Woodward and Thomas Wright - had begun their ministries in the diocese as intruders. Both were intruders from 1650, according to Calamy, Woodward at Peopleton, Wright at Hartlebury; and both continued into the Restoration, Woodward being confirmed in his living in 1660, Wright transferring to Great Witley. Both subscribed to uniformity in 1662, and both retained their parish till death. These two examples - and there could have been more - may imply, like the lack of degrees, a shortage of suitable candidates or, more positively, Morley's accommodating spirit. None of his 38 'appointees' appears among Baxter's or Calamy's lists of martyrs silenced in 1662, however, and this would seem to indicate that they were all prepared to conform to use of surplice and prayer book even before the Act of Uniformity came into force.[53]

The ultimate question is, of course, the pastoral quality of the ministry. Neither degrees nor allegiance, political and religious, would guarantee commitment by the local parish priest to his parishioners. This is the most important requirement, yet the most difficult to measure, and so must be left an open question.

Morley's need to delegate has already been discussed but, in the case of institutions, there were even more limits to his powers. Although the ultimate power to appoint - to 'institute' - to a parish lay with the bishop, Morley appears to have been able to 'collate' - to nominate the candidate as well as to institute him to a parish - only once in his 18 months. Most nominations were in the hands of others such as deans and chapters, academic institutions, the Crown, and an assortment of peers, knights, esquires, and gentry before, during, and after Morley's time as bishop. They nominated and the bishop's role was confined, in these cases, to the formal process of authorising or 'instituting' the clergyman to a parish. For most of the time he did not even do that as he was not there, and either the men to whom he had devolved power carried out the collation or institution or else the chancellor, Baldwyn, took charge.

The effects of this 'alternative' patronage can be measured, again, in terms of qualifications if less easily in other respects. They found some university men but

---

52 See Chapter 4; and Bosher, *Making of the Restoration Settlement*, p. 263.
53 *CR;* Baxter, *Reliquiae,* part 3, pp. 90-93.

nearly half the nominations by laymen were 'mere' clerks; the Dean and Chapter of Worcester were responsible for two more clerks; and the Warden and Fellows of Merton College, Oxford for one. All this shows not only that people other than Morley were also responsible for the quality of the ministry at Worcester but also suggests a scarcity of properly educated candidates rather than a deliberate disregard of academic qualifications by ignorant or careless patrons.

VISITATIONS

Within days of his arrival and enthronement, Morley had turned his attention to a visitation of his parochial incumbents.[54] Common practice was for episcopal visitations to take place every three years[55] and the customary way of proceeding was to summon the clergy - vicars, rectors, and curates - together with churchwardens, deanery by deanery, to a meeting at one of the more central or larger churches, and the bishop, the chancellor or, more often, the latter's surrogate, would travel from one centre to the next over several days or weeks. Clergy credentials - ordinations, institutions, licences (preaching and curates) - were checked. Next articles (questionnaires) were distributed to churchwardens or sometimes, if this had been done in advance, the churchwardens delivered their presentments (allegations of the 'crimes' of their fellow parishioners) at the visitation. The centre piece was a sermon or 'charge' (an uplifting 'mission statement') delivered to the assembly by the bishop or one of the clergy.

There appears to be very little information about diocesan visitations in these early years of the Restoration probably because at this stage (1660-1662) they were waiting upon a national settlement before attempting to draw up articles and impose religious conformity. This did not stop Morley from some initial 'policing' of his clergy, but how far he was alone is difficult to ascertain. Certainly his visitation of 1661 seems, in the early days of the Restoration, to have been a more curtailed affair, concerning the clergy alone, not churchwardens, focusing on their suitability and concentrating consequently on their credentials. The clergy were summoned from the eight deaneries on separate days over three weeks in September and October 1661. It is not clear where clergy in most of the deaneries met and who conducted the business but, certainly the first two groups, from Worcester and Pershore, assembled at the palace and Morley himself was in charge.

---

54 WRO, 802 2951 1 i, eight days over three weeks 25/9/1661 - 18/10/1661.
55 This conclusion is based on a study of visitation books but an exception was Winchester where episcopal (as well as archidiaconal) visitations took place every year, though it is possible to draw the inference that the Bishop would only be expected to attend every three years.

Three quarters of the clergy were present overall which means that over fifty of their number did not attend; and, worse, fewer than half those who came produced all the requisite paperwork. One man was said to be ill,[56] others would have had genuine reasons for absence, and there were, no doubt, the usual sluggards in the system. How far the shortcomings reflect reluctance or even hostility to the revival of episcopal government is difficult to say.

The record is all too often silent also about the response of Morley and his colleagues. Two at least who fell short of the 'bureaucratic' requirements either resigned or were pressured to depart early in 1662.[57] Four curates were 'inhibited': two because they lacked a licence, one because he confessed his lack of ordination, one more because he could not supply proof of ordination.[58] Irregularities were exposed in one vicar's institution and he was subsequently deprived soon after Morley's departure for Winchester.[59]

Morley and his surrogates were more accommodating in other respects. Several curates were allowed to acquire the necessary licence to practise by taking the oath and subscribing on the spot.[60] Preaching licences were issued to a somewhat larger number of parish clergy in the same way.[61] A few cases were referred for further consideration by the bishop.[62] Most importantly, at least twelve whose institutions were in doubt were allowed to undergo a fresh formality during or after the visitation.[63]

Doubts must remain about episcopal control over the parish clergy – the men at the 'frontline' – and in consequence the effectiveness of the Church's mission; but Morley had revived discipline and imposed a measure of control, combining this for the most part with a human approach, at a sensitive, not to say, explosive moment in diocesan history.

---

56 WRO, 802 2951 1 i, f. 13v, Edward Cooke, vicar of Tardebigge; mostly no reasons for absence are given.
57 Joseph Read of Great Witley and Joseph Treble of Church Lench – no action was taken at the time (WRO, 802 2951 1 i, ff. 1v, 7r); the episcopal register shows replacements for them in 2/1662 and 4/1662 respectively and the reason given is 'death' in both cases (WRO, 716 093 2648 10 iii, f. 11r/p. 21) but this must refer to the last 'legal' incumbent, not to Read or Treble who were intruders; and in fact Read had a long subsequent history of dissenting activity to 1712, while Treble conformed elsewhere (*CR*).
58 WRO, 802 2951 1 i, ff. 5v, 7v, 8v, 10v.
59 WRO, 802 2951 1 i, f. 10v (deprivation and replacement).
60 1EI c, 1 (oath of allegiance and supremacy); the Three Articles/Canon 36 (1604) requiring acceptance of the royal supremacy, the book of common prayer, and the Thirty-Nine Articles (e.g. Bray [ed.], *Anglican Canons*, p. 321).
61 e.g. WRO, 802 2951 1 i, f. 16v, William Richardson, vicar of Brailes.
62 WRO, 802 2951 1 i, f. 2v (Sampson Heyward, curate of Tibberton).
63 e.g. William Evett, rector of Madresfield, WRO, 802 2951 1 i, f. 3v; WRO, 716 093 2648 10 iii, f. 9v/p. 18.

DISCIPLINE: THE CONSISTORY COURT

Consistory courts resumed sittings for probate (wills) and instance business (private disputes such as libel) at Chichester, Chester, and York, six months before – at Canterbury nearly a year before – the legislation of July 1661 authorised revival of the church courts;[64] but *ex officio* prosecutions – correction proceedings carried out in the name of the Church – which are far more relevant to the nature of Morley's control over his people and to an understanding of the impact of the Church on society – appear to have been waiting, like visitations, for the outcome of national religious discussions and were slower to restart. Oxford and Chester appear, even so, to have begun 'corrections' five and three months before the legislation, Canterbury in October 1661, Peterborough in August 1662; but it is not until January and July 1663 that *ex officio* records begin at Exeter and Winchester.[65]

It would appear that Morley may have been quicker off the mark than some of his episcopal counterparts with visitations (or, at least, checking his clergy) but slower with *ex officio* proceedings. Coherent recording of the *ex officio* business of the diocesan consistory court only begins at Worcester in September 1661 – the time, coincidentally or otherwise, when Morley arrived in person – and records appear to be complete for the six months from Michaelmas Term 1661 to Hilary Term 1662, the remainder of Morley's term at Worcester and, indeed, to continue well beyond his time, though Morley himself had returned to London by the middle of November 1661.[66]

There is nothing to show that Morley himself ever sat in court and his personal involvement in its proceedings, if any, must have been brief since he spent only some nine weeks in Worcester. The presiding officer is not always specified. Timothy Baldwyn,[67] the diocesan chancellor, known in this capacity as official principal, took charge on four occasions during these last six months of Morley's term, and surrogates sat in his place during the remaining plenaries and most of the sessions *in camera*. Morley, in spite of his 'remote control', would have set the policy and tone of the court.

---

64 For Chichester, Chester, and York, Hutton, *The Restoration*, p. 173; for Canterbury, J. M. Potter, 'Ecclesiastical Courts of the Diocese of Canterbury 1603-1665', unpub. M. Phil. thesis (London, 1973), p. 183.
65 For Oxford and Peterborough, M. D. W. Jones, 'Ecclesiastical Courts before and after the English Civil War: Office Jurisdiction at Oxford and Peterborough 1630-1675', unpub. B. Litt. thesis (Oxford, 1977), p. 44; for Chester, Hutton, *The Restoration*, p. 173; for Canterbury, Potter, 'Ecclesiastical Courts of Canterbury', p. 184; for Exeter, Whiteman, 'Seth Ward', p. 167; for Winchester, HRO, C1/37 (the first surviving *ex officio* book).
66 WRO, 794 011 2513 18 (the relevant court book); hardly any *ex officio* business is recorded before Michaelmas 1661.
67 WRO, 716.093 2648-10 iii, p. 10 or f. 5v (patent).

The court was in full swing by the time of Morley's arrival in the diocese. A total of 187 people – laymen and women, churchwardens, and a clergyman – were summoned to court during the last six months of Morley's reign over the diocese, 86 of them during Michaelmas Term (September–December) 1661 and a further 101 during Hilary Term (January–March) 1662.[68]

A few churchwardens found themselves before the court for such minor matters as failure to take the oath of office; and one clergyman, Thomas James, Curate of Newland, was summoned over a vestment offence and conducting a clandestine marriage. The charges against lay people fall most conveniently into three categories: morality, religion, and church rate. Twenty people were charged with sex before marriage, 30 or so with sexual 'incontinence' (fornication or adultery), another 30 with incest, and no less than 56 with bastardy in the six months under study. Handfuls (all below ten) faced charges of working or playing on the Sabbath and similar numbers of refusing to pay church rate. Conviction rates were even lower. Nine out of 56 people were found guilty of bastardy, for example, and six out of nine for 'play' on the Sabbath; and these were the highest numbers in any particular category.

This low conviction rate was also probably less about the 'virtue' or obedience of his flock, much more about absence. As many as two thirds failed to turn up in court during either Michaelmas or Hilary Term and, if an accused person was missing, there could be no verdict or sentence. In such cases the court could only issue a ways and means order (a 'search warrant'), adjourn proceedings, or pronounce excommunication, and the case remained unresolved (unless or until the accused appeared). In the curate of Newland's case, it issued, in his absence, a suspension which did not, in itself, resolve the matter.[69]

The wholesale ignoring of a summons reveals the impotence of the system in the face of massive absence in 1661/62. It also reveals the extent of the hostility towards the disciplinary machinery of the Church and it helps to explain, moreover, the relatively small number summoned to court in the first place and the balance of the charges against them. Accused people numbering 187 may seem large at first glance but were minute in a population of at least 43,000 adults in the diocese.[70] There was also a clear split – 75 per cent moral, 10 per cent religious – in the balance of the charges. While greater moral virtue was not likely after the 'upside down' world of the 1650s, religious compliance was even less so;[71] and it is more likely also that the

---

68 Eighty-six were summoned during Michaelmas 1661 and 113 in Hilary Term but prosecutions of twelve had begun in the first term and continued into the second.
69 WRO, 794 011 2513 18, f. 40r, 31/10/1661, 'donec... conformaret'.
70 A. Whiteman (ed.), *Compton Census of 1676: a Critical Edition*, (Oxford, 1986), Appendix D, Table D/3, p. ci; estimates for Worcester are problematic.
71 See e.g. C. Hill, *The World Turned Upside Down*, (London, 1972), passim; D. Cressy, *Birth, Marriage and Death: Ritual Religion and the Life Cycle in Tudor and Stuart England* (Oxford, 1997), passim.

smaller proportion of 'religious' prosecutions reflects the caution of the ecclesiastical authorities towards potentially explosive religious sensitivities. Both the relatively small number summoned and the balance of charges away from religion suggest that this was seen as a time for less 'harassment' and more caution by court officials and by Morley himself at the very moment when he was striving in Convocation and the House of Lords for *rapprochement* and a measure of unity with the more moderate religious groups outside the Church.[72]

With few comparable studies of consistory courts in these first two or three years of the Restoration, it is difficult to say how representative were the problems of the court at Worcester in such matters as balance of cases and absence of accused people. The only systematic analysis of *ex officio* cases – for the consistory courts of Oxford and Peterborough – shows that the balance of cases was, like Worcester's, towards morals from 1660 to 1662 and that this changed significantly after the enactment of uniformity, which strongly implies that the respective bishops were, apparently like Morley, awaiting decisions about the religious settlement. Attendance at Oxford appears to have been quite good between 1661 and 1663 – only a quarter failing to attend all sessions – but absence levels at Peterborough were some 70 per cent by 1662-64 – much more like Worcester's – for *ex officio* cases.[73]

To return to Worcester and Morley, reviving and imposing church discipline appears to have run into obstruction from his flock and, in any case, the court seems to have moved with caution at this critical time – the search for a national settlement of religious divisions – all this apparently without much personal direction by Morley; but his officials are likely to have been aware of his approach and unlikely to have flown in the face of his policies.

THE CASE OF RICHARD BAXTER

Richard Baxter proved himself to be the most turbulent of Morley's body of clergy at Worcester. The issues surrounding Baxter, though probably not unique for their time – 1660 – were complex and, while he never had to appear in the consistory court, his business involved him in more than one audience with the ecclesiastical authorities and contact with the Lord Chancellor (Clarendon) and the Secretary of State (William Morice). [74]

---

72 Morley was an active member of Convocation which considered the new prayer book from May 1661 onwards, see G. Bray (ed.), *Records of Convocation,* vol. VIII (Woodbridge, 2006); and of the House of Lords during its deliberations over uniformity, see *Journals of the House of Lords,* vol. 11 (London, 1767-1830).
73 Jones, 'Ecclesiastical Courts', pp. 44-45 (balance), p. 95 (attendance).
74 William Morice (1602-76), Secretary of State for the Northern Department 1660-1668.

The dispute centred on Kidderminster, whether Richard Baxter or George Dance was to be vicar and whether Baxter should be allowed a preaching licence from the bishop. Baxter had been involved at Kidderminster for nearly twenty years by 1660. Arrangements at Kidderminster are none too clear – the only detailed account is Baxter's[75] and precision about such practicalities as terms of appointment or even dates was not his speciality – but it would seem that, at the beginning of the national upheavals of 1640/41, there were complaints from the parish about George Dance (the then vicar of Kidderminster). Dance was allowed to remain as vicar, but Baxter was made lecturer with a stipend, or allowance, of £60 *p.a.* from Dance's income (£200 *p.a.*) and guaranteed by Dance's bond (£500). After further manoeuvres by the parishioners of Kidderminster, the Committee for Plundered Ministers, and the Westminster Assembly, Baxter became vicar in 1647/48 but Dance was allowed £40 *p.a.* by the parish.

The Restoration of 1660 inevitably involved a review of parochial incumbencies. The Act for Confirming and Restoring Ministers enabled 'sufferers' – dispossessed Anglican loyalist incumbents – to return to their former parish.[76] This meant that Dance was able to recover the vicarage but, with his record of incompetence, his return was bound to provoke trouble. Baxter, *parti pris* of course, thought him 'unlearned, ignorant, (and) silly';[77] but it was parochial 'rebellion', endorsed by the parliamentary committee, which had lain at the root of Dance's initial 'reduction' and eventual removal in the 1640s. Baxter had, meanwhile, received offers of a chaplaincy to the king in June 1660 and a bishopric in October 1660 so, although possibly only ordained deacon and without impressive formal academic credentials, these were apparently not seen as obstacles to his preferment.[78] He refused the bishopric, however, and sought return to Kidderminster; but, by this time, while still in London, he had clashed with the 'establishment' – and in particular with Morley – at Worcester House, also in October 1660, and again during Savoy from March to July 1661;[79] and his views on prelacy and ceremonies – especially his opposition to kneeling for communion – were now clear for all, including his new bishop, Morley, to see. Suspicions about his attitude to the Solemn League and Covenant and connection with the Venner Rising (January 1661) provoked questions, furthermore, about Baxter's political allegiance.

---

75 Baxter, *Reliquiae,* part 2, pp. 298-99; 374-81; see also *DNB, ODNB.*
76 12 CII c.17.
77 Baxter, *Reliquiae,* vol. 2, p. 298.
78 Baxter, *Reliquiae,* vol. 2, p. 229 (chaplain); pp. 281, 298 (bishopric); *CR, DNB, ODNB* (ordination), Baxter, *Reliquiae,* vol. 1, p. 85, and N. H. Keeble and G. F. Nuttall (eds), *Calendar of the Correspondence of Richard Baxter,* vol. 2, (Oxford, 1991), no. 225 (education).
79 See Chapter 4.

Dance was, in any case, in lawful possession of the vicarage and enjoyed the support of Morley (by then bishop), Clare (the patron), and Pakington (a local grandee); but Baxter still entertained hopes of return, first, by replacing Dance as vicar, then by retaining the lectureship. There appears to have been a formal meeting 'in the Bishop's Chamber' at Worcester where Baxter faced Morley and Clare and where they clashed particularly over the matter of kneeling for communion.[80] Baxter marshalled support from the parishioners of Kidderminster and, in what looks like desperation, put forward a string of proposals – 'reading Vicar', curate, preaching for nothing, or at least a farewell sermon – but all were blocked by Dance (on the bishop's orders) in spite of Baxter's contacts with Clarendon and Morice,[81] and, at a second meeting of Baxter, this time with dean and bishop, he was refused a preaching licence.[82]

As if to complete their victory, Morley subsequently preached at Kidderminster, denouncing Baxter; Warmestry likewise during two more visits;[83] and Baxter returned to a 'freelance' existence in London where the dispute between him and Morley continued in pamphlet form.[84]

Knowledge of these events relies mainly on Baxter but, if there was any truth in the complaints against Dance, the episode illustrates the elevation of religious and political conformity over 'ministerial' competence. This alone, to the extent that it left Kidderminster in the hands of an incompetent incumbent, would put Morley in a doubtful position; but he put himself in a worse light by indulging in the pamphlet exchange. He labelled Baxter a 'thief', a 'robber', a liar who spoke 'without truth', and a troublemaker who sowed 'the seed of schism'. To add 'colour' he accused Baxter of stealing 'the Fleece as well the Flock' and of blowing 'the Trumpet of Rebellion'.[85] Baxter held different theological views from Morley (about the Book of Common Prayer, for example), his formal qualifications were not impressive, he had no claim at law on Kidderminster, and he too constantly displayed immoderation;[86] but Dance appears to have been totally unsuitable and, in any case, it might have been 'politic' of Morley to have pursued a more conciliatory approach, as exemplified by offers of chaplaincies and bishoprics to Presbyterians, and to have agreed to one of Baxter's more modest final requests, in the interests of church unity. Morley had, after all, been one of the first to suggest offers of preferment to the Presbyterians[87] and, if Baxter

---

80 Baxter, *Reliquiae,* vol. 2, p. 299 – Baxter, typically gives no precise date for the meeting.
81 Baxter, *Reliquiae,* vol. 2, pp. 299, 381 (letter by and meeting with Clarendon), p. 379 (meeting with Morice).
82 Baxter, *Reliquiae,* vol. 2, p. 374 and Morley may be corroborating this meeting – no date or place – in his *Letter to a Friend for Vindication ...from... Baxter's Calumny,* which forms part of *Richard Baxter his Account to his Dearly Beloved the Inhabitants of Kidderminster of the Causes of ... his being Forbidden to Preach.... with The Bishop of Worcester's Letter in Answer thereunto...* (London, 1662), p. 3.
83 Baxter, *Reliquiae,* vol. 2, p. 375 (Morley's visit, presumably while he was at Worcester, 9/1661-11/1661), p. 376 (Warmestry's visits); Morley confirms his own visit in The Bishop of Worcester's Letter, supra, pp. 2, 5.
84 Baxter, again, gives no dates; for the pamphlets (Richard Baxter His Account etc. supra).
85 'The Bishop of Worcester's Letter', supra, pp. 2, 3, 4
86 Baxter himself, in a rare moment of self-recognition, acknowledged something of this and begged to be excused from Savoy (Baxter, *Reliquiae,* vol. 2, p. 303).
87 See Chapter 3; Bod Clarendon MS 72, f. 199r/v (4/5/1660); Clarendon MS 72, f. 357r, (11/5/1660).

was considered good enough for a royal chaplaincy or a bishopric, it is difficult to see why he was unsuitable for Kidderminster. Morley's energetic rebuff, in a deluge of ungenerous and intemperate language, was bound to inflame matters and must have coloured Baxter's attitude. A sense of grievance still rankled, no doubt, on both sides in the 1670s at the time of further attempts at national *rapprochement*.[88]

CONCLUSION

Morley's tenure at Worcester began with the usual flourish - two enthronements, one without him and the other in person - but his record in office was inevitably more mixed. The administrative machinery of the diocese was revived - by Morley - and continued to turn with or without him. Officials, ecclesiastical and secular, were appointed, incumbents were instituted and inducted to parishes, the consistory court came back to life, and renovations to cathedral and palace were begun. He had shown generosity over his institutions and restraint over prosecutions in the consistory court. The one blot on his record was his treatment of Baxter, which was not only questionable at the time, but which may have had long term consequences for church unity.

In view of his short time as bishop and against a background of complex political, religious, and social affairs which consumed most of his attention, it is a wonder he spent as much as two months in the diocese and even more so that any progress was made with the business of the diocese. There were, thus, limits to his achievements at Worcester and, in so far as they were impressive, they must have relied for much of the time on a diocesan machine long used to absentee bishops. Even when working by delegation or through agents, however, Morley presumably set the tone and must be given credit for the revival of the Diocese of Worcester after twenty years of civil wars and interregnum which had, for some fourteen years, overturned and wiped out the whole diocesan structure of the Church of England.

---

88 Letters of Morley and Baxter exchanged in the later 1670s and early 1680s show them jousting with each other over matters 'above 18 years ago' (Keeble and Nuttall, *Correspondence of Richard Baxter*, items 1034, 1093).

CHAPTER 7 : MORLEY AT WINCHESTER: PART 1, RECOVERY

ELECTION AND ENTHRONEMENT

Barely 18 months after his election to Worcester came the climax of Morley's career. Morley's counterpart at Winchester, the ageing Brian Duppa - he was 74 - died in March 1662[1] and Morley's translation from Worcester to Winchester followed.[2] He was also, from October 1663 to February 1668, Dean of the Chapel Royal.[3]

The process of Morley's translation began, within a week or two of Duppa's death, in April 1662. After all the administrative steps - *congé d'élire,* letters missive, election, confirmation, emoluments - came his enthronement. The ceremony took place on Thursday, 22 May.[4] No Bishop of Winchester, it would seem, was enthroned in person from the days of Elizabeth I to the 1820s and Morley, tied up with business in the Lords - the uniformity bill in particular - was forced again, as at Worcester, to rely on a proxy.[5] Like Worcester's, the ceremony was an impressive spectacle and, although the detail inevitably differed, the proceedings were, in the main, much the same.

Henry Bradshawe, one of the canons at the cathedral, assumed the role of proxy this time. He set forth from the cathedral to the church of St Lawrence which lies just outside the outer close of the cathedral, accompanied by distinguished clergy and laymen. He was met on the edge of the close by the Mayor, aldermen, councillors, judges, and other dignitaries, and they continued with him on the short walk to the church. The proxy authorisation was read out and Bradshawe entered the church, the crowd remaining outside while he prayed alone. When he emerged, the whole company processed back to the cathedral where the Dean, Alexander Hyde, and Edward Stanley, another of the canons, received them.

---

1 For his age, G. Isham (ed.), *Correspondence of Bishop Brian Duppa and Sir Justinian Isham 1650-1660,* vol. 17 (Northamptonshire Record Society, 1951-55), p. viii; for date of death, HRO, Chapter Act Book 3, DC/B3/3, p. 47; HRO, 11M59/F/BP/E/B4, point 3; J. Horn, giving his death as the 25 or 26 March, has missed these two sources (J. Horn (ed.), *Fasti Ecclesiae Anglicanae/*Winchester, [London, 1974], p. 82); C. R. Cheney (ed.), *Handbook of Dates,* (London, 1961), Table 9, pp. 100, 101.
2 Horn, *Fasti/*Winchester, p. 82, but the reference to Chapter Act Book 3 should read p. 49, not p. 39; *Forty-Sixth Annual Report of the Deputy Keeper of the Public Records,* (London, 1886), pp. 11, 16.
3 For appointment, 2/10/1663, TNA, SP44/12, p. 34; *CSPD 1663-1664,* p. 285; F. J. Routledge (ed.), *Calendar of Clarendon State Papers,* vol. 5, (Oxford, 1970), p. 635 (letter Morley to Clarendon, April ? 1671); George Morley, *Several Treatises written upon Several Occasions,* (London, 1683), p. xiiii (sic); for dismissal, BL, Verney MS, 636/22, 26/12/1667 (the date of the document, not necessarily his dismissal); R. Latham and W. Matthews (eds), *Diary of Samuel Pepys,* vol. 9 (London, 1983), p. 53 (reported 6/2/1668).
4 HRO, Register of the Common Seal 1660-1671, DC/B5/10, f. 99r.
5 I am grateful to the Very Reverend Trevor Beeson, sometime Dean of Winchester, for drawing my attention to this pattern which has been verified as far as possible from surviving episcopal registers and chapter act books; see also Horn, *Fasti/*Winchester.

Bradshawe produced the letter authorising the enthronement by proxy and the Dean tendered the oath, which Bradshawe took on Morley's behalf, to respect the rights and statutes of the cathedral. Bradshawe produced another letter commissioning the Dean and Chapter to carry out the enthronement and this was read out by the notary public. The Dean processed with Bradshawe through the cathedral to the accompaniment of hymns and canticles. They passed through the choir to the altar where Bradshawe again engaged in private prayer. They all moved to the bishop's throne where the Dean administered the oath of allegiance and another against involvement with foreign powers – these were sworn by Bradshawe on the Gospels – after which the Dean declared Morley, through his proxy, in 'real, actual, and corporal possession of the bishopric'. Bradshawe took his seat on throne, the Dean sitting on his right, Stanley on his left, while the Te Deum rang out from the choir. Bradshawe (in the name of Bishop Morley) then gave the blessing.

To complete proceedings, the Dean and Stanley led Bradshawe to the Chapter House where they assigned to him the customary seat of the bishop. Finally, Bradshawe, still acting for the bishop, ordered John Harfell, the notary public and registrar, to prepare the consequential documents (or 'instruments') recording the whole ceremony.

ADMINISTRATION OF THE DIOCESE

The importance of Winchester at this time cannot be too much stressed. Geographically, in the seventeenth century it stretched from the Thames to the Channel Islands but, mainly comprising the modern counties of Surrey and Hampshire (including the Isle of Wight), it was middling in size, not so small as Bristol or Bangor but not so large as Lincoln. Its population – some 150,000 by the 1670s – gave it weight;[6] but it drew its strength and standing from its enormous wealth. The bishop's income – some £6,500-£7,000 *p.a.* from all sources in the seventeenth century – was probably the largest episcopal income in the land, certainly in the Middle Ages,[7] and was used as remuneration and reward for the great officers of state – hence its prominence, ranking fifth after Canterbury, York, London, and Durham. Winchester gave its bishop a 'platform' from which he could show his colleagues the way, playing a crucial role not just in national religious and secular affairs but also with recovery and reform at diocesan level.

---

6   For population, see A. Whiteman (ed.), *Compton Census of 1676: a Critical Edition*, (Oxford, 1986), Appendix D, Table D/3, p. ci.

7   For seventeenth-century income, e.g. Bod Tanner 140, pp. 33-34; HRO, 11M59/F/BP/E/B4, points 6, 7; for the Middle Ages, M. Page (ed.), *Pipe Roll of the Bishopric of Winchester 1301-1302*, (Hampshire County Council, 1996), p. xxi.

Brian Duppa, Winchester's first bishop of the Restoration,[8] had overseen, nominally at least, the appointment of a host of diocesan officials - stewards, bailiffs, wardens, registrars and apparitors - in the months after he assumed control in Winchester.[9] The leasing of land began in August 1660, the consistory court resumed its instance sessions by October 1661, and much time was spent on the appointment of parochial incumbents because of the usual round of resignations, promotions, and death, and because of the special circumstances of 1660/61 - at least twenty-nine expulsions (out of some 390 rectors, vicars, and perpetual curates).[10] How much of this was his personal work, how far the work of his officials is not clear and nothing survives, moreover, about ordinations and confirmations, functions which were specifically the bishops', or, even more frustratingly, the process of recovering episcopal and cathedral estates. Duppa was an ageing figure, seventy-two at the time of his arrival at Winchester, and within eighteen months he was dead; but he had overseen, however 'distantly', the revival of diocesan machinery, the recovery of church lands, the appointment of parish clergy; these, together with the apparent lack of vindictiveness towards lay or clerical intruders, must be viewed, even without any reform programme, as impressive achievements.

It was at this point that stewardship of the diocese passed to George Morley. Morley was sixty-four and, though somewhat younger than Duppa, his age must have seemed, at first sight, against him. To compensate for this, he brought with him not only high academic credentials from Christ Church Oxford but also considerable experience. He came with twenty years and more as an observer of parliamentary, court, and church politics - a close observer while in exile - and, most recently, two more years of practical and relevant involvement as a bishop running a diocese, as a theologian contributing to the revised prayer book, and as a politician steering the mission of 1660, conducting the conferences of the early 1660s, and dispatching business in the Lords and advising in the Privy Council. His skills as academic, negotiator, and administrator had been tried and tested and it would have been difficult to find anyone more suitable, in theory at least, to oversee the Diocese of Winchester. He had produced initiatives in all his earlier roles, combining them with some degree of flexibility and much energy, and had signalled thereby potential to tackle the challenges of his new post. These were, in the first place, the continuing 'routine business' of ordinations, institutions, visitations, confirmations, and disciplining of his clergy and his lay flock through the consistory

---

8   Horn, *Fasti*/Winchester, p. 82.
9   HRO, A1/32 records patents for e.g. 31 secular posts October/ December 1660.
10 Leasing, HRO, 11M59/D1/2, p. 1; court, HRO, C2/72, C1/37 (earlier books - and therefore court activity - may have been lost); clergy, *Forty-Sixth Annual Report;* TNA, E 331/Winchester 1; *CR;* A. Thomson, 'The Diocese of Winchester before and after the English Civil Wars: a Study of the Character and Performance of its Clergy', unpub. Ph.D. thesis (London, 2004), p. 23.

court and other means. The Restoration of 1660 had raised much hope, moreover, of ecclesiastical reform. Of this the Church was in urgent need: not only had its failings contributed to the showdown of 1640/41 but the 'puritan' reformers of the 1650s had proceeded to point the direction reform should take.

Reform requires separate consideration and will form the basis of a later chapter. This chapter will be confined to the conduct of routine business by Morley and his officials. It will attempt to review the main episcopal activities at Winchester - ordinations, institutions, visitations, confirmations, and the enforcement of discipline through his consistory court - describing and assessing his role with each in turn. Overall the survey will show his achievements - measuring success and failure - as far as day to day management went. Before all this, however, lay the immediate and overriding issue of Uniformity.

DISSENTING CLERGY 1662 AND BEYOND

The enactment of uniformity at Westminster and Morley's enthronement at Winchester took place within days of each other in May 1662 and it fell therefore to Morley, with the prorogation of Parliament, to enforce the terms of the Act within his new diocese.[11] The newly revised Book of Common Prayer annexed to the act made few concessions to the Presbyterians, none to the extremist religious groups, and the act itself required all incumbents to have undergone episcopal ordination and to take oaths giving 'assent and consent' to the new prayer book and renouncing both the Covenant and arms against the king. Enforcement of the new oaths on all parish clergy was therefore at the top of Morley's diocesan agenda.

This was inevitably one of the most delicate and challenging tasks of his ministry but Morley seems at first to have thought the problem slight - his estimate of likely numbers of refusers was 12 - and that offers to discuss outstanding issues with potential opponents 'publicly and privately' would be sufficient to resolve matters peacefully and minimise disruption.[12] If so, he was soon to be disabused. Calamy's account, refined by Matthews, together with a surviving visitation book, suggests at least 54 incumbents baulked at subscription and resigned their livings. There were still over 40 vacancies in 1663/64, far higher than before and after that date.[13]

---

11 14 CII c.4; R. Hutton, *The Restoration: A Political and Religious History of England and Wales 1658-1667* (Oxford, 1985), p. 176; HRO, DC/B5/10, p. 99.
12 Bod Clarendon MS 73, f. 217; 77, f. 307.
13 *CR;* HRO, Visitation Book 1663, B1/35; LMA, DW/VB 1 (1662, 1664); D. L. Wykes, 'Early Religious Dissent in Surrey', *Southern History,* 33 (2011), pp. 54-77, gives, for Surrey Archdeaconry, a somewhat higher figure (40 expulsions of ministers than mine (23), a discrepancy in part because he includes diocesan 'peculiars' and mainly because he combines expulsions of 1660/61 with those of 1662.

This episode shows Morley, initially, as a conciliator, if we trust his version of events, but somewhat ignorant of the mood of his clergy and, when it came to the point and whatever his Calvinist or compromising sympathies, he proved, like Hacket, his counterpart at Lichfield, a faithful executioner of government policy.[14] It also shows that his original estimate was wrong and that his negotiating tactics failed. The scale of known expulsions – 54 out of some 390 incumbents – was a significant disruption but not disastrous and, though a little above the national average (10 per cent), apparently quite moderate compared with percentages of 20 or so in Leicestershire, 33 in London, and possibly as high as 50 per cent in Canterbury.[15]

The effect on clerical relations is difficult to gauge for want of evidence but it was hardly an auspicious start. All the new men were, of course, subscribers to the prayer book, its doctrine and liturgy, and, to judge from the absence of prosecutions of clergy in the church courts for infringements of the Act in 1662 or thereafter, presumably a loyal body of men; but how sincerely or enthusiastically must be left to speculation.

There also remained within the diocese, but outside the church, a residual number of dissenting ministers. Prosecutions continued into the 1660s and 1670s under Morley, and the correspondence of his counterparts at Lichfield and Exeter shows that the existence of such men was not confined to Winchester;[16] but the cases pursued by Morley (or, rather, his agents) seem, from surviving books, to have been few.[17] Six have been traced in surviving court books: Richard Avery, Henry Coxe, Nathaniel Robinson, Samuel Sprint, Samuel Tomlyn, and Robert Whitaker.[18] Charges, when recorded, included teaching without a licence, failing to receive communion, and conducting conventicles.[19] Excommunication was the fate of at least five of them – Robinson, Avery, Sprint, Whitaker, and Tomlyn[20] – during the 1670s, and three, Avery, Tomlyn, and Whitaker, suffered the extreme step of a *significavit* in September 1679.[21] This was in effect an order for their arrest by the secular authorities though there is no indication that any arrests were made.

---

14 Bod Clarendon MS 77, f. 274 (Hacket, 8/1662).

15 Hutton, *The Restoration,* p. 176 (1662, national and London); J. H. Pruett, *Parish Clergy under the Later Stuarts: the Leicestershire Experience* (Urbana, 1978), p. 13; T. Reid, 'Clergy of the Diocese of Canterbury in the Seventeenth Century', unpub. Ph.D. thesis (Kent, 2011), pp. 201-02, 228.

16 Bod Tanner 45, f. 13, June 1665 (Hacket of Lichfield); and Sparrow's reference to pursuit of 'Scandalous Clergy' in his diocese (Exeter) may concern dissenting ministers (Bod Clarendon MS c. 305, f. 231, September 1671).

17 All surviving *ex officio* consistory court books have been examined for proceedings against the clergy of the Archdeaconry of Winchester: they run from 1663 to 1683 but with gaps of up to five, eight, and eleven months; there are no comparable books for Surrey.

18 See *CR* for more on these – it is not clear whether Whitaker was ever beneficed, Averie was an 'outsider', expelled, no date, from 'somewhere in Berkshire', the other four were Hampshire victims: Robinson and Coxe in 1660/61, Sprint and Tomlyn in 1662; G. Lyon Turner (ed. and transc.), *Original Records of English Nonconformity under Persecution and Indulgence,* (London, 1911-1914); note that both *CR* and Lyon Turner contain errors about the prosecutions of Averie, Tomlyn, and Whitaker; see also R. Johnson, 'Lives of Ejected Hampshire Ministers after 1662', in *Southern History,* vol. 36 (2014), pp. 119, 121.

19 These were apparently the charges against Sprint (C1/45, 28/6/1678); if the accused failed to appear in court – e.g. Robinson and Tomlyn – the charge was not usually stated.

20 HRO, C1/42, 9/2/1671 (Robinson); C1/45, 14/3/1679 (Avery); C1/45, 2/5/1679 (Sprint, Whitaker), C1/45, 14/7/1679 (Tomlyn).

21 HRO, C1/45, 17/9/1679 (their names were among seven against whom *significavits* were issued on that day).

The minute number – 5 out of some 48 dissenting ministers who surfaced in the diocese during the Indulgence of 1672[22] – is the most striking feature of these prosecutions. Any number of factors could account for it: from the skill of dissenting ministers in avoiding detection or in perfecting perfunctory compliance to the incompetence of arresting agencies; and there is always the likelihood that Morley suffered the distractions of national politics or pursued a deliberate policy of avoiding trouble within the diocese.

ORDINATIONS

Morley's agenda otherwise, and building on the work of Duppa, was conduct of the routine business of the diocese; and ordination, always important for the supply of future manpower, was made more urgent by the need to replenish the ministry after the wilderness years of the Interregnum. Some of the earliest ordinations were at Oxford and Salisbury from June 1660; while Sanderson (of Lincoln) held an ordination ceremony on the same day as his consecration in October 1660; and at Exeter Gauden began to ordain in January 1661 and Ward (his successor) ordained 57 in 1662.[23] Ordination registers for Duppa and his seventeenth-century predecessors do not survive and the registers under Morley only begin in 1665.[24] These show that Morley ordained between 280 and 290 men as deacon, priest, or both in over a hundred ceremonies during his time as Bishop of Winchester.[25] Only two ceremonies were held in the cathedral: one in September 1668 when he ordained five deacons and five priests; the other three years later in September 1671 when he ordained two deacons and seven priests. He held far more elsewhere: 10 at Whitehall, 22 at Chelsea; and an overwhelming 72 – nearly three quarters of all the ceremonies – at Farnham; in fact Morley held ordinations nowhere else from 1678.

To concentrate on ordinations of priests, as distinct from deacons, the earliest ceremonies show that numbers were a modest 13 in 1666/67, doubling by the mid-1670s, halfway through his episcopate, but declining to earlier and lower levels by the early 1680s. Only half of the earliest group had degrees, four fifths by the mid-1670s, rising to 100 per cent by the early 1680s.[26]

Comparisons with his immediate predecessors, Andrewes, Neile, and Curl, or with Peter Mews, his successor, are not possible as their ordination registers are missing. We know that Andrewes was 'a careful ordainer', Neile a conscientious gatekeeper,

---

22 Lyon Turner, *Original Records,* vol. 2, p. 1035+ (48 is the combined total for the two archdeaconries).
23 A. Whiteman, 'Re-establishment of the Church of England 1660-1663', *TRHS,* 5th series, vol. 5 (1955), pp. 114-15; A. Whiteman, 'Episcopate of Seth Ward Bishop of Exeter 1660-1667 and Salisbury 1667-89', unpub. D.Phil. thesis (Oxford, 1951), p. 204.
24 HRO, A1/34, A1/37.
25 Lloyd of Peterborough, ordaining c. 12 *p.a.* 1679-83, came close to matching Morley (Bod Rawlinson MS, D 1163, f. 16).
26 Ordinations of deacons also took place but have been excluded from this study in the interests of space and because they would add little to the understanding of the quality of the ministry.

so Morley may have ordained more men, particularly in the mid-1670s. Andrewes preferred MAs in his other dioceses and Neile, who had to be more flexible elsewhere, depending on numbers of candidates, would probably have been able to insist similarly at Winchester.[27] Proportions of ordinands with a university education were high in a number of dioceses before the Interregnum and reached levels of 85 and 90 per cent in Salisbury and Leicestershire after the Restoration.[28] Morley may have had difficulty in matching such quality, in common with others, no doubt, in the 1660s, but all his candidates had degrees in his last two or three years.

The drop in numbers and degree standards at Winchester in the early 1660s probably reflects the turbulence of the Interregnum and Restoration and concerns among potential ordinands about the future of the Restoration Church; the subsequent improvement in both respects a growing recovery of interest in the ministry – or greater recruiting efforts by Morley; and, by the same coin, the latter day decline in numbers due possibly to his flagging energies. It should be said, finally, that possession of a university degree is, of course, only one measure of suitability, but little about Morley's – or his contemporaries' – selection procedures, which might have highlighted pastoral concerns, has survived.[29]

INSTITUTIONS

Institution or, alternatively, collation was the point when the bishop transferred the parish, and with it the spiritual care of the parishioners, to the new incumbent.[30] Before this came the right to nominate a suitable candidate. The bishop himself had complete control over the appointment of an incumbent – that is 'collation' or the rights to nominate and to transfer – in barely 50 of the 320 or so rectories and vicarages in the Winchester Diocese. In the remainder – 85 per cent of rectories and vicarages – other patrons, lay and ecclesiastical, enjoyed the right to nominate.[31] The position of the bishop was ambivalent with these latter appointments: he alone possessed powers of institution and no man could take charge of a parish without him, but others were also involved and, while the bishop could reject a candidate, he usually endorsed the patron's choice and would then institute the man to the vacant living. The Bishop of Winchester's 15 per cent was large when compared with his counterpart at Salisbury but small when facing 'alternative' patronage within his own diocese.[32]

---

27 K. C. Fincham, *Prelate as Pastor: The Episcopate of James I* (Oxford, 1990), pp. 179, 183; A. Foster, 'Archbishop Richard Neile Revisited', in P. Lake and M. Questier (eds), *Conformity and Orthodoxy in the English Church 1560-1660,* (Woodbridge, 2000), p. 172.
28 Fincham, *Prelate as Pastor,* p. 182; R. O'Day, *English Clergy: the Emergence and Consolidation of a Profession, 1558-1642* (Leicester, 1979), p. 136; Pruett, *Parish Clergy,* p. 82; Whiteman, 'Seth Ward', p. 210.
29 Whiteman, 'Seth Ward', pp. 209, 235; O'Day, *English Clergy,* pp. 142-43.
30 E. Gibson (ed.), *Codex Juris Ecclesiastici Anglicani,* (Oxford, 1761), p. 813.
31 Calculations, based on examination of Morley's register (HRO, A1/33), are confined to rectories and vicarages (c. 320) because so much information about appointments to perpetual curacies is missing.
32 Whiteman, 'Seth Ward', pp. 351, 449.

Whether a system of appointments, involving so many different types of patron, was good or bad for the Church is also difficult to say. In theory an array of patrons ought to have brought checks, balances, and variety, and Margaret Stieg has discovered in the Diocese of Wells one conscientious layman who listened to the preaching of two rivals before presenting.[33] This must have been exceptional and involvement by lay patrons may be seen, on the other hand, as a threat to the theological integrity of the Church. Lay patronage could have been a gap in its defences, which puritans of the 1630s were only too willing to exploit and which therefore lessened control by the bishop.[34] There was the risk of other patrons buying and selling advowsons (the right to nominate), using posts to reward family, friends, and creditors, failing to check theological soundness or command of Latin, and deterring clergy from speaking out when they ought to have been rebuking the moral behaviour, for example, of their benefactors.[35]

The one aspect where precise comparison of 'appointees' can be made – academic qualifications – shows there was very little difference, however, between bishops' and patrons' nominations during Morley's time as bishop and the pattern did not differ much under Curl and Mews. Vacancies usually arose in seventeen or so rectories and vicarages a year within the diocese during these times and the men chosen by the bishop or patrons to fill them were largely graduate. The pattern varied, inevitably, from year to year and under Morley five 'appointees' of the bishop or his patrons lacked a degree in 1666 but all were graduate in 1683. The spread of degrees remained much the same: mainly arts (BA and MA), with fewer theologians, even fewer lawyers, and a clear majority of Masters of Arts.

If doubts remain about the intrusion of lay patronage and if we can place trust in the bishops, there was one remedy to hand: bishops could always refuse to institute the nominees of others.[36] Andrewes was apparently again a stickler, incurring suits from candidates and patrons alike.[37] One of Morley's registers lists five rejections or postponements of nominees of lay patrons, two of which were the Crown's, between 1675 and 1684, although it has not been possible to establish whether this was exceptional.[38] A chance survival shows he delayed another from the Provost of the Queen's College, Oxford for further scrutiny.[39] Institutions, it would seem, were not automatic under Andrewes or Morley. A survey of the social class of private patrons

---

33 M. Stieg, *Laud's Laboratory: The Diocese of Bath and Wells in the Early Seventeenth Century* (Lewisburg, 1982), pp. 116-17.
34 C. Hill, *Economic Problems of the Church: from Archbishop Whitgift to the Long Parliament*, (London, 1968), p. 252; O'Day, *English Clergy*, p. 92.
35 Ibid., pp. 75, 105, 107, 109, 110; J. Spurr, *Restoration Church of England 1646-1689* (Yale, 1991), p. 195.
36 P. Collinson, *The Religion of Protestants: the Church in English Society 1559-1625* (Oxford, 1982), p. 69; O'Day, *English Clergy*, pp. 79-82.
37 Fincham, *Prelate as Pastor*, p. 185.
38 HRO, A1/36, pp. 11, 12, 13, 65, 67, 75, 77.

in the early 1630s and 1670s suggests theirs would have been the weaker position, as individuals, if the bishop chose to resist them.[40] Peers were relatively few and, while only one private patron confessed to yeoman status, patrons were mostly gentry or esquires whose standing and influence must have been considerably less than the bishop's. A challenge to a nomination, on the other hand, ran the risk of uniting large sectors of influential opposition, so discretion was probably the wiser course.

Stress has been put on the academic qualifications of 'appointees' in part because this is measurable information in the records. Possession of a degree did not guarantee pastoral commitment, of course, but it showed learning among the priesthood and drew respect from the community. To turn from appointments to an overview of Morley's parish clergy in post at particular times, men with a university education formed three quarters of the total body of incumbents in the early 1660s and four fifths by the mid-1670s, a little lower than under Curl (1632-1647) and Mews (1684-1707).[41] Morley's four fifths was apparently lower than Leicestershire's (Lincoln) but higher than Oxford and Hereford and much like Wiltshire, Warwickshire, and Canterbury.[42] Morley had ordained some of his men and he had collated or instituted most of them, but not all, and there were still between 50 and 60 (out of some 290 rectors and vicars) who were in post when Morley arrived in 1662 and who were still there when he left the stage in 1684. John Note, vicar of Leckford (1637-1685), for example, and Henry Beadle, rector of Puttenham (1636-1692), both began their career under Curl (bishop) and Laud (archbishop), both survived the Civil Wars and Cromwell, and both lived to see the Restoration and to outlast Morley. Morley's record may not have been exceptional but it came after a time of great upheaval, and the parish clergy of Winchester formed an impressive body of men when numbers of people as a whole with a university education were so small.[43] Among his institutions or collations, moreover, were several men who were to rise to great heights: for example, Richard Meggott, later Dean of Winchester; Robert Sharrock who, in addition to being 'very knowing in vegetables', was the editor of Lyndwood's *Provinciale,* the ultimate source of canon law and, for a short time, Archdeacon of Winchester; Thomas Ken, future Bishop of Bath and Wells; Henry Compton later Bishop, in turn, of Oxford and London; and George Hooper subsequently Bishop of St Asaph and, after Ken, Bishop of Bath and Wells after Ken.[44]

---

39 B. C. Barker Benfield, 'Scraps from Thomas Barlow's Waste Paper Basket', *Bodleian Library of Record,* 13 (1988-90), p. 85.
40 In 1630 to 1635, of 39 private patrons, 4 were peers, 6 knights/baronets, 20 gentry/armigers; in 1671 to 1675, of 53 private patrons, 3 were peers, 14 knights/baronets, 32 gentry/armigers.
41 HRO, A1/31, E4/1. though different research methods render comparisons with other dioceses inexact.
42 Pruett, *Parish Clergy,* p. 43; W. M. Marshall, 'Administration of the Dioceses of Hereford and Oxford 1660-1760', unpub. Ph.D. thesis (Bristol, 1978), p. 101; D. A. Spaeth, *The Church in an Age of Danger: Parsons and Parishioners 1660-1740* (Cambridge, 2000), p. 51; J. L. Salter, 'Warwickshire Clergy 1660-1714', unpub. Ph.D. thesis (Birmingham, 1975), p. 49; Reid, 'Clergy of Canterbury', p. 19; again comparisons are not exactly like for like.
43 L. Stone, *The University in Society: Oxford and Cambridge from the 14th to the Early 19th Century,* vol. 1 (Princeton, 1975), pp. 94, 103.
44 Meggott, St Olave Southwark 1662-1693; Sharrock, East Woodhay 1668-1669, Bishops Waltham 1669-1684; Ken, Brighstone, 1667-1669, East Woodhay 1669-1672; Compton, Winchester St Faith and St Cross 1669-1676; Hooper, Havant 1671-1672, East Woodhay 1672-1691, Lambeth 1675-1703; for their careers see e.g. *ODNB.*

There is no surviving evidence to indicate the pressures that Morley must have inevitably come under when making his appointments. A little can be surmised, however, about the use he may have made of his powers. Morley may have been putting family connections with the parochial community above academic qualifications when he installed John Waterman – who appears not to have had a degree – at Preston Candover in 1671 and thus left the vicarage in the hands of Watermans for a hundred years. More certainly he used his collations to attract or reward his chaplains: Thomas Ken serving at Brighstone (Isle of Wight) in 1667 then, on becoming a canon, at East Woodhay (on the mainland) in 1669;[45] likewise Thomas Hooper who moved through a succession of appointments in the 1670s from Havant and East Woodhay (both collations) to Lambeth (nomination was in the gift of the Archbishop of Canterbury). Morley appears also to have seen the value of clergymen musicians to the cathedral. One was John Hearsey, a minor canon and song man at the cathedral, whom Morley put in charge of three problematic parishes (Crown livings and a collation) under sequestration in the city and close by the cathedral, where he continued to sing, before appointing him rector of one of them. Two others, Ralph Taylor and David Standish, were minor canons and, in turn, precentor at the cathedral and they combined these with parochial incumbencies in the hands of the bishop or the dean and chapter.[46] Most interestingly of all, Morley made Timothy Goodaker vicar of Wellow in 1681, a year after he had appeared in the consistory court over what may have been a 'uniformity issue'; and Hezekiah Burton, one of the authors of the toleration and comprehension bills of 1668, rector of St George, Southwark, in 1668. Both parishes were held by private patrons but with Morley's final word.[47]

Nothing has so far been said about curates, perpetual curates in particular, as distinct from a number of assistant curates to rectors and vicars, mainly because documentation is far less satisfactory. Perpetual curates were important: they were in charge of a chapel and therefore in effect parochial incumbents; and, with the 120 or so chapels in the diocese, they made a significant contribution to the ministry of Winchester, though their numbers varied from 84 in 1663/4, for example, to 114 in 1675,[48] the former figure probably reflecting vacancies, pluralism, the upheavals of the 1640s and 1650s, and the expulsions of 1662, the latter possibly reflecting successful recruiting by Morley. There are gaps in degree records but it would seem that in the early 1660s, somewhere between a third and a quarter of perpetual curates in the diocese were graduate; by the late 1670s, at least half; and the most usual degree was MA.[49]

---

45 Wood, *Athenae*, vol. 2, col. 189; *JF;* HRO, A1/33.
46 For these parochial appointments see e.g. HRO, A/33; TNA, E 331/Winchester 1; for chaplaincies of Ken and Hooper, see e.g. entries in Wood, *Athenae;* for the musicians, HRO, DC/B3/3, p. 149 (Hearsey, minor canon, 6/1668); pp. 42, 149 (Taylor, minor canon 11/1661, precentor 6/1668); pp. 171, 295 (Standish, minor canon 7/1669, precentor 11/1679).
47 The case of Goodaker in 1680, then curate at Timsbury, turned on 'conformitate' but whether this meant conformity with the beliefs and practice of the Church or merely an instruction to comply with a court order is not clear (HRO, C1/45 - no folios - 15/10/1680); for Burton see the section on toleration and comprehension bills of the late 1660s in Chapter 4.
48 A. Thomson, *The Clergy of Winchester 1615-1698: A Diocesan Ministry in Crisis* (Lewiston, 2011), pp. 183-84.
49 Thomson, *Clergy of Winchester*, p. 34.

Morley took one other step to raise academic standards. He ordered the establishment of a library and left all his books to it and declared that they were specifically for the use not only of the cathedral dignitaries but also for the 'Clergymen and Country Parsons vicars and Curates of my Diocese'.[50]

VISITATIONS

Visitations were opportunities for the bishop to acquire knowledge about his diocese – clergy, people, and buildings – and to instruct, or even inspire, in matters of behaviour, performance, and theology.[51] They could also be sources of irritation with clerking procedures, boredom over lengthy sermons, cynicism at the 'inconsistency' of bishops requiring attendance while themselves failing to attend, and anger at the exactions to finance the bishop's hospitality.[52] Much would turn on the personality and simply the attendance of the bishop. Whatever their shortcomings, visitations could be effective in increasing contact between bishop, clergy, and people of the diocese.

Visitations of the Diocese of Winchester in the name of the bishop and by the two archdeacons took place every year, the bishop's usually in May for the Surrey Archdeaconry, September for Winchester. To concentrate on the triennial visitations, which, if any, the bishop was probably expected to attend, Morley began well in 1662, visiting at least two deaneries on the mainland and crossing to the Isle of Wight.[53] On the surviving evidence 1668 and 1677 were his best years and, though he never again seems to have reached the Isle of Wight, he was present at the visitations of all the other deaneries of the Winchester Archdeaconry and all three Surrey deaneries.[54] He had, meanwhile, been present at the visitations of the Surrey deaneries in 1674 and he appears, finally, to have managed to visit Basingstoke, though no other deanery, in 1680 and 1683. There were gaps in his attendance: he seems to have been entirely absent from Surrey in 1662, 1680, and 1683, for example, but he was present at all three of those deaneries in three other years; present also at many of the ten deaneries of the Winchester Archdeaconry in the 1660s and 1670s for which records survive; but declining, presumably with old age, by the 1680s when he was recorded as only being present once at each visitation.

Morley's attendance at visitations was far better than any of his seventeenth-century predecessors' or his immediate successor's. There is no evidence from surviving visitation books that Bilson, Montagu, or Curl ever appeared in person at

---

50 TNA, 1684 Prob11/377; see Chapter 9.
51 Collinson, *Religion of Protestants*, p. 67; Fincham, *Prelate as Pastor*, pp. 116-17; I. M. Green, *Re-establishment of the Church of England, 1660-1663* (Oxford, 1978), p. 138; Whiteman, 'Re-establishment', pp. 122-23; Bod Clarendon MS 77, f. 307.
52 Collinson, *Religion of Protestants*, p. 68; Fincham, *Prelate as Pastor*, pp. 114, 121; A. Foster, *Neile Revisited*, p. 170.
53 Bod Clarendon MS 73, f. 217.
54 HRO, B1/38, B1/43; Bod Tanner 40, f. 104 (there is a slight discrepancy concerning 1677).

their primary or triennial visitations. Lancelot Andrewes who appeared at a visitation once – Chichester in 1609 – was in fact 'the most persistent absentee', and Richard Neile, who 'rode at the head' of his visitations in Durham, seems to have caught the Winchester disease – neglect – after his translation to the diocese.[55] Mews followed Morley and, in the only (slightly) shorter seventeenth-century tenure than Morley's, visited every deanery in the Winchester Archdeaconry in his Primary Visitation (there is no information about his visits within Surrey). Although he managed all the mainland deaneries once more in 1691, the Isle of Wight again proved too much. Anthony Wood's bold assertion that Morley went 'where had not been a bishop before in the memory of man' must therefore carry considerable justification.[56] There is evidence, scattered among the archives, of visits in person by other bishops (in their diocese) but Morley's personal scrutiny of his diocese was probably far closer than most of his fellow Bishops of Winchester or other contemporaries.[57]

Bishops produced an array of questions – Articles of Inquiry – for their visitations. While their content on issues such as the condition of the church, performance of the incumbent, and attendance of the parishioners often tended to be similar, there was inevitable variation in detail and emphasis. They reflected the religious concerns of their time, for example, the 'Laudianism' of the 1630s, Uniformity in the 1660s, the Treaty of Dover and the Declaration of Indulgence in the 1670s. A comparison of Morley's articles with those of his predecessors reflects these changing concerns.[58] One such difference is length: Neile's list of 1631 ran to 97 articles, Curl's of 1639 to 87, but Morley's of 1662 and 1674 were compressed to 57. This was achieved largely by combining some of the subdivisions, avoiding some of the repetitions, and by removing such marginal matters as sorcery, all of which characterised Neile's articles. It could therefore be said that Morley's inquiries were more manageable and more focused – on the morals of parishioners and their financial support for their church – and thus more effective than Neile's.

---

55 Fincham, *Prelate as Pastor*, pp. 113-14, 322.
56 Wood, *Athenae*, vol. 2, col. 768.
57 Compton (London), E. Carpenter, *Protestant Bishop: Being the Life of Henry Compton, 1632-1713, Bishop of London*, (London, 1956), pp. 208-19; Croft (Hereford), Marshall, 'Hereford and Oxford', p. 116; Fuller (Lincoln), *CSPD 1671*, p. 427; Hacket (Lichfield), Bod Clarendon MS 77, f. 274 and Bod Tanner 43, f. 13; Lloyd (Peterborough), Bod Rawlinson MS, D 1163, ff. 8-11; Sparrow (Exeter), Bod Clarendon MS c. 305, f. 231; Ward (Exeter, Salisbury), Whiteman, 'Seth Ward', pp. 240, 592, Bod Clarendon MS c. 305 f. 156; but for Sheldon, Sancroft, Tenison (Canterbury) see J. Gregory, *Restoration, Reformation, and Reform 1660-1828: Archbishops of Canterbury and their Diocese* (Oxford, 2000), pp. 276-77; see also N. Sykes, *Sheldon to Secker: Aspects of English Church History, 1660-1768* (Cambridge, 1959), pp. 15-16, and Blandford of Worcester's intention to visit in person 'if I can but stand' in 1674 – he died in 1675 (Bod Tanner 42, f. 123 - f. 112 crossed).
58 Neile, *Articles to be Inquired of within the Diocese of Winchester.... 1631*; Curl, *Articles to be enquired of by churchwardens and sworn men in the trienniall visitation of Walter Lord Bishop of Winchester 1639*; Morley, *Articles of visitation and enquiry concerning matters ecclesiastical within the Diocese of Winchester 1662*; and *Articles of visitation and enquiry.... Winchester 1674*.

Of fundamental importance, surely, would have been questions about the authority of kings and bishops. These appear among the questions of Neile and Curl – perhaps obsessively so in Neile's case – but, rather surprisingly, are raised only obliquely in Morley's articles and this may reflect the caution with which people were moving at the Restoration.[59] Another difference between the articles of the 1630s and Morley's of the Restoration is the shift of emphasis over Catholics and dissenters. Neile, Laudian though he was, mentions popery no less than six times and seems determined to distance himself from it.[60] Reference to religious sects appears only once in Neile's articles of 1631, twice in Curl's of 1639, and once each, with specific reference to Quakers, in Morley's of 1662 and 1674.[61] This must reflect a growing concern about such developments just before the Civil Wars and in the aftermath of the Commonwealth and Protectorate.

There remains one of the most interesting differences of all: the credentials of incumbents. In his articles of 1662, Morley enquires about episcopal ordination and institution. There is no mention of these subjects in the articles of the 1630s and Morley's articles of 1674 confine themselves to a relatively innocuous inquiry about induction.[62] At the Restoration, however, substantial numbers of incumbents in post had acquired their parish in the 1650s and the validity of their priestly orders – whether they were episcopally ordained or not – was a major issue.[63] Morley had been centrally involved in this matter, proposing 'Hypotheticall ordination' and even the stratagem of ignoring the problem and of allowing ministers without episcopal orders to 'die out' over time. In 1662, however, after the enactment of uniformity and when loyalty and commitment were such sensitive issues, there was to be no compromise on the provenance and loyalty to Church and Crown of the parish clergy.

A fuller picture of the state of the diocese would be provided by the replies of the churchwardens and clergy, but unfortunately they do not survive. It can be inferred from the visitation articles that Morley's concerns were somewhat different from his predecessors', reflecting the time of his episcopate, and that he was probably less intrusive, more focused, and probably more effective. He exercised, at the same time, a more visible presence through his attendance at the visitations.

---

59 1631 II 8,12, 18, 32, VI 3, 4; 1639 II-27, II-16, V 2, 3; 1662+1674 III-12.
60 1631 II 5, 11, 12, 24, VI 2, 15; 1639 II 20, V 14; 1662+1674 III-10, IV-1.
61 1631 II 32; 1639 II 27, V 3; 1662+1674 III-15, IV-1.
62 1662 III 1; 1662+1674 III-2+3; Whiteman, 'Seth Ward', p. 241.
63 See Chapters 3 and 4.

CONFIRMATIONS

Confirmations were, like ordinations, the duty solely of a bishop and were usually performed during visitations. It was one of the 'rites of passage', allowing parishioners to communicate, and essential for the Church of England in its efforts to retain membership and combat dissent. Patrick Collinson writes of confirmations *'en masse'* before the Interregnum; and after it, Fuller of Lincoln, Henchman of London, Lloyd of Peterborough, Ward of Exeter, and Sparrow of Exeter and Norwich, among others, claimed ceremonies on a similar scale, but there are hardly any details about their – or Morley's – confirmations.[64]

Morley does offer, quite exceptionally, some detail about one round of confirmations in a letter written probably to Lord Chancellor Clarendon in September 1662.[65] He was entertained in some style at Southampton where the mayor and corporation threw a 'very generous...banket'; he was welcomed to the Isle of Wight with a three gun salute, a gift of '2 dozen of partridges', and 'a great supper' of 'meat both flesh and fish'. The crowds swelled, 'half the people of the Town' (Southampton) waving him off to the Isle of Wight where 'the people flock with great devotion'. Earlier at Romsey, Morley claimed to have confirmed two to three hundred and, amid all the celebrations, five to six hundred at Southampton and 'more than a 1000' on the Isle of Wight.

There is no more detail of this kind for Morley or any other seventeenth-century Bishop of Winchester, and whether the numbers of 1662 were usual or exceptional, reflecting the absence of bishops and confirmation ceremonies in the Interregnum, is difficult to be certain. What can be said with some confidence is that Morley did tour the diocese during visitations and he would almost certainly have seized such opportunities to conduct confirmation ceremonies.

DISCIPLINING CLERGY AND LAITY

Proceedings in the consistory court, as well as confirmations, had links with visitations. Confirmation ceremonies took place while the bishop was on visitation and, in the Winchester Diocese, churchwardens delivered their presentments – essentially accusations or charges drawn up against putative offenders – to the bishop's officials during visitation proceedings. These presentments were in response to the bishop's questions and formed the basis of subsequent *ex officio* – or disciplinary – prosecutions in the consistory court. The court also dealt with private disputes – 'instance' cases –

---

64 Collinson, *Religion of Protestants*, p. 51; Fuller (Lincoln), *CSPD 1671*, p. 427; Hacket (Lichfield), Bod Tanner 54, f. 13; Henchman (London), *CSPD 1671-1672*, p. 104; Lloyd (Peterborough), Bod Rawlinson MS, D 1163, f. 21; Ward (Exeter), Bod Clarendon MS c. 305, f. 156 and Whiteman, 'Seth Ward', pp. 250, 268-72; Sparrow (Exeter, Norwich), c. 305, f. 231 (Exeter), *CSPD 1677-78*, p. 400 (Norwich). See also Sykes, *Sheldon to Secker*, p. 13-15 and J. Miller, *After the Civil Wars: English Politics and Government in the Reign of Charles II*, (London, 2000), p. 138 (to both of whom I owe some of these references).

65 Bod Clarendon MS 73, f. 217.

between two 'parties' such as defamation or libel. These latter cases were brought by an individual, one against the other, at his or her choice. The Church, through its officials (bishop, chancellor, and his deputies), was the direct prosecutor in *ex officio* cases in order to safeguard its interests as an institution in such matters as religious observance and public morals. A similar distinction exists in the secular courts of the twenty-first century between 'criminal', or Crown, prosecutions and 'civil' cases.

The consistory court sat in the cathedral to deal with cases within the Archdeaconry of Winchester (Hampshire and the Isle of Wight) and there was parallel 'area' machinery for Surrey, which sat in turn in two or three of its churches.[66] Morley, like others of Winchester and elsewhere and continuing his practice at Worcester, appears never to have sat in his court.[67] He left the conduct of affairs to his Chancellor (known in this capacity as Official Principal). Mondeford Bramston was Morley's first Chancellor during the 1660s and 70s; Charles Morley his second during the 1680s; and they, in turn, mostly left actual conduct of business to surrogates (or deputies).[68] The bishop was, of course, ultimately responsible and his influence probably accounts for changes in the volume and balance (or types) of cases pursued by churchwardens and the courts.

The 'reach' of the judicial arm of the Church was extensive and pursued both clergy and lay men and women. Information about consistory activity in Surrey is too fragmentary and this account will concentrate on proceedings in the Winchester Archdeaconry. Prosecutions against the 'regular' clergy – as distinct from dissenting outsiders – of the archdeaconry averaged fewer than two a year over twenty years.[69] The charges of over half cannot be established; the range of the remainder ranged from dilapidations and licensing to sex, and the largest numbers concerned liturgical irregularities (four) and clandestine marriage (six). Even fewer (six) were found guilty: Thomas Parker, curate of Hawkley, for example, claimed it was too much trouble to contest the issue and was able to commute penance to £20 for fornication, while Benjamin Williams who had performed his own marriage without banns or licence in haste, he said, to sail and fulfil his duties as chaplain with his seaborne employer (a knight) escaped censure.[70]

Ex officio cases against the laity fell mainly into three categories: religious, moral, and financial. Prosecutions concerning finance, usually involving church rate, were few and in the sample years chosen for this study were usually transferred to the 'instance' (private dispute) jurisdiction of the legal system. Disciplinary jurisdiction dealt far more with morality prosecutions from sex before marriage and incontinence

---

66 The best evidence for the legal structure of the Winchester Diocese lies in surviving Consistory Court Books at HRO and LMA (see bibliography).
67 HRO, e.g. C1/35; Whiteman, 'Seth Ward', pp. 170, 181, 591; exceptions were Peirs (Bath and Wells), SHC, D/D/ca, e.g. 313, f. 33r; Stillingfleet (Worcester), WRO, 807 093 2724 ii (list at the back of the book).
68 HRO, A1/32, f. 37; HRO, DC/B5/11, f. 60v.
69 All surviving *ex officio* consistory court books have been examined for proceedings against the clergy of the Archdeaconry of Winchester: they run from 1663 to 1683 but with gaps of up to five, eight, and eleven months; there are no comparable consistory books for Surrey.
70 HRO C1/38 1, 29/11/1664 (Parker); C1/44, 13/5/1674 (Williams); Lloyd of Peterborough claimed suspension of six clergymen in the early 1680s (Bod Rawlinson MS, D 1163, f. 21).

(fornication and adultery) to bastardy, incest, and even desertion (by husband or wife). Incontinence was the commonest misdemeanour and proceedings against George Wither in September 1664 and Peter Rought in October 1673 are good examples of this kind of case.[71] Wither confessed, while Rought denied both the sex act and the consequential bastardy; but both sought to escape prolongation and publicity arising from compurgation (reliance on 'character witnesses') and penance (public confession of sin) by offering to make a charitable donation – in Rought's case £2 of which £1.10 shillings was to be spent on the windows of the consistory court (in the cathedral) and ten shillings to the poor of the parish of St Swithun's Kingsgate (Winchester). There were seventeen proceedings for this kind of offence (sex before marriage, incontinence, and bastardy combined) in 1663/64 for which eleven people were found guilty although, because of absence of the accused or gaps in the records, the rest should not necessarily be considered innocent of the charge.

Moral prosecutions all but disappeared from the court after 1663/1664 but discouragement of divergence, Catholic or Protestant, and enforcement of conformity to the tenets and practice of the Church of England remained the primary objective of the authorities, with Morley in charge, at Winchester. Attendance at church was clearly the central concern. Ninety-three people were charged with this offence in 1663/64 and sixty-seven were pronounced guilty. Numbers shrank noticeably in the early 1670s, but 'attendance' still formed the largest number of prosecutions in all but one of the specimen years. Communion was next and then, in the sample years at least, a few baptism cases.

Offences such as those could have arisen from principle, Protestant or Catholic, but more mundane 'secular' explanations are just as likely. Some explanations such as illness or old age were genuine, no doubt; others arising, less creditably, from laziness (over attendance and communion), ignorance (about baptismal regulations), meanness and hardship (thinking of resistance to church rate). Elizabeth Vinyon blamed her gout, genuinely, no doubt, when charged with attendance and communion offences in July 1681.[72] John Barkham's case is more ambivalent. He was found guilty of baptism irregularities in March 1675 and blamed his wife for a misunderstanding about the need for godparents – which, shifting blame apart, may have arisen simply from ignorance or more fundamentally from objections to baptism according to Anglican rites.[73]

---

71 HRO, C1/37, 7/9/1664 (Wither); C1/43, 29/10/1673 (Rought) – no foliation.
72 HRO, C1/45, 29/7/1681, 'ob infirmitatem et incapacitatem...continuo laborentem tam Chicagra (gout) quam podagra (gout) et aliis infirmitatibus'.
73 HRO, C1/44, 26/3/1675.

Very few were definite dissenters or recusants and some of these, on the scant evidence in the court books, are not without problems. Richard Heckley declared in November 1663 that he was 'noe sectary' and was ordered to attend church.[74] It is not clear, from the sparse notes, whether involvement as a sectary was part of the charge or whether this was just an *'obiter dictum'* volunteered by Heckley as part of his defence. Use of the word 'conformitate' - no less than seven times in 1680/81 - leaves matters doubly uncertain. Were these accused people opponents on principle and, if so, were they Protestants or Catholics? Or were they merely being ordered to comply with, for example, an order to attend church or pay church rate?

Two men did raise 'scruples of conscience' in court during 1664 but, again, the 'opaque' phrase does not make it clear whether they were inclined to Protestant dissent or Catholic recusancy.[75] Two more men were found guilty of 'wearing a hatt in service tyme' at Burghclere parish church in 1664 and another in the same church the next year, and their 'orientation' - Quakerism - is, for once, clear.[76] There can be no doubt about the recusancy of the Tichbornes either. They were prominent Catholics who, together with members of their household, appeared in court in the 1660s, more frequently in the 1680s, and in successive entries excommunication fell first on three lesser figures, then on Lady Tichborne, and finally on Lord Tichborne. A deal, involving requirement to attend church and to receive communion, together with a pledge of £10, was struck *in camera* in January 1683 but the money was declared forfeit in March of the same year.[77]

The survival rates of books of episcopal proceedings are much worse for Surrey than for Winchester, but a series of reports for Michaelmas Term (September-December) 1664 reveals four charged as 'sectary - for not coming to church', together with one 'papist', one 'Anabaptist', and one 'Quaker', while another person, charged with 'calling the church an idolatrous house' looks to have been verging, at the least, on nonconformity.[78] A group of eighteen people were summoned for failing to attend church on one occasion in 1664 and, together with several other similar cases, the total for this kind of offence in Michaelmas Term was twenty-seven;[79] but verdicts and sentencing cannot be established; nor, again, whether the trouble arose from disaffection with the Church or from more 'secular' origins.

---

74 HRO, C1/37, 6/11/1663.
75 HRO, C1/37, Coombes 14/5/1664 and Morrey 31/8/1664.
76 HRO, C1/37, Pearce and Rumbold 26/2/1664; C1/38/1, Winckworth 31/1/1665.
77 HRO, C1/37, 20/4/1664 ('reputed Papists'); C1/45, 7/4/1682 (lesser figures); 28/4/1682 (Lady Tichbourne); 19/1/1683 (Lord Tichborne); 27/1/1683 (deal); 9/3/1683 (forfeit).
78 LMA, DW/VB1, ff. 86v, 87r, 102r, 104r, 108v.
79 LMA, DW/VB1, ff. 64, 65, 67, 87v, 98, 101, 101v.

Conclusions about the nature and extent of Morley's control over his flock – a substantial part of central southern England – become clear. The balance of the main lay prosecutions – financial, religious, and moral – in the Archdeaconry of Winchester inclined towards religion to judge from the consistory court books from 1663 to 1683. The largest number of 'moral' prosecutions – seventeen for fornication or adultery in 1663 – proved exceptional and other numbers were in single figures or zero; while among the 'religious' categories numbers accused of failing to attend church passed 100 in 1663/64, and these alone in nearly every sample year outnumbered – by considerable margins most times – all moral cases put together.[80] The focus of the Church in the Diocese of Winchester – the nature of Morley's control – in these times was clearly religious observance. This was similar to Lloyd's drive against conventicles and recusants at Peterborough in the early 1680s but was not only very different from the emphasis in his court when he was Bishop of Worcester from 1660-62 but also very different from both Worcester and Wells in the 1670s where bishops or their underlings chose, or were forced, to concentrate on moral issues.[81]

The extent of his control appears to have been minimal. Prosecution rates in the consistory court appear to have been minute in comparison with estimates of population and numbers of dissenters and recusants in the Diocese of Winchester. The best estimate of population for the Diocese of Winchester is 150,000 in 1676, 68,200 of them in the Archdeaconry of Winchester, 75,000 in Surrey.[82] Morley himself provides specific estimates of religious divergence in the diocese as a whole – 7,720 conventiclers in 1669 and 8,870 'dissenters' (7,900 Protestant, 968 Catholic) in 1676.[83] Set against these estimates, prosecutions and convictions in the consistory court of the Archdeaconry of Winchester in the 1660s and 1670s were infinitesimal and even if doubled or trebled – somewhat speculatively to take account of the Archdeaconry of Surrey – they would remain so.

It is true that churchwardens' presentments for the Archdeaconry of Winchester show a total of more than 1000 divergent groups (Quakers, Anabaptists, sectaries, and recusants) in 1664 and nearly 400 in the early 1670s;[84] but presentments were only allegations, not even charges, let alone convictions, and there is a striking disjunction between presentments at visitations and prosecutions in the court.[85] It is also true that specific charges are largely missing from the books and that, if charges had been itemised for all the accused (the absent as well as those present), the numbers in all categories, particularly in 1663/64 and 1664/65 would have been considerably higher. Finally it is true that there would have been prosecutions in the courts of the two archdeacons, in the secular courts of magistrates, and in their Quarter Sessions.[86] Prosecutions

---

80 The exceptions were 1673/74 when there were equal numbers of attendance cases and all moral cases (8); and 1672/73 when the Declaration of Indulgence meant suspension of religious prosecutions.

81 Bod Rawlinson MS D 1163, ff. 12-16; C. Evan Davies, 'Enforcement of Religious Uniformity in England 1668-1700', unpub. D.Phil. thesis (Oxford, 1982), Appendix 2, p. 359 (Worcester); SHC, D/D/ca 350, 354 (Wells).

82 Whiteman, *Compton Census,* pp. xcvii, 75.

83 Lyon Turner, *Original Records,* vol. 1, pp. 136-47 (1669); LPL, MS 639, f. 270r; BL, Egerton MS 3329, f. 121r (1676).

84 HRO B1/37 (1664); B1/41 (early to mid 1670s - 1673?).

85 For discussion and sources, see A. Thomson, 'George Morley, Dissenters and Recusants: National and Diocesan Perspectives 1660-1684', *Southern History,* vol. 36 (2014), pp. 92, 97.

and convictions would have been larger therefore than surviving consistory figures for the Archdeaconry of Winchester suggest but, unless the archidiaconal courts were far more active, the extent of ecclesiastical - and certainly direct episcopal - control must still have been small in relation to estimates of divergent religious groups and size of population.

Business was declining, moreover, by some 90 per cent as measured by numbers of people summoned in the course of the seventeenth century - when the population of the Archdeaconry of Winchester (Hampshire and the Isle of Wight) was rising by some 18 per cent.[87] An initial surge in the early 1660s, at least in summoning people, was belied by a paralysis brought about by refusal of accused people to attend - up from 60 to 80 per cent over the century - and, consequently, a failure to complete business - up from 70 to over 80 per cent - inevitably followed. All these factors (minute numbers of prosecutions, decline, and paralysis) strongly imply contraction and that the reach of the court - its grip on society - was weakening in the course of the seventeenth century. Winchester was by no means out of line with developments elsewhere: decline signalled by steep drops of people summoned respectively at Worcester and Wells between the 1610s and the 1670s; and paralysis shown again over the century at Worcester and Wells by high rates of absence and failure to complete business; all very similar to Winchester.[88]

Lack of 'religious' prosecutions in the mid-1670s at Winchester and, no doubt, elsewhere is in part understandable. There was a standstill during Charles II's unilateral declaration of toleration (the Indulgence) of 1672, and restraint would sit well with Morley's efforts - his bill and the talks with Baxter and company - in 1674/75.[89] What is more astonishing is the relatively low level of prosecutions for religious divergence of all types at Winchester in 1665, the year of Morley's famous attack on them on the floor of the Lords; likewise in the early 1680s - the Tichbornes apart - in view of the Popish Plot and his consistent hostility towards Catholics. Possibly he was a true 'ecumenist' where he had a free hand - in his diocese - otherwise old age and ill health must have sapped energy in the 1680s and, ever the pragmatist, it is likely that avoidance of conflict and revolt were prime considerations in both the 1670s and the 1680s.

Separate *ex officio* books cease after May 1683 at Winchester, if not at Worcester and Wells. It must be well-nigh incredible that *ex officio* jurisdiction disappeared from the Diocese of Winchester after that time and the relevant books may have been lost; but the fall in the numbers of people summoned to the court and dispatch of business close to paralysis strongly imply consistory jurisdiction in crisis by the end of Morley's reign at Winchester.

---

86 Documentation for the archdeacons' courts (Winchester and Surrey) is, like Worcester's, missing; for the operation of the secular courts in Hampshire, though the records are again fitful, see A. Coleby, *Central Government and the Localities: Hampshire 1649-89* (Cambridge, 1987), especially pp. 4, 5, 134, 137-38, 201.
87 Whiteman, *Compton Census,* pp. 74-75.
88 These assertions are based on analyses of consistory court books: HRO, C1/33, C1/34, C1/35, C1/45 (Winchester); WRO, 802 2760, 794 011 2722 1 and 2 (Worcester); SHC, D/D/ca 207, 224, 243, 350, 354 (Wells); see also Evan Davies, 'Religious Uniformity', Appendix 2, p. 359.
89 See Chapter 5.

CONCLUSION

George Morley brought fresh drive to the pastoral oversight of the Diocese of Winchester. He combined moderation and firmness in his enforcement of religious uniformity. Building on the work of Duppa, he revived and strengthened episcopal administration - certainly ordinations, institutions, visitations, and confirmations - at Winchester after fourteen years of abolition. Some areas - confirmation and visitations in particular - received far closer scrutiny during his tenure than under his predecessors, his contemporaries, or his successors. An enfeebled and declining consistory court was the one weak link in the machinery and, while this may reflect a tolerant and forgiving Morley, there can be no doubt of the paralysis and decline of the court and its failure, in seventeenth-century terms, to make the bishop's writ run.

Supervision began to suffer in other respects in his later years. He appears to have been absent from his last visitations and, in consequence, confirmations were probably abandoned. Much of this was inevitable. His political role in the House of Lords and the Privy Council forced him to turn his attention all too often from diocesan to national issues in the 1660s and 1670s, and by 1684 he was entering his eighty-seventh year, plagued by such illness that he could hardly see or walk. Ordinations and institutions continued, the former at one of his palaces, the latter with the help of his officials, and neither involving extensive travel.

With a bishop at its head who had a life and responsibilities elsewhere and with key officeholders such as the Chancellor who were largely absentees as well, it must remain a wonder that routine business survived at all. Parochial incumbencies were filled, visitations were organised, clergy were assembled, presentments were received, confirmations were held, and the court sat. When Morley was absent - though less so than his counterparts - he could depend on an army of underlings - surrogates and deputies and clerks - who appear to have manned the pumps and kept the ship afloat when he was not on the bridge.[90]

Those were the later years, and revitalisation was the distinctive feature of the diocese under Morley in his early years at least, purpose and resolve the watchwords of his administration. Momentum slackened towards the end and there never seems to have been much of it in the consistory court; but he equalled and even surpassed his predecessors like Andrewes, his successor, Mews, and counterparts like Ward, Croft, Fuller, and Compton.[91] Thomas Wood may have been singularly neglectful of Lichfield and Coventry[92] but this was an age when most bishops took only an occasional - spasmodic - interest in their diocese and it is significant that even Stillingfleet could only urge episcopal involvement 'sometimes'.[93] Morley should be considered, in this light, a conscientious and humane bishop for the most part among his contemporaries.

---

90 No official 'deeds of delegation', such as those at Christ Church and Worcester (see Chapters 4 and 6), have been found for the Diocese of Winchester.
91 Ward was in turn Bishop of Exeter 1660-1667 and Salisbury 1667-1689; Croft was Bishop of Hereford 1661-1691; Fuller was Bishop of Lincoln 1667-1675; and Compton was Bishop of Oxford 1674-1675 and London 1675-1713; see e.g. *ODNB* for their activities.
92 Bod Tanner 36, f. 185; also e.g. *ODNB*.
93 LPL, MS 1743, p. 115.

CHAPTER 8 : MORLEY AT WINCHESTER: PART 2, REFORM

The Restoration, coming after twenty years of upheaval, ought to have been the moment for reform and Winchester the place where it could have begun. The revolution of 1640/41, the wars, and the overthrow of government in church and state had been provoked or inspired, in part at least, by religion – 'an indictment' of former practice, according to Anne Whiteman[1] – and the regime of Cromwell began the process of addressing the reforms seen as necessary for an effective national church. The Restoration was a time of opportunity. The lesson – that to ignore the problems would lead to disaster – and the answers at diocesan level – a church more in touch with its people and more respected by them – had been made manifest in the preceding twenty years. Obstacles had been removed, reforms begun, and expectations, among some at least, were high. Winchester, with Morley in charge, might have had the potential to become a centre for reform, and it is clear from diocesan and personal records that he made some efforts to tackle two of these – parochial boundaries, and clergy incomes – during his time at Winchester. The other major subject of complaint concerned church discipline and, in particular, its courts. Morley's record in these three vital respects will be described and assessed in turn.

PAROCHIAL RESTRUCTURING

The ordinances in the Interregnum, empowering commissioners to examine and recommend change nationally, together with the orders from Cromwell's Council of State requiring unions and divisions, including the collapsing of five Winchester parishes into two, signalled the problem and pointed the direction reform should take, though little was achieved in the 1650s.[2] Following the Restoration, an Act of Parliament in 1665, encouraged by Sheldon, expressed concerns about 'the great ruine of many churches and parishes...' and the lowly status of preachers 'complying and suiting their...teaching to the humour rather than the good of their Auditors'. The Act empowered, but did not compel, bishops to unite parishes and combine their revenues to achieve 'a competent settled maintenance' – in the region of £100 a year – for the new incumbent, while taking care to protect royal receipt of the annual payments of first fruits and tenths.[3] All this shows that by the 1660s contemporaries were fully aware of the problems.

---

1   A. Whiteman, 'The Episcopate of 'Seth Ward', unpub. D.Phil. thesis (Oxford, 1951), p. 588.
2   C. H. Firth and R. S. Rait (eds), *Acts and Ordinances of the Interregnum 1642-1660,* vol. 2 (London, 1911), pp. 142, 1000, 1132; *CSPD 1657-1658,* p. 376.
3   17 C II c.3; R. Hutton, *The Restoration: A Political and Religious History of England and Wales 1658-1667* (Oxford, 1985), p. 213.

Within the diocese of Winchester as, no doubt, elsewhere, some parishes were too large; there was overcrowding, as at St Saviour's Southwark, where in the 1630s communion had to be arranged in relays, and the solution was subdivision of the parish.[4] More commonly, many parishes were so small that union with a neighbouring parish was the best course to ensure viability. This was an issue in Southampton and Winchester where there had been one or two amalgamations, formal or otherwise, well before the Civil Wars (St Lawrence and St John in the former city and St John and St Peter Soke in the latter).[5] The number of prolonged sequestrations – the process by which a parish in financial difficulties was placed under a 'caretaker' incumbent – was a sure sign of continuing problems of diminished resources to maintain fabric, fittings, and clergyman.[6] Surviving visitation books show three of Winchester's eleven churches under sequestration in 1663 and seven of its ten by 1670.[7]

Following the Act of 1665, Morley petitioned the Crown in May 1670, claiming to have united 'some' smaller 'much decayed' and 'out of repair' churches in the city of Winchester and asking for their release from arrears of tenths due to the Crown – an overhang of debt which a new incumbent would otherwise have had to settle – so that Morley could more easily fill the vacancies. A royal warrant for 'pardon and release' from these arrears in July 1670 was duly applied to nine churches.[8] Two of the churches never appear in contemporaneous visitation books and must have long since been redundant; two others, St Thomas and St Clement, had merged by the 1660s and another (St Peter Colebrook) disappears from the visitation books by the 1680s.[9]

Other minor adjustments, not mentioned in the warrant, can also be inferred from the visitation books: the combining of Nutley with Preston Candover in the 1660s; and Yarmouth's (Isle of Wight) church demolished, under Curl, in 1636 and its incumbent reduced to the status of curate after 1663. Whether these were part of an overall restructuring scheme and on whose initiative is, again, in the absence of any written record, too difficult to say.[10] One definite change was the new parish of Christchurch Southwark, established by Act of Parliament in 1670, because St Saviour's could not accommodate a quarter of its parishioners. The new church was consecrated in October 1671 and the first rector instituted in March 1672.[11]

---

4   J. P. Boulton, 'The Limits of Formal Religion: the Administration of Holy Communion in Later Elizabethan and Early Stuart England', *London Journal*, 10 (1984), p. 136.
5   For Southampton the relationship seems to have been one man as rector for the two, e.g. HRO, A1/29, f. 42v (1615) and in sequestration with no official appointment of rector from 1660 but two sets of different churchwardens, e.g. HRO, B1/27 (1617), /35 (1663), /42 (1677); see also J. S. Davies, *History of Southampton* (Southampton, 1883), p. 371; likewise for Winchester, one rector, e.g. A1/29, f. 34r (1611), sequestration from the 1660s, and two sets of churchwardens (same visitation books).
6   D. M. Owen, *Records of the Established Church of England*, (London, 1970), p. 22.
7   HRO, Visitation Books B1/35 (1663), B1/39 (1670).
8   *CSPD 1670*, pp. 194, 347.
9   Sts Clement and Thomas, HRO, 7M49/3, paper 77 (union 1668) with the same incumbent (Joshua Cooke) and one pair of churchwardens (e.g. HRO, B1/42 and B1/43, Visitation Books for 1677); St Peter Colebrooke is in the Visitation Books for 1682/83 but had gone by 1686 (HRO, B1/48, B1/49, B1/50, B1/51).
10 HRO, B1/35 (1663); A1/31, f. 24v.
11 P. Norman, 'Accounts of the Overseers of the Poor 1608-1671', *Surrey Archaeological Collections*, 16 (1901), p. 60; HRO, A1/33, p. 42.

There cannot be much doubt that parochial restructuring in the diocese of Winchester was on far too small a scale. Parochial boundaries in the diocese stayed much the same throughout the century and into the next. Sequestrations, indicating declining congregations and resources, had risen to eight out of ten churches in Winchester by 1680 - near the end of Morley's stewardship - this time joined by one out of the five in Southampton. By the end of the century and after fifteen years of another episcopate (Mews), sequestrations numbered five out of nine and two out of five respectively;[12] and early in the eighteenth century the Mayor and Corporation were petitioning Anne (Queen and patron) to allow the formal union of the two Southampton parishes (St Lawrence and St John) in question.[13] The opposite was the case at Portsmouth, apparently, as another petition to the Queen, this time from the Bishop of Winchester himself, asserts that the church, overcrowded by the garrison, was 'much to (sic) little for the Inhabitants' and he appears to request the use of the Governor's private chapel for the garrison and 'some of the Inhabitants'.[14]

Progress was piecemeal in Winchester and elsewhere.[15] Attempts to achieve a better correlation between boundaries and parishioners, together with the possibility of improved incomes for their clergy by combining parish resources, remained largely unaddressed. 'It signifies nothing' was the verdict of Seth Ward, Bishop of Exeter, on the Act of 1665.[16] Lack of resources remained the fundamental problem - Ward claimed that the combined income of ten parishes in Exeter would not amount to a decent income for one incumbent - and an injection of cash was clearly necessary. Resistance from lay advowson holders fearful of losing valuable rights of patronage was another obstacle. The reformers of the 1650s had shown the way and the Restoration might have been the moment to carry the reforms forward but the problems were too great, schemes were deferred, action piecemeal, and benefits lost until reforms in subsequent centuries.[17]

---

12 HRO, B1/46 (1680); B1/56 (1699).
13 BL, Addit. MS 61612, ff. 143-44.
14 BL, Addit. MS 61612, f. 75; see also, Bod North MS, b2, no. 41.
15 J. Miller, *Cities Divided: Politics and Religion in English Provincial Towns 1660-1722* (Oxford, 2007), pp. 140-42; T. Reid, 'Clergy of the Diocese of Canterbury in the Seventeenth Century', unpub. Ph.D. thesis (Kent, 2011), p. 92; and see Ward's consecrations at Falmouth and Plymouth 9/1665 (Bod Clarendon MS c. 305, f. 156).
16 Bod Clarendon MS c.305, f. 175 (Ward to Sheldon 2/1667).
17 G. V. Bennett, 'Convocation of 1710: an Anglican Attempt at Counter Revolution', in G. J. Cuming and D. Baker (eds), *Studies in Church History*, 7 (Cambridge, 1971), p. 317; E. L. Woodward, *Age of Reform 1815-1870* (Oxford, 1939), p. 510.

CLERGY INCOMES

Bearing more directly on parish clergy incomes than parochial boundaries were augmentations and impropriations. Clergy incomes were of critical importance for the welfare of the Church and could determine whether a parish had a good pastor or even a pastor at all. Low incomes made it difficult to attract able and learned men and those who did join the ministry were likely to be less effective, their standing in the eyes of their parishioners damaged, their ability to admonish the 'good and the great' compromised. Pluralism and working into old age became all too common – because of lack of money – resulting inevitably in much absence, neglect, and senility. Higher rewards would, conversely, boost the morale and quality of the clergy, enabling them to command respect, to concentrate on the work of the Church, to speak out on public and personal issues and to leave office at a suitable age.

Surviving parliamentary surveys show that incomes of rectors and vicars of Winchester averaged £74 *p.a.*, curates (perpetual and assistant) £20, in the 1650s. This was more than 300 per cent higher than incomes of the 1530s but they had still barely kept pace with inflation.[18] Charles I, no less, had urged a clerical minimum of £80 *p.a* in 1637; the authorities of the Commonwealth and Protectorate had preferred £100 *p.a.* in the 1650s; Charles II ordered a 'competent maintenance' of £80 to £100 to achieve 'a learned and godly ministry', in almost identical terms as his father, twenty-three years later in 1660; and an Act of Parliament echoed the aim of a 'competent... maintenance' for the parish clergy in 1665.[19] Even if the parliamentary surveys of the 1650s are not entirely representative, many clergy incomes must have fallen well short of those targets.[20] These 'guidelines' – £80 and £100 – show, once again, contemporary awareness and concern for clergy incomes and the welfare of the Church.

The simpler method of reform was augmentation and, in line with Charles I's request, Winchester Cathedral was raising incomes – or requiring their lessees to do so – before the Civil Wars for parishes within its gift.[21] During the Commonwealth and Protectorate commissions of inquiry into clergy incomes, overlapping with those reviewing parish boundaries, were set in train, assets of bishops and cathedrals were 'nationalised' to provide funds, and augmentations begun.[22] This process came to an end with the Restoration but, the problem having been highlighted, there were some spasmodic efforts to address the issue. Charles II's letter of 1660 urged bishops, deans, and chapters, under threats to promotion prospects, to make provision from their

---

18   See E. H. Phelps Brown and S. V. Hopkins, 'Seven Centuries of Prices of Consumables', *Economica*, 23, 1956, pp. 305, 306; P. J. Bowden, 'Economic Change: Wages, Profits, and Rents 1500-1750', in J. Thirsk (ed.), *Chapters in the Agrarian History of England 1500-1700*, (Cambridge, 1990), p. 14; A. Thomson 'The Diocese of Winchester before and after the English Civil Wars: A Study of the Character and Performance of its Clergy', unpub. Ph.D. thesis (London, 2004), p. 234.
19   HRO/Winchester CL, T4 3/7/3; Firth and Rait, *Acts and Ordinances*, vol. 2, p. 142; D. Wilkins (ed.), *Concilia Magnae Britanniae,* (London, 1737), p. 556; *CSPD 1660-1661,* p. 183; 17 C II c.3.
20   The incomes of 69 per cent of the rectors and vicars of Canterbury fell below £100 in 1667 (Reid, 'Clergy of Canterbury', p. 122).
21   HRO, DC/B5/7, DC/B5/10.
22   LPL, Commonwealth Surveys, XII/A/7, 14, 15, 16, 21; TNA, C94/4; HRO, DC/J10/2/1, 2; Firth and Rait, *Acts and Ordinances,* vol. 1, p. 879, vol. 2, p. 81; *CSPD 1650s, passim;* W. A. Shaw, *History of the English Church,* vol. 2 (London, 1900), p. 496.

endowments, before granting them away in leases, to augment the incomes of their poorer parish clergy.[23] Several subsequent documents of the 1660s urged enforcement of the royal letter and the Act of Parliament of 1665 required owners of church property to bestow at least part of it on their vicar or curate.[24].

In response to these pressures there appears to have been some increase in augmentations after the Restoration. Morley himself augmented a number of parishes within the diocese. He purchased a manor in 1671 for £816, producing income of £51 *p.a.,* some of which was assigned to the vicar of Whitchurch and the lecturer at West Cowes. A larger purchase in 1681, at a cost of £1065 and generating £56 *p.a.,* was to be shared between the parishes of Binstead (Isle of Wight), Holy Rood (Southampton), and St Maurice (Winchester).[25] Finally, in his will, the income of Farnham was augmented by £20 *p.a.,* Horsell by £10 *p.a.*; and the Guildford parishes, St Mary and Holy Trinity, were to be united and to receive an extra £20 *p.a.*[26] This was a case of so far so good but it fell short of transformation. One thing he could have done to enable augmentation on a more meaningful and effective scale would have been to increase rents from his enormous diocesan property portfolio, but instead he and his officials allowed rents to languish at levels of the 1530s.[27]

Evidence also exists of a few other modest augmentations. The dean and chapter claimed to have spent between £470 and £537 *p.a.* on augmentations in the 1660s and 1670s;[28] private patrons made modest payments at Andover and Combe; while at Bisley the rector obliged.[29] It is not possible to establish how widespread this policy was[30] and whether it had been inspired by Morley's efforts, but, if the attempts so far discovered to increase clergy incomes – fewer than twenty rectories, vicarages, and curacies (out of some 450 altogether) and only eight of them linked to Morley himself – bear any resemblance to the total, they were miniscule. The stream of augmentations in his and other dioceses apparently remained thin; so much so that more legislation and another memorandum appeared in the late 1670s and early 1680s. The Act of 1677 did not compel or increase augmentations but tried to bring a degree of permanence and security to existing augmentations; and Archbishop Sancroft's memorandum of 1681, just like Charles II's letter of 1660, called – again – upon all higher clergy in the Southern Province to act this time upon the legislation of 1677, by 'augmenting the livelihood of poor vicars and curates'; but to what effect is not clear.[31] These renewed efforts only went to show how feeble progress had been to date with augmentations.

---

23 Wilkins, *Concilia,* p. 556; *CSPD 1660-1661,* p. 183.
24 Bod Tanner 280, f. 189; Tanner 300, f. 143; Tanner 315, ff. 98, 102; 17 C II c.3.
25 HRO, DC/H4/1, pp. 6-7, 11-12; see Chapter 9 for discussion of Morley's benefactions.
26 TNA, Prob 11/377, 1684.
27 A. Thomson, 'Estate Management in the Winchester Diocese before and after the Interregnum: A Missed Opportunity', *Hampshire Studies,* 61 (2006), p. 193.
28 HRO, DC/C15/1 (numerous loose folios); Bod Tanner 140, ff. 117, 123.
29 HRO, E15/3, E15/26; LMA, DW/PC/5/1712/15.
30 For examples of augmentations elsewhere, Bod Tanner 128, f. 57; 130, f. 66; 141, f. 101; 144, ff. 8, 9; Whiteman, 'Seth Ward', pp. 589, 592; I. M. Green, *Re-establishment of the Church of England* (Oxford, 1978), pp. 109-10.
31 29 CII c.8; Bod Tanner 282 f. 115; reproduced in E. Cardwell (ed.), *Documentary Annals of the Reformed Church of England,* vol. 2 (Oxford, 1844), p. 345.

More complex was the question of impropriation – the diversion of the endowments of a parish from the incumbent (the vicar) to 'outsiders' (the 'rector', otherwise known as the impropriator), who enjoyed the revenues and either paid the vicar a small sum from the profits or allowed him to receive the lesser tithes. Before the Reformation the monasteries had been the usual impropriators; after the Reformation the impropriators in the Diocese of Winchester were the dean and chapter of the cathedral, together with numerous laymen, not the bishop; but responsibility for reform of the practice lay with him. Winchester Cathedral, possessor of numerous properties, leased out its rectory (with lands) at Christchurch (Hampshire), for example, at regular intervals for a lump sum (the 'entry fine') of £450 at each renewal, together with an annual rent of £58 *p.a.*, the lessee enjoyed profits of some £880 *p.a.*, and the vicar, last in the queue, received £8 *p.a.*[32] Profits, similarly, among lay impropriators were as high as £500 *p.a.* at Kingston.[33] If transferred to the local clergy, such sums would have improved parochial salaries out of all recognition and would have done much to raise their standing and independence.

The critical questions are the numbers and the values of impropriations. Numbers totalled about a third of rectories and vicarages and a quarter of the chapels in the Diocese of Winchester and, while Canterbury apparently had the highest proportions of impropriations in the Southern Province, these proportions were similar to the Elizabethan Diocese of London and to Restoration Salisbury.[34] A contemporary calculation valued impropriations nationally – all dioceses – at £129,000 but it is not possible to give an individual estimate for the Winchester Diocese.[35]

Contemporaries were fully aware of the 'issue'. It had been 'on the agenda' of William Laud in the 1630s, on the agenda of the parliamentary revolutionaries in the 1640s, and it was still on the agenda of such reformers as Leoline Jenkyn in the 1660s;[36] but nothing had been done – certainly not at Winchester – when Morley assumed control of the diocese, and even a savage attack in a draft bill at this time proposed, as a remedy, not abolition but merely provision by impropriators (ecclesiastical, not lay) of enough from their 'Proffits' to bring the incomes of impoverished vicars and curates to £80 *p.a.*[37]

---

32 HRO, DC/B5/6-12; HRO, DC/C1/etc.; HRO, DC/J10/2/1, 2; HRO, E15/23; also F. R. Goodman (ed.), *Diary of John Young,* (London, 1928), pp. 121, 148; the vicar also received from the cathedral, stipend of £26 and augmentation of £54, plus e.g. Easter Offerings (total c. £90 *p.a.*).
33 LPL. Commonwealth Survey X11/a/21/7.
34 e.g. BL, Harleian MS 595, ff. 213-250 (1603) is one of the best survivals and numbers do not seem to have changed much over the century; Reid, 'Clergy of Canterbury', p. 131; H. G. Owen, 'London Parish Clergy in the Reign of Elizabeth I', unpub. Ph.D. thesis (London, 1957), p. 359; Whiteman, 'Seth Ward', p. 287.
35 Bod Addit. MS, c. 302, f. 29r (written as £129000440!)
36 W. Scott and J. Bliss (eds), *The Works of the Most Reverend Father in God William Laud,* 7 vols (Oxford, 1847-60), vol. 3, p. 255; H. Trevor Roper, *Archbishop Laud,* (London, 1962), pp. 107-09; Shaw, *English Church,* vol. 2, p. 477; Bod Tanner 315, f. 102; Laud was Archbishop of Canterbury 1633-1645; Jenkyn was an academic, MP, minister, and judge under Charles II.
37 Bod Tanner 447, f. 126 (no author or date – 1667 and 1668 appear in the text).

With augmentations, at least there was progress; not so with impropriations which appear to have continued, cathedral and lay, intact, to the end of the century and beyond. To give two further examples – one an ecclesiastical impropriator, the other lay – at Nether Wallop the vicars choral of York shared £300 *p.a.*, while the vicar had to make do with £40 *p.a.*; and at Okewood Chapel the lay impropriator received £200, leaving John Evelyn's brother to pay the curate.[38] A swarm of impropriators continued to exploit parochial revenues and significant amounts of money continued to bypass vicars and curates.

With no impropriations of their own to manipulate, the guilt of the bishops, including Morley, lay in their failure to challenge those who did. Instead all was thwarted, by discreet pressure, if not howls of anguish, from the impropriators; and buying them out or simply abolishing them was not an option in Laudian, Cromwellian, or Morleyian times.

The outcome was that, by the end of the century, clergy incomes were still too low. Evidence assembled for 127 rectories and vicarages in the Diocese of Winchester suggests the average of £74 *p.a.* for the 1650s had hardly changed.[39] Furthermore, perpetual curates faced the ultimate challenge of living on some £30 *p.a.*[40] On Gregory King's general scale of incomes, £70 or £80 would have placed the clergy of Winchester between greater and lesser freeholders, £50 into the realms of farmers and tradesmen, £20 on the level of servants and labourers.[41] All would have come well below merchants, gentry, and lawyers, let alone knights and peers – the people with power and influence in the community. Winchester's lower incomes were, moreover, far from unique.[42] Starved of their true remuneration, the only relief was that inflation appears, fortunately, to have stabilised at this time, arresting the decline of purchasing power.[43]

Failure over impropriations denied so many parishes of the true wealth of their 'livings' and, together with miniscule augmentations, drove the clergy of Winchester (and elsewhere) to pluralism and working into old age. A quarter of rectors and vicars of 1675 in the Diocese of Winchester had two parishes either inside or outside the diocese and, likewise, a quarter continued to serve their parish beyond the age of

---

38　HRO, E15/89; J. Aubrey, *Natural History and Antiquities of the County of Surrey,* vol. 4 (Dorking, 1975), p. 82.
39　Aubrey, *Natural History, passim;* J. Ecton (ed.), *Liber Valorum et Decimarum,* (London, 1711); LPL, *Notitia Parochialis,* MS 960 (1705); by way of caution, the last two sources were compiled specifically to demonstrate the existence of poorer parishes; in 1682 the incomes of 73 per cent of rectors and vicars at Canterbury were below £100 (Reid, 'Clergy of Canterbury', p. 122).
40　HRO, B1/55.
41　C. Davenant, *Political and Commercial Works,* vol. 2 (London, 1771), p. 184.
42　Whiteman, 'Seth Ward', p. 321; J. H. Pruett, *Parish Clergy under the Later Stuarts: the Leicestershire Experience* (Urbana, 1978), p. 82; J. Gregory, *Restoration, Reformation, and Reform 1660-1828: Archbishops of Canterbury and their Diocese* (Oxford, 2000), pp. 161-62; D. A. Spaeth, *The Church in an Age of Danger: Parsons and Parishioners 1660-1740* (Cambridge, 2000), pp. 34-38; note especially D. Robinson (ed.), *Diary of Francis Evans,* (Worcestershire Historical Society, 1903), p. 24.
43　Phelps Brown and Hopkins, 'Seven Centuries of Prices', pp. 305, 313; Bowden, 'Economic Change', p. 189.

seventy. There is not enough information for comparisons with old age elsewhere but, within the diocese, the proportions were somewhat lower before Morley's time, and stayed much the same afterwards; while rates of pluralism were, again, much the same in Winchester and comparable in Leicestershire and the Dioceses of Oxford, Worcester, and Salisbury throughout the century.[44]

Morley did augment a handful of vicarages; but did nothing about impropriations and appeared to accept the consequential existence of pluralism within his diocese. Pluralism, like augmentations and impropriations, if not working into old age, was an 'issue' of the times raised most notably by Sheldon, Jenkyn, and Stillingfleet.[45] Sheldon seems merely to have thought in terms of enforcement of regulations set out in canon law and, while Stillingfleet vaguely aspired to 'lessen' pluralism, it was Jenkyn who proposed a limit of two benefices per person. An anonymous bill of the 1660s, though full of sound and fury about the 'scandall' of pluralism, applied the same limit; but another bill of the 1670s required potential pluralists to choose between benefices.[46] All of these reformers, except the last, either considered a certain amount of pluralism necessary or were fearful of the wrath of the practitioners and refrained from advocating abolition. None was truly radical and no sign has been found of any interest by Morley in the subject: except that he once confessed to Sancroft that business was held up because of the absence of his pluralist Archdeacon and 'I know not where he is nor how to write to him.'[47] It must be said, in Morley's defence, that he and Winchester were not alone – the problems were universal – and vested interest was a powerful obstacle to reform. Small wonder that Burnet and Sharp continued their campaign for augmentation which culminated in Queen Anne's Bounty; small wonder that impropriations continued to provoke the outrage of Aubrey, Evelyn, and Ecton.[48]

THE CONSISTORY COURT

The church courts, the first part of the traditional ecclesiastical apparatus to be attacked and destroyed by the Long Parliament,[49] were abolished in the political revolution of 1640/41. It was the *ex officio* oath, strictly speaking, which was abolished but the courts suffered discredit and soon disappeared during the early 1640s. They were revived in

---

44 A. Thomson, *The Clergy of Winchester 1615-1698: A Diocesan Ministry in Crisis* (Lewiston, 2011), p. 69 (pluralism); p. 60 (age).
45 See, for contemporaneous condemnation, Bod Tanner 447, f. 126, also Thomson, *Clergy of Winchester*, pp. 67-79; for the three commentators see, concerning Sheldon, Bod Addit. MS c. 308, f. 32r, Bod Tanner 240, f. 84, Tanner 282, f. 58, all identical and reprinted in Wilkins, *Concilia*, p. 582; LPL, MS 1743, pp. 111-18 (Stillingfleet); Bod Tanner 315, f. 102 (Jenkyn).
46 Bod Tanner 447, f. 126 (no author); LPL, MS 929, item 133.
47 Bod Tanner 37, f. 9 (Morley to Sancroft 1/4/1680); Pearson was Rector of Wigan, Archdeacon of Surrey, and Bishop of Chester and ironically Morley had sanctioned his elevation (Horn, *Fasti/* Winchester, p. 88).
48 A. Savidge, *Foundations of Queen Anne's Bounty* (London, 1955), pp. 12, 16; G. F. A. Best, *Temporal Pillars: Queen Anne's Bounty, The Ecclesiastical Commissioners, and the Church of England* (Cambridge, 1964), p. 30; Aubrey, *Natural History*, vol. 3, p. 126 (Aubrey himself); ibid., vol. 4, p. 82 (Aubrey quoting Evelyn); J. Ecton, *Thesaurum Rerum Ecclesiasticarum* (London, 1742), p. 4.
49 16 Cl c.11.
50 13 CII c.12.

1660[50] and, although use of the oath remained a voluntary possibility, the procedure was in fact 'dead'. This reduction of procedure and, indeed, the disappearance of the church courts, albeit temporary, is striking testimony to the strength of hostility towards the Church and its judicial arm.

This hostility, accompanied by demands for reform, continued into the Restoration. The papers of Sir Leoline Jenkyn, the bills of Sir Matthew Hale, and reports of debates in Parliament by John Milward and John Nicholas, all show that the earlier concerns, expressed so drastically in the 1640s, persisted into the 1660s and 1670s.[51] They were shared by Sheldon, Sancroft, Stillingfleet, and Tillotson;[52] and Francis Atterbury, Bishop of Rochester, revived the campaign in the last years of the reign of Queen Anne.[53]

Proposals for reform ranged from removing 'reversions' which tied posts to families and descendants,[54] to tackling corruption by public display of fees[55] and to confining trials to four law terms for the completion of a case.[56] Some of these proposals such as time limits and displaying of fees were, without any specific means for enforcement, purely aspirational. Excommunication, the fourth issue, arose most frequently in the documents and was clearly a central concern; but again the response was disappointing. The proposal from Jenkyn, that excommunication should be made in writing, for example, was merely administrative.[57] Another proposal from Jenkyn and revived, *mutatis mutandis,* by Stillingfleet and Atterbury, concerned people who refused to pay church rate or court fees. They were no longer to face the procedure *de excommunicato capiendo* but instead a writ *de contumaci capiendo*. They would, thus, escape excommunication and be pronounced in contempt, which meant they could still expect a church burial; but the distinction appears technical, and the destination - prison - would have been the same, while the list of excommunicable offences would have remained almost as fearsome as ever.[58]

---

51 Bod Tanner 315, e.g. ff. 66, 102, 109 (Jenkyn); Bod MS B. 14. 15. Linc, pp. 11, 13 (Hale); BL, MS 2539, f. 168; C. Robbins (ed.), *The Diary of John Milward, esq. Member of Parliament for Derbyshire, September 1666-May 1668,* (Cambridge, 1938), pp. 191, 215, 218, 222 (several speakers); BL, Egerton MS 2539, f. 168 (Nicholas, clerk to the Privy Council).

52 Sheldon: Bod Addit. MS c. 308, f. 114r; Bod Tanner, f. 102; Sancroft: Sykes relies on Bod Tanner 300, f. 143 but this has no date or author (N. Sykes, *Sheldon to Secker: Aspects of English Church History, 1660-1768,* [Cambridge, 1959], p. 188); while Jones relegates him to annotations of Sheldon's efforts (M. D. W. Jones, 'Ecclesiastical Courts before and after the English Civil War: Office Jurisdiction in the Dioceses of Oxford and Peterborough 1630-1675', unpub. B.Litt. thesis [Oxford, 1977], p. 247); Stillingfleet: LPL, MS 1743, pp. 111-18; Tillotson: ibid., pp. 151-54.

53 LPL, MS 929, no. 107; the index gives the date '1713' and Gareth Bennett links the bill to Atterbury (Bennett, 'Convocation of 1710', p. 316).

54 Bod Tanner 300, f. 143r; Tanner 315, f. 102.

55 Canon 136 (1604) in e.g. G. Bray (ed.), *Anglican Canons 1529-1947,* (Woodbridge, 1998), p. 441; Bod Tanner 315, ff. 66r, 88r.

56 Bod Tanner 315, f. 75r.

57 Bod Tanner 315, f. 66r.

58 Bod Tanner 300 f. 143r; Tanner 315 ff. 102r, 109r; LPL, MS 929, documents 107, 119; Bennett implies the change was an improvement but Outhwaite condemns its introduction in 1813 (Bennett, 'Convocation in 1710', p. 316; R. B. Outhwaite, *The Rise and Fall of the English Ecclesiastical Courts 1500-1860* [Cambridge, 2006], pp. 103, 128); see also Jones's comment that reforms, producing more robust courts, might have precipitated an earlier downfall (Jones, 'Ecclesiastical Courts', p. 250).

The church courts suffered from many other inherent failings which received less or no attention from Jenkyn and the other reformers but which may have been of greater concern to the 'common people'. Several historians[59] have claimed that compurgation was abolished at the same time as the *ex officio* oath in 1641-60, but examples of its use can be found at Winchester and elsewhere after the Restoration.[60] It is not clear how far faith in the procedure, which either patently relied on the biased testimony of friends and neighbours or collapsed because of the expense involved in bringing the witnesses to court, may have been a cause of contemporary concern.[61] Two other features – penance and class discrimination – are likely to have met with more mixed responses. The humiliation of penance would have been hated by the victims but welcomed by many observers.[62] Pursuit of defenceless widows and pregnant women, while the sins of the noble or gentry classes were apparently ignored, are likely, again, to have provoked conflicting views.[63] Certainly fees,[64] usually reckoned in shillings in an age when a typical wage was likely to have been no more than a shilling a day,[65] would most likely have been top of the list of their objections.

---

59 E. Gibson (ed.), *Codex Juris Ecclesiastici Anglicani*, (Oxford, 1761), p. 1042, implies abolition and laments its passing; C. R. Chapman, *Ecclesiastical Courts, Officials, and Records* (Dursley, 1997), p. 51; S. F. Hockaday, 'The Consistory Court of the Diocese of Gloucester', *Transactions of the Bristol and Gloucestershire Archaeological Society,* XLVI (1924), p. 224; R. A. Marchant, *Church under the Law; Justice, Administration, and Discipline in the Diocese of York 1560-1640* (Cambridge, 1969), p. 225; A. Tarver, *Church Court Records* (Chichester, 1995), p. 2; B. D. Till, *Church Courts 1660-1720: the Revival of Procedure* (Borthwick, 2006), p. 20.

60 HRO, C1/37, no folios, 5/10/1663 (Aldridge), 5/12/1663 (Misslebrook); SHC, D/D/ca 350, no folios, 3/10/1671 (Balch), 10/11/1675 (Shattock); WRO, 807 093 2724 ii, ff. 70r (Yate), 78v (Cordell), 110r (Dilworth), 114r (Brookes), 117r (Payn), 157r (Lloyd), 159r (Grove) – all in the 1690s; for examples of its use in the 1660s, see Till, *Church Courts 1660-1720,* p. 20 and J. M. Potter, 'Ecclesiastical Courts of the Diocese of Canterbury 1603-1665', unpub. M.Phil. thesis (London, 1973), p. 194.

61 See G. R. Quaife, *Wanton Wenches and Wayward Wives,* (London, 1979), p. 191; C. Hill, *Society and Puritanism in Pre-Revolutionary England* (London, 1969), pp. 299-300; R. A. Houlbrooke, *Church Courts and the People during the Reformation 1520-1570* (Oxford, 1979), p. 46; Potter, 'Ecclesiastical Courts of Canterbury', p. 102; Thomson, 'The Diocese of Winchester before and after the English Civil Wars', p. 282; but for a different view see E. J. Carlson, *Marriage and the English Reformation* (Oxford, 1994), pp. 148-49; M. Ingram, *Church Courts, Sex and Marriage* (Cambridge, 1987), pp. 332-33.

62 See M. Ingram, *Church Courts,* pp. 3, 258; Jones, *'Ecclesiastical Courts',* pp. 110; Outhwaite, *Ecclesiastical Courts,* p. 11; Thomson, 'The Diocese of Winchester before and after the English Civil Wars', p. 288.

63 Houlbrooke, *Church Courts,* p. 79; M. Stieg, *Laud's Laboratory: The Diocese of Bath and Wells in the Early Seventeenth Century* (Lewisburg, 1982), p. 271; M. E. McIntosh, *A Community Transformed: the Manor and Liberty of Havering 1500-1620* (Cambridge, 1991), p. 251; K. Wrightson and D. Levine, *Poverty and Piety in an English Village: Terling 1525-1700* (London, 1979), pp. 120, 136, 140, 156, 164; M. Ingram, *Church Courts,* p. 331; Marchant, *Church under Law*, pp. 145, 217; Jones, 'Ecclesiastical Courts', p. 14; Thomson, 'The Diocese of Winchester before and after the English Civil Wars', pp. 259-61.

64 See Bod Clarendon MS 92, f. 95r (I owe this reference to John Miller, *After the Civil Wars: English Politics and Government in the Reign of Charles II* [London, 2000], p. 138); Houlbrooke, *Church Courts,* p. 51; Ingram *Church Courts,* pp. 57-58, Jones, 'Ecclesiastical Courts', pp. 88-89; Marchant, *Church under Law,* p. 145; J. Spurr, *Restoration Church of England 1646-89* (Yale, 1991), p. 217.

65 Bowden, 'Economic Change', pp. 19, 29, 166, 192, 193, 369.

Morley acknowledged, in a rare comment on ecclesiastical justice, the overuse of excommunication when he wrote to 'Mr Cressey' in 1662 that it was pointless 'to draw the sword...of Excommunication to cut nothing but the Aire or by striking it upon a rock to blunt and break the Edge of it and consequently to make it the lesse powerfull...'[66] The voice of Morley was not heard, otherwise, in the company of either complainers or reformers. No more was said or done by him and the most notable features of the consistory court - paralysis and decline - only grew worse, apparently to the point of the extinction of *ex officio* business, during his time at Winchester.

Separate *ex officio* books cease after May 1683.[67] It is difficult to believe that *ex officio* jurisdiction disappeared from the Diocese of Winchester after that time and the relevant books may have been lost; but the fall in the numbers of people summoned to the court and dispatch of business close to paralysis strongly imply consistory jurisdiction in crisis by the end of Morley's reign at Winchester. Decline is therefore as definite as can be in light of evidence available.

Morley must take some share of the blame for the absence of reform and the consequent decline of the consistory court at Winchester. Inns of Court registers show the admission of Morley, together with Humphrey Henchman, Bishop of London, as a member of Lincoln's Inn in March 1664; and a few days later, he and Gilbert Sheldon, Archbishop of Canterbury, to Gray's Inn, likewise.[68] These were presumably honorific appointments and he acknowledged his lack of expertise when he wrote to Sheldon, during an appeal from Jersey to Winchester, 'I dare not rely upon mine own Judgement...having soe little skill...in the Ecclesiastical Law'.[69] He seems never to have proposed a scheme for reform, unlike Seth Ward, his counterpart at Salisbury;[70] nor to have sat in person, unlike Edward Stillingfleet, Bishop of Worcester in the 1690s[71] Baxter reports that Morley believed in excommunication and imprisonment;[72] and, although Morley's letter to Cressey contradicts this, his lack of further action probably encouraged an impression of his conservatism towards church courts and discipline.[73]

---

66 BL, Addit. MS, 21630, f. 10.
67 HRO, C2/84 (back of the book - upside down - no folios) contains a handful of uninformative *ex officio mero* cases heard on 23 May 1679 and, although the stream of instance books continues, they appear to contain only instance and *ex officio promoto* cases.
68 J. Foster (ed.), *Register of Admissions: Gray's Inn 1521-1887,* (London, 1889), p. 296; *Records of the Honourable Society of Lincoln's Inn,* vol. 1, Admissions 1420-1799 (Lincoln's Inn, 1896), p. 292.
69 Bod Tanner 38, ff. 20-21 (no date).
70 Whiteman, 'Seth Ward', p. 181 - the document is lost and no details survive.
71 The chancellor occasionally and deputies usually sat in the court, according to the Winchester consistory court books, but never the bishop himself; for Stillingfleet, WRO, 807 093 2724, there is a list of his attendance, unfoliated, at the back of the book.
72 Baxter, *Reliquiae,* part 3, p. 128.
73 BL, Addit. MS, 21630, f. 10.

He may even have been guilty, in one way, of damaging his court when he replaced his late diocesan chancellor, Mondeford Bramston, with his nephew, Charles Morley, in 1679. Charles Morley's immediate predecessors – Thomas Ridley, Robert Mason, and Mondeford Bramston – had all been men in their thirties and forties at the time of their appointment[74] – men with substantial experience – and all three had been LLD.[75] The new chancellor of 1679 barely scraped the minimum age limit of 26 and was newly LLB.[76] The court books reveal little of his record, though it is clear that he rarely sat, and it was while he was in charge that *ex officio* business appears to have declined nearly to nothing. Morley's oversight of the court appears, thus, to have been characterised by lack of interest, ignorance, and nepotism.

The problems of ecclesiastical justice were not confined, however, to the Diocese of Winchester. A majority of historians – Ralph Houlbrooke, Martin Jones, William Marshall, Brian Outhwaite, Donald Spaeth, Barry Till, and Anne Whiteman – all believe that the church courts in fact suffered decline during the seventeenth and eighteenth centuries.[77] Evan Davies, Anne Tarver, and William Jacob are three historians who insist on the vitality of the courts they have examined;[78] but none of the three brings to the discussion a perspective based on comparisons with court activity before the upheavals of the 1640s and 1650s, none is able to deny decline of *ex officio* business in the end, and Tarver and Jacob must leave historians wondering, moreover, why such a robust system was in need of reform by the mid-nineteenth century.[79]

Nor were Morley and his fellow bishops alone to blame, neglectful though many of them may have been, and several other factors sapped the strength of the church courts after the Restoration. The mission of the church courts, newly restored in 1660, was to uphold traditional authority and to ensure traditional religious and moral conformity. By 1660 people had enjoyed freedom from the courts for nearly twenty years and, for this reason alone, it was difficult for the courts to recover their authority. The nation

---

74 For date of birth of these chancellors (Ridley, Mason, Bramston, Morley) see *JF; Venn*.
75 For appointments to the Winchester Diocese and qualifications see HRO, 11M59/A3/1/2, f. 19r (Ridley and Mason); HRO, A1/32, f. 32r (Bramston); HRO, DC/B5/11, f. 60v (Morley).
76 Canon 127 (1604), e.g. Bray (ed.), *Anglican Canons*, p. 427.
77 Houlbrooke, *Church Courts*, pp. 262, 263, 266, 267, 269, 270; Jones, 'Ecclesiastical Courts', pp. 65, 83, 91-98, 234-36; W. M. Marshall, 'Administration of the Dioceses of Hereford and Oxford 1660-1760', unpub. Ph.D. thesis (Bristol, 1978), pp. 74-77; Outhwaite, *Ecclesiastical Courts*, p. 83; Spaeth, *Church in Danger*, pp. 59-64; Till, *Church Courts 1660-1720*, p. 30; A. Whiteman, 'Re-establishment of the Church of England 1660-1663', *TRHS*, 5th Series, vol. 5 (1955), p. 120.
78 C. Evan Davies, 'Enforcement of Religious Uniformity in England 1668-1700', unpub. D.Phil. thesis (Oxford, 1982), Abstract II, pp. 3, 4; 'methodology' – different years, lengths of time, and classifications of charges, inclusion or not of *promoto* cases, the way of calculating percentages – produces different figures from mine but they agree, in the main, about the trend; W. M. Jacob, 'In Love and Charity with your Neighbour', *Studies in Church History*, vol. 40 (2004), pp. 205, 212; A. Tarver, 'Consistory Court of the Diocese of Lichfield and Coventry', unpub. Ph.D. thesis (Warwick, 1998), pp. 128, 131, 134, 438.
79 Instance business underwent statutory abolition in the nineteenth century, e.g. 6+7 W IV c.71; 18+19 Vic c.41; 20+21 Vic c.77; 20+21 Vic c.85; and this was in addition to demolitions of *ex officio* business.

underwent, moreover, a revolution in attitudes – political, religious, and social – in the 1650s.[80] The origins of the disregard and defiance of the church courts – and their consequent paralysis – in the 1660s and 1670s undoubtedly lay in these developments.

Change of this kind could and did generate rebellion from time to time. The Lambert, Venner, and Yorkshire revolts, together with conspiracies such as Rye House and the Popish Plot, simmered either above or below the surface throughout the reign of Charles II. Governments from at least the time of Henry VIII had placed more trust in the secular courts, which could fine and imprison, rather than in the church courts which could not, for enforcement of 'religious' statutes. The Cavalier Parliament appears to have continued this policy and the 'Clarendon Code' and the Test Acts of the 1660s and 1670s relied in the same way on the secular courts. Andrew Coleby has shown something of the scale of secular judicial involvement in 'religious' cases by the 1670s and 1680s.[81]

All those factors encouraged decline of the church courts and, even if Morley and his fellow bishops had expressed interest in reform, any attack on fees and even time limits on cases would have provoked instant resistance, reversions likewise, from lawyers with livelihoods at stake. The vested interests of officialdom are clearly revealed in the largely blocking response of 'judges and advocates' to the remit they received from Sheldon in 1668 to consider a gamut of reforms.[82]

In the case of the church courts, then, there was no reform at Winchester, only decline, and the 'suspicion', at least, of extinction; and Morley must take some of the blame. Decline was not confined to Winchester, however, nor blame to Morley. The Grand Jury of Buckinghamshire charged the church courts with 'usury' in the 1660s; and 'oppressing the people', 'dilatory', 'fraudulent', as well as 'expense' and 'corruption' were the damning comments of another bishop, Gilbert Burnet, no less, on the whole system towards the end of the century.[83]

---

80 C. Hill, *The World Turned Upside Down*, (London, 1972), *passim;* D. Cressy, *Birth, Marriage and Death: Ritual Religion and Life Cycle in Tudor and Stuart England* (Oxford, 1997), e.g. pp. 174, 181, 185, 332-34, 416, 418.
81 A. Coleby, *Central Government and the Localities: Hampshire 1649-1689* (Cambridge, 1987), especially pp. 4, 5, 134, 137, 138, 201.
82 Bod Tanner 315, f. 88.
83 Bod Clarendon MS 92, f. 95r (no date but they refer to 'his majesty's Restoration' and 'the selling of part of his dominions' – Dunkirk?); H. C. Foxcroft, *Supplement to Burnet's History of My Own Time* (Oxford, 1902), pp. 331, 503 (his comments refer to his time as Bishop of Salisbury, 1689-1715).

CONCLUSION

Hopes were raised at the Restoration of a fresh start in religion. A new national settlement might have brought at least the main Protestant groups together and opened the prospect of religious peace within the kingdom; while reforms within the dioceses raised parallel hopes of a more sensible parish structure, a better rewarded ministry, and a more humane system of ecclesiastical justice. All this would have ensured a stronger Protestant church, united and reformed, and, hence, capable of an altogether more effective ministry. The Restoration turned out, in terms of religion, however, to mean restoration, not reform. It meant, at the national level, uniformity and, at the diocesan level, a return to the old parish boundaries, the old parish clergy incomes, and, though shorn of the *ex officio* oath, the old consistory court.

Morley was a leading bishop in the 1660s and 1670s and a central figure on the national stage; a man, moreover, of initiatives and with the energy to see them through. All the more disappointing, then, was the outcome of his efforts. Restructuring of parochial boundaries was confined to unions of a few defunct parishes mainly in Southampton and Winchester. Augmentations were relatively few, impropriations survived untouched, clergy incomes remained, for the most part, low, and parochial pluralism and working into old age continued to weaken the Church. Nothing at all was done about the consistory court and it seems to have declined to the point of extinction.

Morley was blocked by others: an army of vested interests from lessees, patrons, and impropriators to the clerks, apparitors, advocates, and notaries public in his consistory court. Morley himself must take some of the blame, nonetheless, for this dismal record. His neglect of the consistory court - ignorance and nepotism particularly - mar his record in this respect. He was, otherwise, vigorous in his sixties but too heavily involved with the government and with parliamentary activity to give his full attention to his diocese; and he was dogged, by his late seventies, with old age and ill health.

All this is true; but it means that George Morley cannot be counted a reforming visionary. Stillingfleet and Tillotson both sketched schemes, not always original and sometimes vague on detail, for diocesan reform ranging from the consistory courts to the residence of bishops and the pluralism of incumbents; but no such list or plan survives for Morley and his approach was more that of a pragmatist and survivor than a reformer.

CHAPTER 9 : DEATH AND BENEFACTIONS

George Morley died at Farnham Castle in the small hours of 29 October 1684.[1] His funeral took place two weeks later on 13 November 1684.[2] He was buried in the cathedral, a little to the north west, on the 'congregational' side of the screen which divides the nave from the choir. His tomb is marked by a slab with a suitable inscription.[3]

Morley appears to have spent most of his time, when in the diocese, at Farnham. Well over half his traceable letters were written from Farnham, nearly three quarters of his ordination ceremonies took place there, and that was where he died.[4] Morley wrote in one of his surviving letters that 'mine own house at Chelsy (is) lent out...' which shows that he was not always in a position to occupy at least one of his three main residences.[5] He remained a bachelor all his life.[6] His daily routine, according to Anthony Wood, Morley's contemporary, had both pattern and austerity about it. He went to bed at about 11 in the evening and rose at 5 o'clock in the morning, summer and winter, 'never' having a fire even in the coldest of mornings; and never more than one meal a day. He enjoyed good health – sound in wind and limb apparently – 'never' had gout, stone, or headache and was laid low with 'sicknes' only twice in his life.[7]

All that – certainly his health – began to change in the course of the 1670s. Wood continues that towards the end 'his grinders began to cease...and other infirmities followed'. Morley had in fact been having eyesight trouble in his fifties and in one of his letters, written in exile, he comments *en passant* that he had 'bin fayne to use spectacles above these 2 years'.[8] By the 1670s these problems were clearly worsening. In one letter in 1672 he wrote of 'greater dimness in my left eye...the light of the other...quite gone'. In another of 1676 he mentions 'a great defluxion from my head which settled on the weaker of my eyes'. A veritable cascade of ailments pours from yet another letter written, presumably, about this time: some of them 'above six yeares', starting with 'a great cold in my head' and continuing with 'disptemper...losse of sight of one of mine eyes wholy and the decaying of the other... the skirvy and the dropsy...ackeing of my legs and shinns...shortness of breath...' and ending with 'cataract (and) the swelling of my feet and ankles...'[9]

---

1 Memorial Inscription, Winchester Cathedral; Bod Tanner 32, f. 165 (letter of the Bishop of Ely 30/10/ 1684); O. Airy (ed.), *Burnet's History of My Own Time,* vol. 2 (Oxford, 1897), p. 431; W. Kennett, *Register and Chronicle Ecclesiastical and Civil,* (London, 1728), p. 686.
2 HRO, DC/D1/1, *Register of Burialls, Christenings, and Marriages in the Cathedral of Winton since....1539* (no folios).
3 See Chapter 1.
4 Examination of 76 letters written between 1662 and 1684 with a date and an address on them shows that 42 (55 per cent) were written at Farnham, 34 (45 per cent) from an array of other addresses; for ordinations the calculation is based on HRO, A1/34, A1/37.
5 Bod Tanner 43, f. 32 (7/9/1672).
6 Morley's life was 'spent all in celibacy' (Wood, *Athenae,* vol. 2, col. 774); and there is no reference to marriage or wife in Foster's entry on Bishop Morley *(JF)*; but his entries for Francis Morley senior and George Morley junior confuse the issue by describing them as 'probably son' and 'grandson' respectively of the bishop; Christ Church rules required bachelorhood (see Chapter 1); no wife or children appear in his will.
7 Wood, *Athenae,* vol. 2, col. 771.
8 BL, Harleian MS 6942, f. 142r (25/1/1654).

All this was by no means unique to Morley. At least two of his predecessors, Bilson and Andrewes, suffered illness;[10] and there are as many references to the health - particularly eyesight and 'fitts' - of Sheldon, Morley's friend and metropolitan, in surviving documents as there are to Morley's.[11] Working into old age and death in harness were commonplace in the age before the pension plans of the Church Commissioners. Neil's short reign at Winchester was crowned by promotion - the only one from Winchester in the seventeenth century - to York in 1632 at the age of seventy; Montague's was cut short by his early death at fifty in 1618; and Curl's likewise in his sixties by the wars of the 1640s. The remaining five of the century all passed seventy while still in post, Morley and Mews reaching eighty-six and eighty-seven respectively, and all died in office.[12]

Occupation of such key posts as the bishopric of Winchester by elderly figures may have brought, on the positive side, a wealth of experience to the diocese. Questions must arise, however, about the quality of stewardship by bishops clinging to office in their seventies and eighties. Ill health and old age must have had inevitable consequences for effective episcopal governance. Even if the grinding workload of the consistory court and management of estates were usually devolved to others, the exacting toll of routine duties - ordinations, institutions, visitations - must have forced ageing bishops to forego personal oversight and to pass much, if not all, of the work to subordinates, clerical and lay, competent or otherwise. Reading and writing are fundamentals underlying all administration, and yet Morley was forced to admit, more than once, that he found it 'hurtfull and painfull...to write and read' and that he would be doing 'as little as possible' of it.[13] He achieved, nonetheless, in 1677 the remarkable feat of visiting all the deaneries of the diocese, except for the three islands (Wight, Guernsey, and Jersey), in 'my 5th and as I verily believe my last Trienniall'. His pessimism turned out to be mistaken and he lived through two more triennials (in 1680 and 1683), but Basingstoke was the only deanery he managed on those occasions. This was a remarkable feat in itself but confinement of his tour to one deanery close to Farnham is a sign of his diminishing oversight of the diocese as he grew older and weaker.[14] Sheldon was dead by then but the earlier correspondence between him and Morley paints a graphic - and depressing - picture of the leader of the Church and his right hand man barely able to read, write, and move about, let alone to endure the rigours of travel round extensive dioceses.

9 Bod Tanner 43, f. 27 (10/1672); Tanner 40, f. 34 (11/1676); Tanner 40, f. 87 (March/no year); other comments by Morley himself or contemporaries include more on his eyes (Tanner 40, f. 199); the odd cold (Tanner 40, f. 104; BL, Addit. MS 17017, f. 157r; Bod Clarendon MS 73, f. 217); 'ilness' (BL, Verney MS 636/24); 'feavour' (BL, Harleian MS 7377, f. 40v).
10 K. C. Fincham, *Prelate as Pastor: The Episcopate of James I* (Oxford, 1990), p. 113 (Bilson); *CSPD 1625-1626*, pp. 8, 172, 356 (Andrewes).
11 Bod Tanner 40, ff. 34, 41; BL, Harleian MS 7377, ff. 47v, 55v, 56r, 58r, 62v; Harleian MS 3785, f. 262, Bod Addit. MS c. 308, ff. 14r, 109r.
12 See for these e.g. *JF; Venn;* J. Horn (ed.), *Fasti Ecclesiae Anglicanae*/Winchester, (London, 1974).
13 Bod Tanner 40, ff. 34, 87.
14 See Chapter 8 for his visitation and, in particular, Bod Tanner 40, f. 104.

Morley's descent from public – certainly political – office took effect in the late 1670s. He made his last appearance in the House of Lords in March 1679;[15] he fell victim to a 'reshuffle' of the Privy Council in April 1679;[16] and it looks as if this was the critical moment when, at the age of eighty-one, he withdrew from court and politics due in part, no doubt, to his physical disabilities. Morley himself appears to have announced, in a letter to Ormond twelve months earlier, his intention to withdraw as he had 'the King's leave to quit my attendance upon all public businesse' and to begin 'my retreat' at Farnham in order to prepare for 'my neer approaching dissolution'.[17]

Old age and his afflictions were no doubt decisive in his withdrawal from national politics and his diminishing role as diocesan. Plenty of other factors – 'so many engagements' was how Morley himself put it on one occasion in 1677[18] – ensured a heavy, not to say intolerable, workload and help to explain the failure of his schemes at the time and his decline towards the end.

His involvement in the general business of the House of Lords, over and above uniformity or comprehension, took a huge amount of time. One apparent protégé comments, *en passant,* in 1670 that 'the Bishop (of Winchester) daily attends Parliament at Westminster'.[19] Reference has already been made to his attendance during the passage of the bill of uniformity – twenty-seven out of thirty-one sessions[20] – and historians of the House of Lords calculate that Morley was present at all but four sessions of the House in the reign of Charles II, 90 per cent of the time in seven of them, and 70 per cent in four more. He was named during these sessions to 280 of its committees to consider a wide range of subjects – from trade to plague, from foreign affairs, to recusancy – though for much of this there is no evidence of attendance or speeches.[21] This problem – distraction from their 'spiritual' work – raised concerns at the time and at least one bill or motion appeared 'that Bishops ought not to vote in Parliament...because it is a very great hindrance to the exercise of their Ministerial function... and because they do vowe and undertake (to) give themselves wholie to that vocation.'[22]

Other issues were set to 'deflect' him further from his diocesan remit and indeed from his attempts at *rapprochement* with the Protestant dissenters. Among these were his roles as preacher at the Chapel Royal, as visitor to several institutions, and as adviser of the Duchess of York, for example, together with occasional crises such as the flight and impeachment of Clarendon.

---

15 *Journals of the House of Lords,* vol. 13 (London, 1767-1830), p. 449; R. Paley (ed.), *House of Lords 1660-1615,* (Cambridge, 2016), article by R. Paley and B. Adams, p. 327.
16 TNA, PC/64, p. 468 (appointment); PC/68, p. 1 (departure).
17 *HMC, 14th Report,* Part 7, *Ormond MSS,* 1st Series, vol. 1 (London, 1895), p. 101 (26/4/1678).
18 *CSPD 1677-1678,* p. 288.
19 *CSPD 1670,* p. 514.
20 See Chapter 4.
21 Paley and Adams, *House of Lords 1660-1715,* p. 319.
22 Bod Addit. MS c. 307, ff. 54r, 56r (no date).

Morley was deeply involved in the fall of Clarendon in November/December 1667. Impeachment proceedings, ultimately abortive, passed to and fro between the two Houses for sixteen days. Morley was present every day and was a member of a joint conference of both Houses which considered technicalities. He was famously one of the messengers from the king advising Clarendon 'speedily to be gone'.[23] The Lords then turned to banishment and Morley was again present for the ten days of the bill's first reading to royal assent. There is no information about what was said but there can be no doubt that Morley would have been on the side of his old friend.

The Catholicism of James Duke of York and Anne, his wife, was a problem which concerned Morley as deeply and which recurred from time to time over the twenty-five years or so of Charles II's reign and Morley's episcopate.[24] The issue was particularly acute in 1670/71 and again in 1679. The conversion first of James and then of Anne provoked a lengthy letter in 1671 from Morley to the Duchess in which he urged her to declare the 'falsity' of such rumours.[25] It became clear that James was likely to succeed his brother and the Popish Plot and Exclusion propelled the issue centre-stage again in 1679 when William Sancroft, the Archbishop of Canterbury no less, sought Morley's involvement in a meeting with James. The 'agenda' is not clearly specified but Morley emerged from 'retreat' at Farnham and a meeting of the two of them with James duly took place in February 1679 but without effect.[26]

Another, more regular commitment in the 1660s was his role as Dean of the Chapel Royal for five years from 1663 to 1667.[27] One at least of his sermons, preached on 5 November 1667 and climaxing in one of his many attacks on popery, 'whilst... Dean of the Chappel-Royal', has survived.[28] This commitment came to an end with the Clarendon debacle presumably because the king, although complicit in the flight, wished to appease critics and to distance himself from Clarendon's friends such as Morley and from any suggestion of subversion of the will of Parliament.[29]

---

23 *Life of Edward Earl of Clarendon.... in which is included a Continuation of the History of the Grand Rebellion,* vol. 3 (Oxford, 1827), p. 332.
24 See e.g. Airy (ed.), *Burnet's History,* vol. 1 (1897), pp. 299, 552, 557.
25 F. J. Routledge (ed.), *Calendar of Clarendon State Papers,* vol. 5, (Oxford, 1970), pp. 633, 635; Bod Clarendon MS, 87, ff. 74-87; George Morley, *Several Treatises written upon Several Occasions,* (London, 1683); Evelyn claims to have encouraged Morley to 'set forth his vindication' – done in *Several Treatises* – against criticisms of his role as spiritual adviser to Anne (E. S. de Beer (ed.), *The Diary of John Evelyn,* vol. 4, [Oxford, 1955], p. 283).
26 Bod Tanner 39, f. 178; Tanner 39, f. 184.
27 TNA, Entry Book, State Paper 44/12, p. 34; *CSPD 1663-1664,* p. 285, (appointment 2/10/1663).
28 *Sermon Preached before the King at Whitehall November 5 1667 by...George Morley...Bishop of Winchester...*(London, 1683); *CSPD 1666-1667,* p. 242, records a sermon the same day in 1666; Pepys reports a sermon by Morley at the Chapel Royal 25/12/1662 and the editors imply, mistakenly, that Morley was already Dean (R. Latham and W. Matthews [eds], *Diary of Samuel Pepys,* vol. 3 [London, 1971], pp. 292-93).
29 BL, Verney MS 636/22, 26/12/1667; Latham and Matthews (eds), *Pepys Diary,* vol. 8, p. 587, 25/12/1667; vol. 9, p. 53, 6/2/1668 (these are the dates on the documents and not necessarily of Morley's dismissal); also *Calendar Clarendon SP,* vol. 5, p. 635.

Yet another was his position, *ex officio,* as visitor to the Cathedral and to several Oxford Colleges.[30] Duties involved formal visits with lists of questions and answers about the state of the cathedral or college in question and intervention in an appeal or when problems arose. Visitation of the cathedral was meant to take place every three years according to the cathedral statute of 1638 but, except for the bishop's judgement in a dispute between Thomas Gumble,[31] one of the canons, and the Dean and Chapter in 1674/75, there is no evidence of action by Morley.[32] He was visitor to five Oxford Colleges: Corpus Christi, Magdalen, St John's, Trinity, and New College. Morley held two visitations of the five colleges. The first, in 1664, took six days;[33] the second, in 1674, was carried out by delegation to two canons of Winchester Cathedral.[34] Surviving documents show numerous occasions when a ruling or guidance by Morley was necessary. At Trinity College, for example, it was a dispute over the precedence of fellows in 1664 and over the admission of scholars in 1665; at New College a dispute between one of the fellows and an undergraduate in 1671; at Magdalen College disputes between the fellows and the president in 1665; between the fellows and the 'Master' of their school at Wainfleet (Lincolnshire) in 1675; and between the bishop himself and the body of fellows in 1684.[35]

These problems and pressures have considerable bearing on any assessment of Morley's achievements and at once explain his failures and make all the more impressive his successes. The particular concerns of this book have been his strivings for church unity and his work as a bishop of two dioceses; and his achievements in both these respects should be seen as the triumph of stamina and commitment over a host of obstacles.

His death leads inevitably to a review of his benefactions.[36] The range of Morley's munificence – in his lifetime and in his will – is truly astonishing: five bishops' palaces; three cathedrals, three schemes to augment clergy incomes; education (both buildings and scholars); an assortment of charities from 'the poor' to clergy widows and victims of the plague.

---

30 A. W. Goodman and W. H. Hutton (eds), S*tatutes Governing the Cathedral Church of Winchester,* (Oxford, 1925), p. 78; R. K. Pugh, 'Post-Restoration Bishops of Winchester as Visitors of Oxford Colleges', *Oxoniensia,* XLIII (1978), p. 170.
31 Horn, *Fasti*/Winchester, p. 96.
32 Chapter Act Book 3 1660-1695, HRO, DC/B3/3, pp. 283-86; W. R. W. Stephens and T. F. Madge (eds), *Documents of Winchester Cathedral, Vol. 2, 1636-1683,* (London, 1897), p. 169.
33 Wood, *Athenae,* vol. 2, col. 771; A. Clarke (ed.), *Life and Times of Anthony Wood,* vol. 2 (Oxford, 1892), pp. 16-18; note there is a discrepancy in the two accounts – Wood records in *Athenae* a confrontation between Morley and a Fellow at Christ Church (where he was not visitor but where he lodged for the visitation), and in *Life and Times* one – the same or different – at Corpus.
34 New College, MS 1087.
35 Trinity College, HRO, J4/2/6, J4/2/10; New College, MS 1013; Magdalen College, HRO, J6/4/8, J6/4/63, Bod Tanner 32, f. 121.
36 For lists of his benefactions see HRO, DC/H4/1; LPL, MS 943; Portsmouth HC, 179/1/9/1/3; BL, Stowe MS 541.

To highlight some of the more spectacular benefactions: one was in the field of education. The right to receive rent of £68 *p.a.* from a particular property was bought for £1,107 in July 1671 by Morley and used to finance five scholars from the Channel Islands with £10 a year each plus board and lodging (£2 apiece) at Pembroke College, Oxford. A board of trustees was set up to oversee the scheme in May 1678 and, with typical attention to detail, the list of the trustees, provision of an administrator, distribution of the moneys, selection of the scholars, procedures for vacancies, and disposal of an 'overplus' are among the matters prescribed in the relevant document.[37] Morley is thought, on top of that particular scheme, to have spent £500 a year – £11,500 over twenty-three years – to support other scholars at the university.

Bishop's palaces form another set of benefactions. This was an urgent problem. The Bishopric had four palaces remaining in the seventeenth century: Wolvesey (Winchester), Bishops Waltham, Farnham, and Southwark. They were more than a luxury: they were important for entertainment, in the interests of the Church, of 'the good and the great'; and as hubs of diocesan administration or centres of 'command and control'. The position was truly daunting at the Restoration, after eleven years without a king and fourteen without a bishop. Farnham and Wolvesey had suffered badly from damage and neglect, Bishops Waltham was in ruins, and Southwark had undergone 'redevelopment' – 'divers Tenements Shops Warehouses and other Edifices' – by its lay purchasers.[38] Brian Duppa, the first Bishop of Winchester after the Restoration, commenting on the state of his palaces at the start of his episcopate, wrote that they were 'for the most part so demolish'd that of the 4 houses I have not the fourth part of one left...'[39]

Morley's attention appears to have centred in the 1660s on the overhaul of Farnham and the purchase of a new house at Chelsea to replace Southwark. Finance for these projects was to come from entry fines and rents arising from the leasing of the tenements built on the site of the palace at Southwark and from episcopal properties at Bishops Waltham and several other places in Hampshire. All episcopal properties had been restored to the bishopric in 1660;[40] there were no doubts about ownership and, ordinarily, it would have been the bishop's business alone to lease out land and to dispose of rents and fines, but on this occasion Morley secured an Act of Parliament in 1664 for the purpose.[41] There was nothing unusual about the lengths of the terms – forty years for leasing a tenement and twenty-one years for land – laid down in the Act. Some of the properties in question – certainly the tenements built on the site

---

37 Pembroke College, Oxford, PMB/P/5/2/3; HRO, DC/H4/1, p. 4.
38 15 CII 17, 1664 (private Act); HRO, 11M59/E/2/Z/249389 (copy of the Act), 11M59/F/BP/E/B4 (Case of Dilapidations in the Court of Arches); for Farnham in particular, see also L. J. Redstone, 'Farnham Castle', in R. S. Rait (ed.), *English Episcopal Palaces*, (London, 1910), pp. 147-48.
39 G. Isham (ed.), *Correspondence of Bishop Brian Duppa and Sir Justinian Isham 1650-1660*, (Northamptonshire Record Society, 1951-55), p. 187.
40 J. Thirsk, 'Restoration Land Settlement', *JMH*, 26, no. 1 (1954), p. 319; H. J. Habakkuk, 'Landowners and the Civil War', *Econ HR*, 2nd Series, 18 (1965), p. 130; ibid., 'Land Settlement and the Restoration of Charles II,' *TRHS*, 5th Series, 28 (1978), pp. 212, 217.
41 15 CII 17, 1664 (private Act); HRO, 11M59/E/2/Z/249389 (copy of the Act); see also Wood, *Athenae*, vol. 2, col. 771; HRO, DC/H4/1, p. 31 (Chelsea), p. 33 (Farnham); LPL. MS 943, p. 812 (Farnham), p. 814 (Chelsea); Portsmouth HC, 179A/1/9/1//2 (Chelsea, Farnham); BL, Stowe MS 541, f. 138r (Farnham), f. 139r (Chelsea).

of the palace and possibly the park at Bishops Waltham – had never been 'demised' before and it may therefore have been felt necessary to legislate. Careful reading of the none-too-coherent Act, however, reveals the real reason for legislation: to guarantee the 'finishing and completing' of the project. If Morley enjoyed freedom to offer leases and spend the income, his successor(s) would have the same freedom to divert the money elsewhere and, in case Morley should die or undergo translation before completion of the scheme, legislation establishing the accountability of his successors to a body of trustees was therefore necessary. A further problem was the location of the new palace – in London – outside the diocese, unlike the bishop's other residences, including Southwark; and the Act declared the palace exempt from the jurisdiction of the Bishop of London and the Dean and Chapter of Westminster Abbey. The Act established, thus, the legal framework for the scheme: it defined the relations of the Bishops of Winchester with other authorities in extra-diocesan territory; and it ensured completion of the scheme in the 'notional' absence of Morley.

The larger amount – nearly £11,000 and much more than the £3,000 originally envisaged in the Act – was spent on Farnham which became his chief residence. The original estimate for the London residence was £4,000 but the acquisition of Chelsea came to £4,250 and more than £1,000 was spent on repairs and improvements. Wolvesey was maintained outside this scheme throughout the 1660s and 70s, with sums ranging from £3 in 1666 to £300 in 1671; but, towards the end of his time, incentivised, possibly, by Charles II's scheme for a new royal palace at Winchester in the 1680s[42] – never finished – building and spending increased dramatically with £2,200 for refurbishment and a further £500 left in his will to finish the project.[43]

One of his most important charities was the establishment of a home for the 'perpetual sustentation' of clergy widows, Morley College, in the Outer Close of the cathedral. This plan was first outlined in an entry with some detail in the Cathedral Chapter Act Book in December 1672.[44] The 'concurrence' of the dean and chapter was necessary partly because they were allocating a stretch of land on the northern edge of the Close for the building itself, raising the possibility of conflict with the cathedral statutes which banned 'new erections' in the Close; partly because they were involved in financing the maintenance of the buildings and widows; partly also because cathedral officials were required to administer the scheme. The cathedral must have passed the land to Morley in 1672 but there appears to be no record of the transaction.[45] The cathedral was involved in financing the scheme when Morley bought from Charles II in

---

42 J. Hare, 'Why so many Houses? The Varied Functions of the Episcopal Residences of the See of Winchester c. 1130-c.1680', in D. W. Rollason (ed.), *Princes of the Church: Bishops and their Palaces*, (London, 2017), p. 205.
43 There is no date for the increased spending on Wolvesey in the relevant documents (HRO, DC/H4/1, p. 29; LPL, MS 943, p. 815; Portsmouth HC, 179A/1/9/1/1; BL, Stowe MS 541, f. 139v); the date '1684' is on the building apparently (N. Pevsner and D. Lloyd, *Hampshire and the Isle of Wight* [London, 1967], p. 687); will TNA, Prob 11 1684 377.
44 HRO, DC/B3/3, Winchester Cathedral Chapter Act Book 3 1660-1695, pp. 249-50.
45 The entry in the relevant cathedral chapter act book 12/1672 refers to 'ground', the boundaries of which it carefully identifies, to be 'conveyed by Lease' to the bishop to maintain the college (HRO, DC/B3/3, pp. 249-50) but no lease has been traced in the cathedral lease books for the 1670s and no exemption seems to have been made to the statute; a search of the relevant Chapter Act Book for the 1870s (the time of rebuilding) gives no details of any lease relating to Morley College in the 1670s (HRO, DC/B3/10-11, DC/F6/2/1/11).

1674 for about £2,040 the right to receive an annual payment of £160 or so which the cathedral had in the past customarily paid to the king.⁴⁶ Morley then had the further outlay of about £980 to build the 'college'.⁴⁷

The buildings were ready for occupation by 1674, the constitution was composed in 1675 and, to ensure permanent management of the college, a body of trustees was established in 1677.⁴⁸ The meticulous regulations in the constitution are, like parts of his will and so many of his official documents, characteristic of Morley's approach. They specify the number of widows (ten), their age (fifty and upwards), and the locations which qualified – the Diocese of Winchester or, if that left vacancies, the Diocese of Worcester – and one place was reserved for a clergy widow from Taunton, Somerset, where the Bishops of Winchester owned property. Other sections deal with the day to day life of the college: payments to the widows and servants, repairs to the buildings, commitments of the widows, duties of the servants, and responsibilities of 'the Chanter' (the precentor who was to act as administrator). Detail bordered on the minute. The widows, who were to show 'exemplary ...Devotion towards God', were told to walk two by two twice a day for prayers at the cathedral; the servants were told to open and close the gates at specific times; the 'chanter' was told when and how to issue the numerous payments to the widows and for repairs, and he was required to take an inventory at a changeover of occupants. Discipline went so far as to insist that the widows, not the charity, should pay for broken windows 'to make them more carefull'.

Parish clergy incomes in the Diocese of Winchester averaged c. £74 *p.a.* in the 1650s and by the turn of the century c. £80/90.⁴⁹ Attempts to augment some of the incomes below these levels formed another of Morley's charitable acts. He established three schemes, two in his lifetime and one in his will, to purchase rents costing either slightly above or below £1,000 apiece and each yielding £50 or so a year to be shared among a string of diocesan vicarages. Once again, proportions for each incumbent were prescribed, likewise alternative arrangements in case some part of the scheme should fail, together with disposal of any 'overplus', and provision of bodies of trustees.⁵⁰ In a fourth scheme he used a fine levied at the Taunton Assizes to augment the income of one of the town's churches.⁵¹

---

46   The cathedral had 'agreed' to pay Henry VIII and his successors c. £160 *p.a.* in lieu of First Fruits and Tenths (FF+T); for the purchase of this 'ffee ffarme Rent', HRO, DC/B5/11, *Register of the Common Seal* 18, f. 31v; for FF+10, HRO, DC/B5/11, f. 81r and HRO DC/H3/1/3, f. 4r.
47   HRO, DC/H4/1, p. 8; LPL, MS 943, p. 807; Portsmouth HC, 179/1/9/1/3; BL, Stowe MS 541, f. 137.
48   For completion of the buildings, e.g. HRO, DC/H4/1, p. 23; for the constitution, e.g. HRO, DC/B5/11 (Register 18), ff. 81r-85r or HRO, DC/H3/1/3, ff. 4-10; for the trustees, HRO, DC/H4/4 (DC/H4/1, p. 8 is a summary).
49   See Chapter 8; also A. Thomson, *The Clergy of Winchester 1615-1698: A Diocesan Ministry in Crisis* (Lewiston, 2011), pp. 85, 86.
50   See Chapter 8; two schemes are outlined in detail (HRO, H4/1, pp. 6-7; 11-12); a third scheme, in his will (TNA, Prob 11/377, 1684), apportions augmentations and mentions the possibility of trustees for Farnham but is vaguer for Guildford ('upon such conditions as I shall propose unto them') and silent for Horsell; perhaps he hoped to carry out arrangements before his death?
51   Bod Tanner 37, f. 9; Tanner 140 f. 71, 4/1680; one of the diocesan properties lay at Taunton and the bishop was apparently entitled to fines from the Assizes; the money was 'to be settled upon him (the Vicar or Taunton and his successors interlined) by due Form of law by the Att(orney) gen(eral)...'

To return, finally in this section, to education. Morley left, in his will, 'all my bookes' to Winchester Cathedral for the use of the parish clergy as much as the men of the cathedral. The cathedral already possessed a library which numbered, by the 1640s, some 190 volumes and which was valued at £200 in 1652. The books were dispersed, mainly to Winchester College in the 1650s and the college returned its share to the cathedral in 1669. Morley's donation was thought to be worth £1000, so must have formed a substantial addition, probably some 2,000 volumes, and his will went on, typically, to lay out a scheme, including opening hours and the stipend of the librarian, in considerable detail.[52]

This account is not, so far, the sum total of his wealth or giving. Other 'odd' acts of charity sometimes come to light, such as the gift, mentioned in Bulstrode Whitelocke's Diary, of between £5 and £10 *p.a.* from Morley to the widow of an extra-diocesan clergyman. He gave in his will another £1,000 in gifts and legacies (i.e. where the value is given) outside the strictly charitable category; together with gifts with no value specified including clock, cabinets, vestments, plate, and bible. There was, on top of this, a substantial estate left, with no value put upon it, to his executor (Francis Morley).

There is an extraordinary moment where Pepys retails in his Diary gossip that Morley 'doth not spend one groate to the poor himself'.[53] On the contrary, as the editors comment, Morley gave on a huge scale. The total value of Morley's charitable benefactions in his lifetime and in his will came to £45-50,000 (in seventeenth-century values). The range - cathedrals, palaces, churches, universities, schools, clergy incomes, clergy widows, the poor far and wide - is enormous. The schemes were marked, moreover, by their foresight and detail. Careful funding of schemes such as Pembroke and Morley College and the augmentations of clergy incomes, by purchasing incomes from the land of bodies other than the bishop's estates, looked to the future and avoided tying up the income of future Bishops of Winchester. The detail in the regulations for Pembroke College, Morley College, and the cathedral library reveal how Morley wished his schemes to run and tried to ensure efficient management of his bequests.

---

52 Winchester College Fellows' Library, MSS 202, 215 (number and value of the books), MS 202, f. 43r (return of books); I owe this information to Richard Foster, Fellows' Librarian of Winchester College.
53 Latham and Matthews, *Pepys Diary*, vol. 3, p. 293.

It was the enormous income received and enjoyed by the Bishops of Winchester which made possible giving on so lavish a scale. Based largely on a portfolio of sixty properties, their regular rental income, together with an 'invisible', but almost certainly large, income from entry fines, was likely to have come to at least £6,500 and probably passed £7,000 *p.a.* and was in fact the largest ecclesiastical income in the country and one of the largest in Europe.[54] As Morley himself once wrote, however, 'I never was nor ever will be a hoarder of money, but as it comes in, soe it goes out......'[55]

The generosity of his immediate predecessors and successors at Winchester came nowhere near this scale of giving.[56] Among these, Montagu's £5,100 was the highest and, incidentally, Curl's £20 the lowest. The difference can be explained partly by the hazards of document survival. These are exceptionally good for Morley - at least two identical inventories, a will, and a mass of documents about Morley College - while his fellow bishops have only a will or nothing at all; so he has had good publicity.

Morley was also in post for twenty-two years, just beating Mews, and completing the longest reign over the diocese in the seventeenth century, which gave him the time to accumulate and distribute.[57] He was also a bachelor; but so were Montagu and Andrewes and, in any case, bachelors have relations - Morley lists nineteen in his will - and, according to their wills, while Duppa (married) had the most (at least forty-one), Andrewes (another bachelor) had twenty-four. The Civil Wars, the overthrow of the Church of England, and the casting aside of the bishops in the middle years of the seventeenth century probably help to explain Curl's minute gift to the poor, and possibly Duppa would have given more the £4,500, if he had not lost Salisbury, though he lived to enjoy for seventeen months a bonanza of riches from re-leasing and entry fines on an industrial scale at the Restoration.

---

54 HRO, 11M59/B1/315 and B1/323 (Pipe Rolls); HRO, 11M59/F/BP/E/B4 (dilapidations case); A. Thomson, 'The Diocese of Winchester before and after the English Civil Wars: a Study of the Character and Performance of its Clergy', unpub. Ph.D. thesis (London, 2004), pp. 213-19; ibid., 'Estate Management in the Winchester Diocese before and after the Interregnum: a Missed Opportunity', *Hampshire Studies* No. 61 (2006), pp. 193-94; Duppa's income from entry fines, admittedly in a 'bonanza' of re-leasing at the Restoration, was £17,900 over the eighteen months of his episcopate according to Morley's lawyer.
55 Bod Tanner 140, f. 134.
56 Bod Addit. MS c. 308 f. 151v is an impressive list of episcopal benefactions in the 1660s - eighteen bishops and thousands of pounds - but it takes no account of such factors as length of time in office, family commitments, or of need/state of disrepair; and Sheldon and Morley are not on the list.
57 Morley reigned for twenty-two years and five months, Mews, his successor, for twenty-two years exactly (Horn, *Fasti/* Winchester, p. 82).

CONCLUSION

Morley lived to a great age and his life and work took him through the vicissitudes of a turbulent century. His early years – school, university, and teaching career – were conventional enough and, though he excelled more than most, he was in his sixties before his career took flight. It was the upheavals of the 1640s and 1650s which propelled him to prominence and he might, otherwise, have remained an academic with little wider 'public' impact in the relatively closed world of an Oxford College. It must, furthermore, have looked like disaster when he embarked at Gravesend for the continent in 1649, but he was fortunate in his contacts, noble and royal, which enabled him to survive and which put him in the right place at the right time when, ten years later, the wheels of fortune turned in the Royalists' – and his – favour. Luck, together with his moderate churchmanship and the trust he engendered from both sides, Royalist/Anglican and republican/Presbyterian, thrust him onto the 'public' stage; and the offices he held thereafter gave him the opportunity to take the initiative and play a leading role in the political and religious problems of the 1660s and 1670s.

Morley was a key figure in the main steps towards the Restoration itself in 1660; in the several attempts at a religious settlement with the Protestant dissenters in the 1660s and 1670s; in the revival of diocesan machinery first at Worcester and then at Winchester; in his attempts at reform – to improve and strengthen – the Church within his diocese; and, finally, in the scale of his benefactions.

He failed in two of these projects. His attempts at reform within his diocese, in the hope, no doubt, that they would inspire wider efforts along the same lines among his fellow bishops, proved timid and piecemeal. His even grander designs for a measure of church unity with the more moderate Protestants, whether in 1660-62 or 1674/75, came to nought, and there was no *rapprochement* let alone true comprehension. These schemes failed for much the same reasons: the numerous 'distractions' – committee work in the House of Lords, 'visiting' Oxford Colleges, preaching at the Chapel Royal, advising the Duchess of York, defending the Lord Chancellor – together with his increasingly failing health and, more particularly, vested interests blocking the diocesan reforms and the heat – not to say bigotry – generated by conscience and belief which doomed his attempts to achieve a religious settlement.

True fulfilment proved unattainable but, concerning both issues, the attempts were still important. The subjects of his reforms within the Diocese of Winchester – parochial boundaries and clergy incomes – were fundamental to the life and success of the Church and, modest as they were, it was Morley who identified the problems and produced answers.

His proposals for a national religious settlement were, indeed, none too precise. A 'mist' hangs over the 'hypotheticall ordination' of 1660, for example, and over the practicalities of waiving assent and consent to the Book of Common Prayer in 1674. The scope of these proposals appears narrow, moreover, when comparing his Bill of 1674 with Baxter's ambitious schemes of 1673-75. The fact is, however, that he was the source of a string of proposals for a settlement: possibly the Black Rubric; certainly 'hypotheticall ordination'; concessions at Worcester House to do with the surplice and ceremonies which were revived and combined with an offer of 'redundancy payments' to expelled clergy during the passage of uniformity in the Lords in 1660s; and, most strikingly, he appeared to be willing to accept optional use of the prayer book in the 1670s. All these initiatives failed but, where he had a free hand, he showed flexibility and generosity: by his acceptance of 'intruders' in the parochial ministry nationally through his work on Clarendon's 'committee' in 1660 and while at Worcester from 1660 to 1662; by his restraint in prosecutions of clergy and laity alike in his consistory court during his time at Winchester; and by his promotion of Hezekiah Burton, a key supporter of comprehension and toleration bills in the 1660s, to a Southwark parish. He shone a light in these ways on the problems and showed the way forward. He did more than anyone else for the cause of church unity, and it was his tragedy and the nation's loss that so few were able or willing to share his vision and support his ideas.

In at least three other respects Morley did in fact enjoy considerable success. He was vitally important, though not the only person, in the initial moves to restore the king. He was the figure acceptable to both religious camps, the Anglicans and the Presbyterians. He undertook the mission to England. He assessed the mood and proposed the tactics during the contacts; and all this smoothed the way for the return of the king. At diocesan level, likewise, he was responsible, often by his personal presence, for the revival of the administrative machinery – ordinations, visitations, confirmations, the consistory court, the officials in the 'estates office' – in two dioceses. He ensured that the manpower of clergy and officialdom was there. He made certain the discipline of clergy and people alike. He was, thus, the central agent in the revival of the life and work of the Church at 'ground level' after twenty years of upheaval and fourteen of abolition. He was the source, finally, of multiple benefactions either during his lifetime or at his death. He put to work the exceptional resources of his diocese and distributed tens of thousands of pounds, in terms of buildings, for the repair of palaces, cathedrals, and churches; and in terms of the advancement of scholarship and protection of the poor.

There can be little doubting the greatness of Morley. He had his failings: being guilty of nepotism in advancing relations such as Charles Morley to the Winchester Consistory Court; of repression in his treatment of Richard Baxter; of hostility to Catholicism; of intemperance at moments - critical moments - such as Worcester House and Savoy; and these all had less than fortunate consequences for the disciplinary machinery at Winchester, in the case of Charles Morley, and for the cause of unity in religion with the other matters. He has been traduced by some as a deceiver and as part of an Anglican conspiracy bent on outwitting and destroying the dissenters. A case can certainly be made for inconsistency in his attitude towards the latter - making offers at one time, urging repression at another. It must also be said, however, that he was only human; it would be surprising to find in anybody cast iron consistency over a lifetime - of more than eighty years in his case - and, when circumstances changed, he - sensibly some would say - changed as well.

Morley was, then, a great bishop; and one of the greatest in the long line of bishops of Winchester. He could not match Wykeham for the munificence of his building projects nor Andrewes for saintliness. He had spent twenty years and more in the realms of theology and philosophy at an Oxford College and he could easily have remained an academic in relative obscurity for the rest of his life. Although these powers never left him and he was always capable of producing academic tracts and sermons, another, far more practical, side emerged when he entered the more public, episcopal, stage in the 1660s. A conservative by 'default', Morley showed himself essentially a practitioner and a pragmatist who strove more than any of his contemporaries to modernise the Church at diocesan level and to heal the divisions of the Protestants in a national settlement. In these grand designs he failed; but he helped to restore the king to his throne, he directed the affairs of his diocese in person, and he left in the 'castle' at Farnham and in the accumulation of buildings around the cathedral close - Morley College, Wolvesey Palace, and the Cathedral Library - impressive reminders to this day of his reign - its pragmatism and its benevolence - in the Diocese of Winchester.

APPENDICES

1. Summary of Morley's Movements on the Continent in the 1650s

Gravesend/The Hague	3/1649	*HMC*, 12th Report, p. 38; Wood, *Athenae*, 2, col. 769
Brussels	1649	*Several Treatises* (Conference with Darcy 6/1649)
Paris Brown's household	1649	*Several Treatises*, p. viii
Caen Lady Ormond's household	9-10/1649	*Several Treatises*, p. viii; Harleian 6942, f.138, 9/1649; Harleian 7190, f. 146, 10/1649
Paris/Louvre Henrietta Maria	1649/50	Evelyn Diary, 2, pp. 251-52; Harleian 6942, f. 138, 9/1649, (2/1650?); Harleian 7190, 10/1649; *HMC* Bath MSS, vol. 2, p. 92, 6/1650
Breda	1650	*Several Treatises*, p. ix; Wood, *Athenae*, 2, col. 769
The Hague	1650	Wood *Athenae*, 2, col. 769
Antwerp Cottrells	1650	Wood, *Athenae*, 2, col. 769; BL, Harleian 6942, f. 140, 11/1650, f.141, 11/1650
Antwerp Hydes	1650-54	Harleian 6942, f. 152, 5/1652; f. 148, 7/1652; f. 147, 11/1652; Harleian 7190, f. 147, 11/1652; *HMC*, Bath MSS, vol. 2, pp. 96, 110, 112, 5/1651, 9/1653, 11/1653; *HMC*, 7th Report, pp. 458, 460, 11/1652, 1/1653; *Several Treatises*, p. v; Wood, *Athenae*, 2, col. 770
The Hague Elizabeth of Bohemia	1654-56	Calendar *CSP*, vol. 2, 4/1654; ibid., vol. 3, 4/1655; *Several Treatises*, pp. vii, ix; Wood, *Athenae*, 2, col. 770
Visits to: Breda		*Calendar Clarendon SP*, vol. 2, pp. 333, 339, 4/1654; vol. 3. p. 7, 1/1655; Camden, vol. 2, pp. 244, 251, 4/1655
Dusseldorf/Dort(mund?)/Palatinate		Camden, vol. 2, p. 156, 1/1655; *Calendar Clarendon SP*, vol. 3, p. 26, 3/1655
Heidelberg? in the Palatinate		Harleian 6942, f. 149, 7/1655?
Cologne a free city		Cottrell MSS, 6 letters 9/1655
Breda (visits to Antwerp, Brussels, Bruges)	1656-60	*Several Treatises*, p. ix; Ad Cl. Virum Janum Ulitium Epistolae Duae, pp. 6, 67; Wood, *Athenae*, 2, col. 770; *Calendar Clarendon SP*, vol. 4, 19 letters 11/1658-4/1660; Clarendon MS 59, 60, 62, 65, 4 letters 1/1659-10/1659; Surtees Society, vol. LII, p. 291, 2/1660

2. Morley's Benefactions

CATHEDRALS		
Worcester	200	
St Paul's	1700	
Christ Church	2300	(cathedral or college?)
PALACES		
Wolvesey	3937	repairs and new buildings including. £500 *in his will*
Farnham	10948	repairs and new buildings and enhancement/land purchase £300
Chelsea	5695	purchase £4,250 + £76 cost + £454 improvements + £914 repairs
Worcester	950	£800 plus sum to an interloper to quit Worcester Palace 1660 £150
Hartlebury	500	
CHURCHES		
Southwark St Saviour	50	repairs
B Waltham	50	repairs
E Meon	190	repairs
Lymington	10	repairs
Newport	10	'to the church'
Farnham	10	'to the church'
Chelsea	100	towards the building of the church
Hamilton chapel	10	repairs
AUGMENTATIONS		
scheme 1	816	purchase yielding £51 rent shared between the lecturer at W Cowes, the vicar of Whitchurch (and the schoolmaster at Bishops Waltham – see below) 1671/79
scheme 2	1065	purchase yielding £56 shared between St Maurice Winchester, Holy Rood Southampton, Binstead (IofW) 1681/83
scheme 3	*1000*	*purchase yielding £50 p.a. rent to be shared by HT Guildford, Farnham, Horsell*
scheme 4	500	fine due to GM from a case at Taunton Assize to the vicar – amount p.a.? 1680
EDUCATION		
Scholars Channel Islands	1107	purchase land to finance 5 scholars Channel Islands 1671
Scholar support	11500	mainly to scholars – £500 p.a. over 23 years
New College, Oxford	100	new buildings
Cathedral Library	*1000*	*this is the value of books plus salary of librarian*
Farnham Schoolmaster's house	250	probably where the schoolmaster taught 1679
Note B Waltham above		See above scheme 1
CHARITY		
Morley College	3022	building, £980; purchase of rent worth £160 *p.a.* for 10 Widows, £2,042; *plus a £20 (£2 per widow) single payment at his death*
Poor of Southwark	350	investments in rents and coal to produce income
Poor generally	80	*sundry places, including £10 to the poor of Farnham, all in his will*
Plague	70	in 'severall places'
Chelsea Hospital	*500*	*contribution to the military hospital*
French Protestants	100	
Algiers	500	
College in Bohemia	100	
MISCELLANEOUS		
benevolence	800	benevolence, or grant, to the king
bridge at Winchester	290	bridge at Winchester
	49810	

Notes:
Entries in italics: are benefactions in his will; the rest were in his lifetime.
Sources:
Summaries: HRO, DC/H4/1; LPL, MS 943, pp. 805-09; Portsmouth HC 179A/1/9/1/1-4; BL, Stowe MS 541.
Will: TNA, Prob 11/377 1684
Bod Tanner 37, ff. 9, 14; Tanner 140 f. 71 (Taunton)
Pembroke College, Oxford, PMB/P/5/2/3
NB. R. Spalding (ed.), *Diary of Bulstrode Whitelocke 1605-1675,* (Oxford, 1990), p. 180, in which Bulstrode Whitelock records a gift of £5-10 a year from GM to an extra diocesan clergy widow, 5/1673)

BIBLIOGRAPHY

ORIGINAL DOCUMENTS

BRITISH LIBRARY
Addit. MSS 20058; 21630; 28053.
Egerton MSS 2539; 3329.
Harleian MSS 6942; 7190; 7377; 17017.
Lansdowne MS 459.
Stowe MS 541.
Verney MSS 636/22; 636/24.

BODLEIAN LIBRARY OXFORD
Addit. MSS.
B.14.15.Linc.
Carte MSS.
Clarendon MSS.
Rawlinson MS D 1163.
Tanner MSS.

CHRIST CHURCH OXFORD.
Dean and Chapter Act Book i.b.2; i.b.3.
Disbursement Book xii.b.65; xii.b.85; xii.b.103.

HOUSE OF LORDS
HL/PO/LB/1/36/1+2 (Book of Common Prayer 1662).
HL/PO/JO/10/135 (Morley's comprehension bill 1674).
15 CII 17 1663 (Morley's private Act for palaces).

HAMPSHIRE RECORD OFFICE
7M49/3 (union of parishes).
11M59/A1/2/14 (parliamentary survey).
11M59/A3/1/etc. (patent book).
11M59/B1/315, 323 (pipe books).
11M59/D1/etc. (bishops lease books).
11M59/E 2/Z/249389 (copy of Morley's Bill).
11M59/F/BP/E/B4 (dilapidations document).
21M65/A1/etc. (episcopal registers).
21M65/B1/etc. (visitation books).
21M65/C1/etc. (consistory court books).
21M65/E15/etc. (bishops' terriers).
35M48 (archdeacons' terriers).
DC/B/3/etc. (chapter act books).
DC/B/5 etc. (registers of the common seal).
DC/C1/etc. (treasurers' books).
DC/C3/etc. (audit books).
DC/C4/etc. (compotus rolls).
DC/C15/1 (accounts).
DC/D1/1 *Register of Burialls Christenings and Marriages in the Cathedral of Winchester since 1539.*
DC/F5/1/1-7 (catalogues of Morley's books).
DC/H3/1/3 (Morley College constitution).
DC/H4/1 (copy of Morley's benefactions).
DC/H4/4 (Morley College trustees).
DC/J10/2/etc. (parliamentary surveys).
DC/K4/12/2 (typescript of Cottrell letters).
DC/K11/5/1 (*Winchester Cathedral Memorials*, ed. by T. D. Atkinson, typescript, 1937).
J4/2/6, 10, 13; J6/4/8, 63 (visitations of Oxford Colleges).
T4 3/7/3 (letter CI to D+C).

LONDON METROPOLITAN ARCHIVES
DW/PC5/1712/15.
DW/S -73.
DW/VB1 etc.

LONGLEAT
Coventry MS vol. 7.

LAMBETH PALACE LIBRARY
Archbishops' Registers.
Commonwealth Surveys.
MS 639.
MS 903.
MS 943 (copy of Morley's benefactions).
MS 1743.
Notitia Parochialis.

NATIONAL LIBRARY OF SCOTLAND
Wodrow MS, Folio XXXII, no. 9.

NATIONAL LIBRARY OF WALES
SA-MB-15.

NEW COLLEGE OXFORD
MS 1013, 1087.

OXFORDSHIRE HISTORY CENTRE
Oxford Diocesan Papers d. 70, d. 78, d. 106.

PEMBROKE COLLEGE OXFORD
PMB/P/5/2/3.

PORTSMOUTH HISTORY CENTRE
179A/1/9/1/etc. (copy of Morley's benefactions).

SOUTHAMPTON CIVIC CENTRE
PR6/9/1.

SOMERSET HERITAGE CENTRE
D/D/ca/etc. (consistory court books).

TNA
C94/4 Commonwealth Surveys.
E 331/institutions.
E 334/compositions.
Liber Institutionum.
PC2/etc. (Privy Council Registers).
PCC 1667 Prob 11 324 (Wren); 1684 Prob 11 377 (Morley).
PRO Transcript 31/3/107.
SP 29/8; 29/31; 44/12.

WORCESTER CATHEDRAL LIBRARY
A26, A73, A76, D197.

WORCESTERSHIRE RECORD OFFICE
716 051 2697 (subscriptions).
716 093 2648 10 iii (episcopal register).
7322 2049 (ordinations); 778 7322 2448 (calendar of ordinations).
802 2760; 794 011 2513 18; 794 011 2722 1 and 2; 807 093 2724 ii (consistory court books).
802 2951 1 and 2 (visitation books).

PRIVATE COLLECTION
Cottrell MSS, see NRA 996 (and typescript HRO, DC/K4/12/2).

PRIMARY SOURCES IN PRINT

Airy, O., (ed.), *Burnet's History of my Own Time*, 2 vols (Oxford, 1897-1900).
Aubrey, J., *Natural History and Antiquities of Surrey*, (Dorking, 1975).
Barwick, P., *Life of John Barwick*, (London, 1724).
Baxter, R., *Reliquiae Baxterianae*, ed. M. Sylvester (London, 1696).
Bray, G. (ed.), *Anglican Canons 1529-1947*, (Woodbridge, 1998).
Bray, G. (ed.), *Records of Convocation*, vol. VIII (Woodbridge, 2006).
Browning, A. (ed.), *English Historical Documents, 1660-1714*, vol. 8 (London, 1953).
Bruce Bannerman, A. M. (ed. and transc.), *Register of St Matthew Friday Street London 1538-1812*, Harleian Society Register, vol. 63 (London, 1933).
Burrows, M. (ed.), *Register of the Visitors of the University of Oxford 1647-1658*, (Camden Society, 1881).
Calendar of State Papers Domestic (series).
Cardwell, E. (ed.), *Documentary Annals of the Reformed Church of England*, (Oxford, 1844).
Cardwell, E. (ed.), *History of Conferences*, (Oxford, 1841).
Cardwell, E. (ed.), *Synodalia*, (Oxford, 1842).
Cheney, C. R. (ed.), *Handbook of Dates*, (Cambridge, 1945/1961/1996).
Clarendon, *Life of Edward Earl of Clarendon...in which is included a Continuation of the History of the Grand Rebellion*, 3 vols (Oxford, 1827).
Clarendon, Henry Earl of and Gale, S. (eds), *History and Antiquities of the Cathedral Church of Winchester*, (London, 1715).
Cobbett, W. (ed.), *Parliamentary History of England*, vol. 4 (London, 1808).
Davenant, C., *Political and Commercial Works*, (London, 1771).
De Beer, E. S. (ed.), *The Diary of John Evelyn*, (Oxford, 1955).
Ecton, J. (ed.), *Liber Valorum et Decimarum*, (London, 1711).
Ecton, J. (ed.), *Thesaurum Rerum Ecclesiasticarum*, (London, 1742).
Firth, C. H. and Rait, R. S. (eds), *Acts and Ordinances of the Interregnum 1642-1660*, 2 vols (London, 1911).
Forty-Sixth Annual Report of the Deputy Keeper of the Public Records, The, (London, 1886).
Foster, J. (ed.), *Alumni Oxonienses*, (Oxford, 1891/92).
Foster, J. (ed.), *Register of Admissions: Grays Inn 1521-1887*, (London, 1889).
Gibson, E. (ed.), *Codex Juris Ecclesiastici Anglicani*, (Oxford, 1761).
Goodman, A. W. and Hutton, W. H. (eds), *Statutes Governing the Cathedral Church of Winchester*, (Oxford, 1925).
Goodman, F. R. (ed.), *Diary of John Young*, (London, 1928).
Gould, G. (ed.), *Documents Relating to the Settlement of the Church of England by the Act of Uniformity 1662*, (London, 1862).
Granger, J., *Biographical History of England*, vol. 3 (London, 1804).
HMC, 5th Report, (London, 1876).
HMC, 7th Report, (London, 1879).
HMC, 9th Report, (London, 1884).
HMC, 10th Report, Appendix, Part VI (London, 1885).
HMC, 11th Report, Appendix, Part VII (London, 1888).
HMC, 12th Report, Appendix, Part IX (London, 1891).
HMC, 14th Report, Appendix, Part VII, Ormond MSS, vol. 1 (London, 1895).
HMC, 15th Report, Appendix, Part VII, Somerset MSS, (London, 1898).
HMC, Bath MSS, vol. 2 (London, 1907).
HMC, Hastings MSS, vol. 4 (London, 1928-1947).
Horn, J. (ed.), *Fasti Ecclesiae Anglicanae*, (London, numerous volumes/dates).
Isham, G. (ed.), *Correspondence of Bishop Brian Duppa and Sir Justinian Isham, 1650-1660*, Northampton Record Society, 17 (1951-55).
Journals of the House of Commons, vols 2, 3, 8, 9 (London, 1803).
Journals of the House of Lords, vols 9, 11, 12, 13 (London, 1767-1830).
Keeble, N. H. and Nuttall, G. F. (eds), *Calendar of the Correspondence of Richard Baxter*, (Oxford, 1991).
Kennett, W., *Register and Chronicle Ecclesiastical and Civil*, (London, 1728).
Kitchen, G. W. and Madge, T. F. (eds), *Documents Relating to the Foundation of the Chapter of Winchester Cathedral*, (London, 1889).
Latham, R. and Matthews, W. (eds), *Diary of Samuel Pepys*, (London, 1970-1983).
Lincoln's Inn, *Records of the Honourable Society of Lincoln's Inn: Vol. 1, Admissions 1420-1799*, (Lincoln's Inn, 1896).
Lyon Turner, G. (ed. and transc.), *Original Records of Early Nonconformity under Persecution and Indulgence*, 3 vols (London, 1911-14).

Macpherson, J. (ed.), *Original Papers Containing the Secret History of Great Britain,* (London, 1775).
Macray, W. D. (ed.), *Calendar of Clarendon State Papers,* vol. 2 (Oxford, 1869).
Macray, W. D. (ed.), *Calendar of Clarendon State Papers,* vol. 3 (Oxford, 1876).
Macray, W. D. (ed.), *The History of the Rebellion and Civil Wars in England...1642,* 6 vols (Oxford, 1888).
Matthews, A. G. (ed.), *Calamy Revised,* (Oxford, 1934).
Matthews, A. G. (ed.), *Walker Revised,* (Oxford, 1948).
Morley, George, *Several Treatises written upon Several Occasions,* (London, 1683).
Notestein, W. (ed.), *Journal of Sir Simons D'Ewes,* (Yale, 1923).
Routledge, F. J. (ed.), *Calendar of Clarendon State Papers,* vol. 5 (Oxford, 1970).
Peckham, W. D. (ed.), *Acts of the Dean and Chapter...of Chichester 1545-1642,* (Sussex Record Society, 1959).
Page, M., *Pipe Roll of the Bishopric of Winchester 1301-1302,* Hampshire Record Series, 14 (1996).
Page, M., *Pipe Roll of the Bishopric of Winchester 1409-10,* Hampshire Record Series, 16 (1999).
Polhill, E. O., *Samaritan,* (London, 1682).
Porter, S., Roberts, S. K., Roy, I. (eds), *Diary and Papers of Henry Townshend 1640-1663,* (Worcestershire Historical Society, 2014).
Robbins, C. (ed.), *Diary of John Milward Member of Parliament for Derbyshire, September 1666-May 1668,* (Cambridge, 1938).
Robinson, D. (ed.), *Diary of Francis Evans,* (Worcestershire Historical Society, 1903).
Routledge, F. J. (ed.), *Calendar of Clarendon State Papers,* vol. 4 (Oxford, 1932).
Routledge, F. J. (ed.), *Calendar of Clarendon State Papers,* vol. 5 (Oxford, 1970).
Russell Barker, G. H. and Stenning, A. N. (eds), *Record of Old Westminsters,* (London, 1928).
Scott, W. and Bliss J. (eds), *Works of...Wm Laud,* (Oxford, 1847-1860).
Scrope, R. and Monkhouse T. (eds), *State Papers collected by Edward Earl of Clarendon,* 3 vols (Oxford, 1767-86).
Spalding, R. (ed.), *Diary of Bulstrode Whitelocke 1605-1675,* (Oxford, 1990).
Stephens, W. R. W. and Madge, T. F. (eds), *Documents Relating to the Cathedral Church of Winchester in the Seventeenth Century,* (London, 1897).
Venn, J. and J. A. (eds), *Alumni Cantabrigienses,* (Cambridge, 1922-27).
Visitation Articles: Neil 1631, Curl 1639, Morley 1662, 1674; see *STC,* Pollard and Redgrave *STC;* Wing *STC.*
Walton, I., *Lives of Donne, Wotton, Hooker, Herbert, and Sanderson,* (London, 1825).
Warner, G. F. (ed.), *Correspondence of Sir Edward Nicholas,* 2 vols (Camden Society, 1886-92).
Welch, J. (ed.), *Alumni Westmonsterienses,* (London, 1852).
Whiteman, A. (ed.), *Compton Census of 1676: A Critical Edition,* (Oxford, 1986).
Wilkins, D. (ed.), *Concilia Magnae Britanniae,* (London, 1737).
Williams, J. W. (ed.), *Diary of Henry Townshend,* (London, 1920).
Wood, A. (ed.), *Athenae Oxonienses 1500-1695,* (London, 1721).
Wood, A., *History of the Visitation of the University of Oxford by a Parliamentary Commission 1647-1648,* (Oxford, 1873).

SECONDARY SOURCES: ARTICLES/ESSAYS

Abernathy, G. R., 'English Presbyterians and the Stuart Restoration 1648-1663', *TAPS,* vol. 55, part 2 (1965).
Atherton, I., 'Dean and Chapter, Reformation and Restoration 1541-1660' in P. Meadows and N. Ramsey (eds), *History of Ely Cathedral,* (Woodbridge, 2003).
Atherton, I. and Holderness, B. A., 'Dean and Chapter Estates since the Reformation' in *Norwich Cathedral, City, and Diocese 1096-1996,* ed. I. Atherton (London, 1996).
Barker Benfield, B. C., 'Scraps from Thomas Barlow's Waste Paper Basket', *Bodleian Library of Record,* 13 (1988-90).
Beddard, R. A., 'Restoration Oxford and the Remaking of the Protestant Establishment' in N. Tyacke (ed.), *History of the University of Oxford,* vol. 4 (Oxford, 1997).
Beddard, R. A., 'A Reward for Services Rendered: Charles II and the Restoration Bishopric of Worcester, 1660-1663', *Midland History,* vol. XXIX (2004).
Bennett, G. V., 'Convocation of 1710: An Anglican Attempt at Counter Revolution' in G. J. Cuming and D. Baker (eds), *Studies in Church History,* (Cambridge, 1971).
Berlatsky, J., 'Elizabethan Episcopate' in F. Heal and R. O'Day (eds), *Princes and Paupers in the English Church 1500-1800,* (Leicester, 1981).
Boulton, J. P., 'Limits of Formal Religion: The Administration of Holy Communion in Later Elizabethan and Early Stuart England', *London Journal,* 10 (1984).
Bowden, P. J., 'Economic Change: Wages, Profits, and Rents 1500-1750' in J. Thirsk (ed.), *Chapters in the Agrarian History of England 1500-1700,* (Cambridge, 1990).
Bowker, M., 'Historical Survey 1450-1750' in D. M. Owen (ed.), *History of Lincoln Minster,* (Cambridge, 1984).
Bussby, F., 'Anglican in Exile', *Church Quarterly Review,* 1965.
Bussby, F., 'Early Life of George Morley', *Winchester Cathedral Record,* 1970.
Bussby, F., 'George Morley Bishop of Winchester 1662-1684', *Church Quarterly Review,* 1967.
Clay, C., 'The Greed of Whig Bishops', *Past and Present,* 87 (1980).
Cuming, G. J., 'The Prayer Book in Convocation November 1661', *JEH,* vol. 8 (1957).
Fincham, K. C. and Taylor, S., 'Restoration of the Church of England 1660-1662: Ordination, Re-ordination, and Conformity' in S. Taylor and G. Tapsell (eds), *The Nature of the English Revolution Revisited,* (Woodbridge, 2013).
Foster, A., 'Archbishop Richard Neile Revisited' in P. Lake and M. Questier (eds), *Conformity and Orthodoxy in the English Church 1560-1660,* (Woodbridge, 2000).
Greenslade, S. L., 'Faculty of Theology' in J. McConica (ed.), *History of the University of Oxford,* vol. 3 (Oxford, 1986).
Gwynn, R., 'Strains of Worship: the Huguenots and Non-Conformity' in D. J. B. Trim (ed.), *The Huguenots: History and Memory in Transnational Context,* (Leiden and Boston, 2011).
Habbakuk, H. J., 'Landowners and the Civil War', *Econ HR,* 2nd Series, 18 (1965).
Habbakuk, H. J., 'Land Settlement at the Restoration of Charles II', *TRHS,* 5th Series, 28 (1978).
Hare, J., 'Why So Many Houses? The Varied Functions of the Episcopal Residences of the See of Winchester, c.1100-c.1680' in D. W. Rollason (ed.), *Princes of the Church: Bishops and their Palaces,* (London, 2017).
Hockaday, S. F., 'Consistory Court of the Diocese of Gloucester', *Transactions of Bristol and Gloucester Archaeological Society,* XLVI (1924).
Horwitz, H., 'Protestant Reconciliation in the Exclusion Crisis', *JEH, XV,* No. 2 (October 1964).
Jacob, W. M., 'In Love and Charity with your Neighbour', *Studies in Church History,* 40 (2004).
Johnson, D., 'Estate Income 1540-1714' in D. Keene, A. Burn, and A. Saint (eds), *St Paul's: The Cathedral Church of London 604-2004,* (London, 2004).
Johnson, R., 'Lives of Ejected Hampshire Clergy after 1662', *SH,* 36 (2014).
Mason, J. F. A., 'A Brief History of Christ Church Oxford' in C. Hibbert (ed.), *Encyclopaedia of Oxford,* (Oxford, 1988).
Norman, P., 'Accounts of the Overseers of the Poor, 1608-1671', *Surrey Archaeological Collections,* 16 (1901).
Paley, R. and Adams B., 'Morley' in R. Paley (ed.), *House of Lords 1660-1715,* (Cambridge, 2016).
Phelps Brown, H. E. and Hopkins, S. V., 'Seven Centuries of Prices of Consumables', *Economica,* 23 (1956).
Pugh, R. K., 'Post-Restoration Bishops of Winchester as Visitors of Oxford Colleges', *Oxoniensia,* XLIII (1978).
Ratcliffe, E. C., 'Savoy Conference', in G. F. Nuttall and O. Chadwick (eds), *From Uniformity to Unity,* (London, 1962).

Redstone, L. J. 'Farnham Castle', in R. S. Rait (ed.), *English Episcopal Palaces,* (London, 1910).
Robbins, C., 'The Oxford Session of the Long Parliament', *BIHR,* 1946-48.
Seaward, P., 'Circumstantial Temporary Concessions: Clarendon, Comprehension, and Uniformity' in N. H. Keeble (ed.), *Settling the Peace of the Church: 1662 Revisited,* (Oxford, 2014).
Spurr, J., 'The Church of England: Comprehension and the Toleration Act of 1689', *EHR,* CIV, 413 (1989).
Thirsk, J., 'Restoration Land Settlement', *JMH,* 26, 1 (1954).
Thomas, R., 'Comprehension and Indulgence' in G. F. Nuttall and O. Chadwick (eds), *From Uniformity to Unity 1662-1962,* (London, 1962).
Thomson, A., 'Continuity and Change', *SH,* 30 (2008).
Thomson, A., 'Estate Management in the Winchester Diocese before and after the Interregnum: a Missed Opportunity', *Hampshire Studies,* 61 (2006).
Thrush, A. and Ferris, J. P. (eds), *House of Commons 1604-1629,* vol. IV (Cambridge, 2010).
Till, B. D., *Church Courts 1660-1720: the Revival of Procedure* (Borthwick, 2006).
Till, B. D., 'Worcester House Declaration and the Restoration of the Church of England', *Historical Research,* vol. 70 (1997).
Titow, J. Z., 'Lost Rent', *Agricultural History Review,* 92 (1994).
Tomlinson, H., 'Restoration to Reform' in G. Aylmer and J. Tiller (eds), *Hereford Cathedral,* (London, 2000).
Tyacke, N., 'Religious Controversy' in N. Tyacke (ed.), *History of the University of Oxford,* vol. 4 (Oxford, 1997).
Whiteman, A., 'Re-Establishment of the Church of England 1660', *TRHS,* 5th Series, vol. 5 (1955).
Whiteman, A., 'Restoration of the Church of England' in G. F. Nuttall and O. Chadwick (eds), *From Uniformity to Unity 1662-1962,* (London, 1962).
Wykes, D. L., 'Early Religious Dissent in Surrey', *SH,* 33 (2011).

SECONDARY SOURCES: MONOGRAPHS

Best, G. F. A., *Temporal Pillars,* (Cambridge, 1964).
Bill, E. G. W., *Education at Christ Church Oxford 1660-1899,* (Oxford, 1988).
Bill, E. G. W. and Mason, J. F. A., *Christ Church and Reform 1850-1867,* (Oxford, 1970).
Bosher, R. S., *Making of the Restoration Settlement,* (London, 1951).
Carlson, E. J., *Marriage and the English Reformation,* (Oxford, 1994).
Carpenter, E. F., *Protestant Bishop: Being the Life of Henry Compton, 1632-1713, Bishop of London,* (London, 1956).
Chapman, C. R., *Ecclesiastical Courts, Officials, and Records,* (Dursley, 1997).
Clarke, A., *Life and Times of Anthony Wood,* (Oxford, 1892).
Coleby, A., *Central Government and the Localities: Hampshire 1649-89,* (Cambridge, 1989).
Collinson, P., *The Religion of Protestants,* (Oxford, 1982).
Cressy, D., *Birth, Marriage and Death: Ritual Religion and the Life Cycle in Tudor and Stuart England,* (Oxford, 1997).
Curthoys, J., *The Cardinal's College,* (London, 2012).
Curtis, M. H., *Oxford and Cambridge in Transition 1558-1642,* (Oxford, 1959).
Davies, J. D., *History of Southampton,* (Southampton, 1883).
Fincham, K. C., *Prelate as Pastor: the Episcopate of James I,* (Oxford, 1990).
Foxcroft, H. C., *Supplement to Burnet's History of My Own Time,* (Oxford, 1902).
Greaves, R. L., *Deliver Us from Evil,* (Oxford, 1986).
Green, I. M., *Re-establishment of the Church of England,* (Oxford, 1978).
Gregory, J., *Restoration, Reformation, and Reform 1660-1828: Archbishops of Canterbury and their Diocese,* (Oxford, 2000).
Haller, W., *Liberty and Reformation in the Puritan Revolution,* (New York, 1955).
Heal, F., *Of Prelates and Princes: A Study of the Economic and Social Position of the Tudor Episcopate,* (Cambridge, 1980).
Hembry, P., *Bishops of Bath and Wells 1540-1640,* (London, 1967).
Hill, C., *Economic Problems of the Church,* London, 1968.
Hill, C., *Society and Puritanism in Pre-Revolutionary England,* London, 1969.
Hill, C., *The World Turned Upside Down,* (London, 1972).
Houlbrooke, R. A., *Church Courts and the People* (Oxford, 1979).

Hutton, R., *The Restoration: A Political and Religious History of England and Wales 1658-1667* (Oxford, 1985).
Ingram, M., *Church Courts, Sex and Marriage in England 1570-1640,* (Cambridge, 1987).
Lehmberg, S. E., *Cathedrals under Siege 1600-1700,* (Exeter, 1996).
Lister, T. H., *Life and Administration of the First Earl of Clarendon,* 3 vols (London, 1837).
McIntosh, M. E., *A Community Transformed: The Manor and Liberty of Havering, 1500-1620,* (Cambridge, 1986).
Marchant, R. A., *Church under the Law,* (Cambridge, 1969).
Miller, J., *After the Civil Wars: English Politics and Government in the Reign of Charles II,* (London, 2000).
Miller, J., *Cities Divided: Politics and Religion in English Provincial Towns 1660-1722,* (Oxford, 2007).
Nuttall, G. F. and Chadwick, O. (eds), *From Uniformity to Unity 1662-1962,* (London, 1962).
O'Day, R., *English Clergy: The Emergence and Consolidation of a Profession 1558-1642,* (Leicestershire, 1979).
Ollard, R., *Clarendon and his Friends,* (London, 1987).
Outhwaite, R. B., *The Rise and Fall of the Ecclesiastical Courts 1500-1860,* (Cambridge, 2006).
Owen, D. M., *Records of the Established Church of England,* (London, 1970).
Paul, R. S., *Assembly of the Lord,* (Edinburgh, 1985).
Pevsner, N. and Lloyd, D., *Hampshire and the Isle of Wight,* (London, 1967).
Pruett, J. H., *Parish Clergy under the Later Stuarts,* (Leicestershire, 1978).
Quaife, G. R., *Wanton Wenches and Wayward Wives,* (London, 1979).
Savidge, A., *Foundation of Queen Anne's Bounty,* (London, 1955).
Seaward, P., *Cavalier Parliament and the Reconstruction of the Old Regime 1661-1667,* (Cambridge, 1985).
Shaw, W. A., *History of the English Church,* (London, 1900).
Simon, W. G., *Restoration Episcopate,* (New York, 1965).
Spaeth, D. A., *The Church in an Age of Danger: Parsons and Parishioners 1660-1740,* (Cambridge, 2000).
Spurr, J., *Restoration Church of England 1646-1689,* (Yale, 1991).
Stieg, M., *Laud's Laboratory: The Diocese of Bath and Wells in the Early Seventeenth Century,* (Lewisburg 1982).
Stone, L., *The University in Society: vol. 1, Oxford and Cambridge from the 14th to the Early 19th Century,* (Princeton, 1975).
Stoughton, J., *History of Religion in England,* vol. 3 (London, 1901).
Sutch, V. D., *Gilbert Sheldon: Architect of Anglican Survival,* (The Hague, 1973).
Sykes, N., *From Sheldon to Secker: Aspects of English Church History, 1660-1768,* (Cambridge, 1959).
Tarver, A., *Church Court Records,* (Chichester, 1995).
Thomson, A., *The Clergy of Winchester England 1615-1698: A Diocesan Ministry in Crisis,* (Lewiston/Mellen, 2011).
Trevor Roper, H., *Archbishop Laud,* (London, 1935).
Tyacke, N., *Anti-Calvinists and the Rise of English Arminianism c.1590-1640,* (Oxford, 1987).
Usher, R. G., *Reconstruction of the English Church,* (New York, 1910).
Wood, A. H., *Church Unity without Uniformity* (London, 1963).
Wrightson, K. and Levine, D., *Poverty and Piety: Terling 1525-1700,* (London, 1979).

UNPUBLISHED THESES

Christopher, R. A., 'Social and Economic Background of the Surrey Clergy 1520-1620', Ph.D. (London, 1975).
Evan Davies, C., 'Enforcement of Religious Uniformity in England 1668-1700', D.Phil. (Oxford, 1982).
Jones, M. D. W., 'Ecclesiastical Courts Before and After the English Civil War 1630-1675', B.Litt., (Oxford, 1977).
Marshall, W. M., 'Administration of the Dioceses of Hereford and Oxford 1660-1760', Ph.D. (Bristol. 1978).
Owen, H. G., 'London Parish Clergy in the Reign of Elizabeth I', Ph.D. (London, 1957).
Potter, J. M., 'Ecclesiastical Courts of the Diocese of Canterbury, 1603-1665', M.Phil. (London, 1973).
Salter, J. L., 'Warwickshire Clergy 1660-1714', Ph.D. (Birmingham, 1975).
Reid, T., 'The Clergy of the Diocese of Canterbury in the Seventeenth Century', Ph.D. (Kent, 2011).
Tarver, A., 'Consistory Court of the Diocese of Lichfield and Coventry 1680-1830', Ph.D. (Warwick, 1998).
Thomson, A., 'Diocese of Winchester Before and After the English Civil Wars: a Study of the Character and Performance of its Clergy', Ph.D. (London, 2004).
Whiteman, A., 'Episcopate of Seth Ward, Bishop of Exeter 1662-1667 and Salisbury 1667-1689', D.Phil. (Oxford, 1951).

INDEX

A

Acts, Confirming and Restoring Ministers (1660) 39, 78; Uniformity (1662) 41, 45, 49, 55n, 66, 72, 77, 78n, 84, 117, 126; Five Mile (1665) 50, 51; Conventicle (1670) 51, 57n ; Test Acts (1673) 54, 55; (both 1673, 1678) 59, 60, 113; Toleration (1689) 12, 62
Andrewes, Lancelot 86, 87, 88, 92, 100, 116, 124, 127
Anne, Duchess of York see York
Atterbury, Francis 109
Augmentation (clergy incomes) 104, 105, 107, 108, 114, 122n, 123, 129

B

Baldwyn, Timothy 66, 67, 72, 75
Baxter, Richard, Worcester House 41-5, 78; Savoy 46-7, 48, 52, 65, 78, 79n; bill (1673) 54; talks with Stillingfleet and Tillotson (1674-75) 56, 58; Kidderminster 77-80
Bills for comprehension (1667-68) 13, 50, 90; (1673) 54, 55; (1674), 54, 56, 60
Bills for toleration (1668) 50, 90; (1673), 54, 55; (1675) 56
Bishops Waltham Palace 120, 121, 129
Bilson, Thomas 91, 116
Black Rubric 13, 48, 126
Book of Common Prayer 13, 34, 43, 44, 46, 47, 48, 49, 50, 52, 55, 56, 60, 72, 74n, 77n, 84, 85, 126
Bouchard 26
Bramston, Mondeford 95, 112
Burnet, Gilbert 16, 45, 47, 48, 61, 108, 113

C

Calamy, Edward 35, 44, 62, 70, 71, 72, 84
Census (1676) 56, 58, 76, 82, 98, 99
Charles II, exile 22, 28; campaigns 1650s 22; Presbyterian delegation 1660 30; Catholicism 33, 35, 52; Restoration 29, 30; declarations see declarations below; Worcester House 42; Savoy 46; motives 33 (mission), 34, 45 (Worcester House), 52 (Savoy); skill 37; clergy incomes 104; Winchester scheme 121
Chelsea Palace 120, 121, 129
Christ Church, Morley's posts 9, 13, 20, 38; degrees 16; regulations 16-17; his contemporaries 18; expulsions 21; receipt of largesse 129
Clarendon (Hyde), identity 13; views on Morley 18, 33; exile 23, 128; mission of 1660 32-34; clergy appointments 40; Worcester House 41-44; Black Rubric 48; uniformity bill 49; motives 45, 52; chancellor of Oxford 65; fall 117, 118
Compton, Henry 11, 89, 92n, 100, and see census
Convocation 11, 12, 13, 46, 47-8, 49, 51, 52, 55, 65, 66, 77, 101, 109
Cosin, John 22, 46, 47, 62
Consistory courts see Morley
Curl, Walter 86, 88, 89, 91, 92, 93, 102, 116, 124
Cromwell, Richard 28, 29, 30, 31; Oliver, 29, 30, 32, 41, 101

D

Danby (Thomas Osborne) 56, 57, 60
Darcy 26, 128
Declarations, Breda 30, 33, 37, 41; Worcester House, September 1660 41, 43, 45; October 1660 41, 43, 45; Indulgence (1672) 54, 55, 59, 86, 92, 98n, 99
Duppa, Brian 63, 67, 71, 81, 83, 86, 120, 124

E

Elizabeth, Queen of Bohemia 23, 27, 28, 128
Evelyn, John 22, 108, 118n, 128
Exclusion Crisis 9, 58, 118

F

Fearne, Henry 47
Farnham Palace 86, 115, 117, 118, 120, 121, 127, 129
Frewen, Accepted 63

G

Gauden, John 46, 48, 86
Great Haseley 38, 39

H

Hale, Matthew 35, 50, 62, 109
Hartfield 18, 19
Henrietta Maria 22, 28
Huguenots 24, 60
Hyde, Edward see Clarendon

I

Impropriations (clergy incomes) 106-108, 114
Incomes, episcopal see Morley; parochial see parish clergy

J

James, Duke of York see York
Jenkyn, Leoline 106, 108, 109, 110

K

Kidderminster see Baxter; parish clergy incomes
Ken, Thomas 89, 90
Kennett, White 16, 38, 45, 47, 48, 61, 63n, 64

L

Laud, William 17, 18, 89, 106
Laudian/Laudianism 9, 11, 26, 32, 40, 41n, 52, 92, 93, 106, 107
Lambert, John 11, 31, 113

M

Mews, Peter 86, 88, 89, 92, 100, 103, 116, 124
Mildenhall 18, 19, 21, 38
Monck, George 28, 29, 30, 31, 32, 37
Morley, Charles 95, 112, 127
Morley, George **Appointments,** Christ Church, stipendiary studentship 16, canon 20, dean 38; Bishop of Worcester 63-64; Bishop of Winchester 80-81; dean of the Chapel Royal 38; **Baxter,** see Baxter; **benefactions,** 119-124, 129; **Birth,** 15; **BCP,** Worcester House 43-44, Savoy 46, Convocation 47, Black Rubric 48, bill 1674 54, 60; **Calvinism,** 16, 26, 48, 61; **clergy appointments committee 1660,** 40-41; **Compton Census,** see census; **Conferences,** see BCP; **Confirmations,** at Winchester 94, 100; **Consistory court,** at Worcester 75-77, at Winchester 58, 59, 62, 83, 85, 90, 94-99, 100, 108-113, 114, 126, 127; **Convocation,** see BCP; **Death,** 15, 115; **Education,** school 16; university see Christ Church; **Ejections of clergy,** see legislation below; **Enthronements,** see appointments above; **Exile,** 14, Chapter 2 passim, 128; **Health,** 99, 114, 115; **Income,** Worcester 68; Winchester 82, 124; **Institutions,** Worcester 66, 67, 70-73; Winchester 87-91; **Legislation,** Uniformity, enactment 48, 49, 52, 66, enforcement 49, 53, 84-86; Five Mile 50; Conventicle 51, 57n; Comprehension Bill of 1674 54, 56, 60; Palaces Act 1664 120; **Library at Winchester,** see benefactions above; **Morley College,** see benefactions above; **Motives,** Mission of 1660 33, 34; Worcester House 45; uniformity 1662 52-5; Census 1676 56-58; overall 58-62; **Ordinations,** of Presbyterians 34, 35, 36, 42, 43, at Worcester 73, 74, at Winchester 86-87, 93; **Oxford University,** visitations 119, see benefactions; **Palaces,** see Bishops Waltham, Chelsea, Farnham, Wolvesey;

Parishes, see Hartfield, Mildenhall, Pennant, Great Haseley; **Popery,** 19, 25, 59, 61, 118; **Privy Council,** membership 11, 46, 48, 117; action 48-49; **Reform,** see parish boundaries, parish clergy incomes, consistory court; **Sermons,** 19, 118; **Treaties,** at Uxbridge, Newmarket, Newport 20; **Tomb,** 15, 115; **Visitations,** Worcester 73-74; Winchester 91-93, 98; **Writings,** 24, 25, 35, 59, 79, 118

P

Pakington, Sir John 63, 79
Parish boundaries, general 101-103, 114, 126; under the Commonwealth 101; legislation 1660s 101, 103
Parish clergy incomes, origins 28; general 104-108, 114, 126; Mildenhall 18; expellees 49; Kidderminster 78; Winchester clergy 104, 107; directives 101, 104, 105; legislation 104, 105; see augmentations, impropriations
Pembroke (Philip Herbert) 19, 20, 21, 23n, 30
Pennant 18, 19
Penruddock's rebellion 29
Popish Plot 9, 10, 58, 99, 113, 118
Presbyterians, Scottish 20, 22, 66; structure 26; 1650s 31, 41; delegates in 1660 34; hopes 39; Worcester House 41-45; Savoy 46-47; BCP 48; bill 1673 54; talks 1674-75, 56, 58; leaders 62
Privy Council 11, 12, 46, 48, 49, 51, 52, 55, 64, 83, 100, 117

R

Rye House Plot 59, 113

S

Sancroft, William 62, 92n, 105, 109, 118
Sanderson, Robert 18, 46, 47, 63, 67, 86
Savoy 11, 44, 46-7, 48, 49, 52, 65, 78, 79n, 127
Sharrock, Robert 89
Sheldon, Gilbert, Tew 18; consecration 11, 63; clergy appointments committee 40; Worcester House 45; Savoy 46; uniformity 49, 62; Five Mile Act 58; organising attendance House of Lords 51, 55-56; census 56-58; reform of parishes 101, of pluralism 108, of church courts 109, 113; health 116
Stillingfleet, Edward 56, 58, 62, 95n, 100, 108, 109, 111, 114

T

Tew 18
Tichborne Lord and Lady, 97, 99
Tillotson, John 42n, 56, 58, 62, 109, 114

V

Venner Risings 10, 29, 31, 46, 78, 113

W

Ward, Seth 11, 56, 67, 75n, 86, 87, 92n, 93, 94, 95n, 100, 103, 105n, 106, 107n, 111
Westminster Assembly 20, 35n, 78
Wren, Matthew 47, 62, 63
Wolvesey Palace 120, 121, 127, 129
Worcester repairs (cathedral, palace, houses) 68-69, 129
Worcester House 11, 41-5, 52, 65, 78, 126, 127

Y

York, Anne Duchess of 23, 42, 65, 117, 118, 125
York, James Duke of 9n, 23, 48, 54, 59, 61, 118
Yorkshire Rising 10, 31, 46, 113

ABOUT THE AUTHOR

Andrew Thomson read History at King's College London in the 1950s and taught the subject, as head of department, at sixth form college level from which he took early retirement to devote himself to research. He gained a Ph.D. from the University of London in 2004 and has continued to research and to produce articles and books on the bishops, clergy, and church courts of the seventeenth-century Church of England.

www.ingramcontent.com/pod-product-compliance
Lightning Source LLC
Chambersburg PA
CBHW081134170426
43197CB00017B/2856